Social and Cultural
Issues of the
New International
Economic Order

Pergamon Titles of Related Interest

Laszlo/Kurtzman/Bhattacharya RCDC (REGIONAL COOPERATION AMONG DEVELOPING COUNTRIES)
Nicol/Echeverria/Peccei REGIONALISM AND THE NEW INTERNATIONAL ECONOMIC ORDER

UNITAR-CEESTEM Library on NIEO

Laszlo & Kurtzman	Eastern Europe and the New International Economic Order
Laszlo & Kurtzman	Western Europe and the New International Economic Order
Laszlo & Kurtzman	Political and Institutional Issues of the New International Economic Order
Laszlo & Kurtzman	The Structure of the World Economy and the New International Economic Order
Laszlo & Kurtzman	The United States, Canada and the New International Economic Order
Laszlo et al.	The Implementation of the New International Economic Order
Laszlo et al.	World Leadership and the New International Economic Order
Laszlo et al.	The Objectives of the New International Economic Order
Laszlo et al.	The Obstacles to the New International Economic Order
Lozoya & Bhattacharya	The Financial Issues of the New International Economic Order
Lozoya & Cuadra	Africa, Middle East and the New International Economic Order
Lozoya & Bhattacharya	Asia and the New International Economic Order
Lozoya & Green	International Trade, Industrialization and the New International Economic Order
Lozoya & Estevez	Latin America and the New International Economic Order
Lozoya & Birgin	Social and Cultural Issues of the New International Economic Order
Lozoya et al.	Alternative Views of the New International Economic Order
Miljan, Laszlo & Kurtzman	Food and Agriculture in Global Perspective

Related Journals*

HABITAT INTERNATIONAL
INTERNATIONAL JOURNAL OF INTERCULTURAL RELATIONS
SOCIO-ECONOMIC PLANNING SCIENCES
TECHNOLOGY IN SOCIETY

*Free specimen copies available upon request.

PERGAMON
POLICY
STUDIES

ON THE NEW INTERNATIONAL
ECONOMIC ORDER

Social and Cultural Issues of the New International Economic Order

Edited by
Jorge A. Lozoya
Haydee Birgin

A Volume in the New International
Economic Order (NIEO) Library
Published for UNITAR and the
Center for Economic and Social
Studies of the Third World

Pergamon Press
NEW YORK • OXFORD • TORONTO • SYDNEY • PARIS • FRANKFURT

Pergamon Press Offices:

U.S.A.   Pergamon Press Inc., Maxwell House, Fairview Park,
Elmsford, New York 10523, U.S.A.

U.K.   Pergamon Press Ltd., Headington Hill Hall,
Oxford OX3 0BW, England

CANADA   Pergamon Press Canada Ltd., Suite 104, 150 Consumers Road,
Willowdale, Ontario M2J 1P9, Canada

AUSTRALIA   Pergamon Press (Aust.) Pty. Ltd., P.O. Box 544,
Potts Point, NSW 2011, Australia

FRANCE   Pergamon Press SARL, 24 rue des Ecoles,
75240 Paris, Cedex 05, France

FEDERAL REPUBLIC   Pergamon Press GmbH, Hammerweg 6, Postfach 1305,
OF GERMANY   6242 Kronberg/Taunus, Federal Republic of Germany

Library of Congress Cataloging in Publication Data
Main entry under title:

Social and cultural issues of the new international
economic order.

(Pergamon policy studies on the new international
economic order)
"A volume in the New international economic order
(NIEO) library."
Includes index.
1. International economic relations--Addresses,
essays, lectures. 2. International economic relations--
Social aspects--Addresses, essays, lectures.
I. Lozoya, Jorge Alberto. II. Birgin, Haydee.
III. United Nations Institute for Training and
Research. IV. Centro de Estudios Economicos y Sociales
del Tercer Mundo. V. Series.

HF1411.S55 1981   337'.09'048   81-2028
ISBN 0-08-025123-4   AACR2

Printed in the United States of America

Contents

CHAPTER

Preface to the UNITAR-CEESTEM NIEO Library

The present volume is one in a series of 17 books which make up the UNITAR-CEESTEM NIEO Library. While each volume covers a specific aspect of the issues that comprise the New International Economic Order and can be read independently of the others, it seems useful to provide a brief introduction to outline the scope of the entire undertaking and put this volume in its proper context.

In the winter of 1976-77, UNITAR (the United Nations Institute for Training and Research) initiated with CEESTEM (the Centro de Estudios Economicos y Sociales del Tercer Mundo, Mexico) a series of inquiries into problems and opportunities associated with the establishment of the New International Economic Order (NIEO). Both institutions agreed that the NIEO constituted one of the highest priority items on the international agenda, and that independent, objective and scholarly investigation of its objectives, obstacles, opportunities, and indicated strategies may be of great value both to the decision makers directly concerned with the negotiation of the issues, and to the international community at large. The UNITAR-CEESTEM NIEO Library is a result of the research that was undertaken by the central professional staffs of the institutes, and by their jointly formed international network of collaborators and consultants.

What are some of the reasons behind this assessment of the importance of the NIEO in contemporary economic and world affairs? Although most people know that the world economy is encountering serious difficulties on both national and international levels, few people outside a small circle of experts realize the seriousness of the problems and the breadth of their scope. Contrary to some current perceptions, the NIEO is neither a passing pressure of the poor countries on

the rich, nor merely a demand for more aid and assistance. It
is a process which has deep historical precedents, and an
undisputed historical significance.

We need not go back further than the end of World War II
to find an entire array of historical events which set the stage
for the later emergence of the call for the NIEO. While these
events arose from their own historical antecedents, they
themselves produced the setting for the breakdown of the
post-war economic system, and the widening gap between rich
and poor nations.

The first and perhaps most decisive event was the
liberation of the oppressed peoples of Africa and Asia, in the
great wave of decolonization that swept the world in the years
following World War II. The newly independent states were
said to be sovereign and equal to all other states, old and
new, large and small. Their admittance to the U.N.
underscored this. However, the fresh political and juridical
status of the new countries was far from matched by their
actual economic conditions. The majority felt that their de
jure political colonization ended only to be replaced by a de
facto economic colonization.

The historical process which gave the majority of the
world's population the status of citizens of sovereign and equal
states, but left them at the same time in a situation of
economic underdevelopment and dependence, triggered the
"revolution of rising expectations". Desires for rapid economic
growth led Third World governments into ambitious plans and
programmes of national development. Most of the plans
envisaged a quick repetition of the industrial growth processes
of the developed world, following a path already long trodden
by the countries of Latin America. When the unintended
side-effects of traditional patterns of industrialization became
evident -- uncontrolled growth of cities, relative neglect of
rural areas and agriculture, threats to the environment, and
the increasing stratification of people in modern and traditional
sectors, often with serious damage to social structure and
cohesion -- many of the original development strategies
underwent modification. The goal of rapid economic growth
was not surrendered, however. Quantitative growth targets
were formally included in the official development strategies of
the First and Second U.N. Development Decades (for the 1960s
and the 1970s, respectively).

However, the mid-term review of the achievement of the
Second Development Decade's goals showed mixed results. The
greatest disappointment came in the area of agricultural
production and official development aid. On the average, the
U.N. official development aid targets have not even been half
achieved. At the same time service charges on past loans
began to put enormous pressures on developing countries'

balance of payment, and world poverty showed no signs of diminishing. There was insufficient progress in commodity trade, inadequate access to the markets of developed countries, particularly for agricultural products; tariffs have escalated, especially for semi-processed and processed products, and new tariff and nontariff restrictions were introduced by many developed countries on a number of items, including textiles and leather goods. The plight of the least developed, island and land-locked developing countries, gave rise to additional concern. While some progress was achieved, for example, through the introduction of a generalized system of preferences by the developed countries, and the proposals of the Tokyo Declaration concerning multilateral trade negotiations, the negative developments weighed more heavily in the balance and created widespread dissatisfaction in the developing world.

Another set of factors came into play as well. This was the sudden and unexpected rise of Third World economic and political power. The Middle East oil embargo of 1972-73, and the subsequent fourfold increase in the price of oil created a world energy crisis. It affected all oil-importing nations, developed as well as developing. It also exhibited the dependence of the developed countries on the developing world for several major natural resources, and proved the ability of the Third World to wield economic and political power effectively. The consequences included rises in the price of food, due to the increased cost of chemical fertilizers, and further tensions between producers and consumers of raw materials. But the OPEC-type exercise of Third World economic and political power proved unable to improve the condition of the developing countries as a whole. Despite significantly higher gross resource flows from the oil-exporting to the oil-importing developing countries, the economic plight of the latter worsened due to the higher cost of energy. Developed countries found themselves beset by economic problems of their own, including not only higher oil prices but inflation, unemployment, and unused industrial capacity. Economic rates of growth slowed, while in most countries balance of payment deficits grew. Even where surpluses could still be generated, concerns focused on the domestic economy, and the political will to increase levels of aid and assistance to the Third World faltered.

Compounding the economic difficulties of the developed nations were signs of breakdown in the international monetary system which affected all countries, developed as well as developing. Amidst growing tensions between the United States, Japan, and the European Community over matters of trade, the Bretton Woods system collapsed and gave rise to a system of floating exchange rates. The value of the U.S.

dollar began to erode, creating serious difficulties for those countries which, like most of the Third World, held their reserves in dollars. The creation of Special Drawing Rights provided some access to foreign exchange independently of dollar holdings, but such access favored the countries already developed, and the rest remained seriously dissatisfied with the workings of the international monetary system. It became evident that some of the fundamental tenets of the post-war world economy were being called into question, and indeed that some had already collapsed.

The NIEO made its appearance as an international political issue in the context of this series of events. Encouraged by the success of OPEC but fearful of splintering Third World solidarity through the newly won wealth of a few of its countries, Presidents Boumedienne of Algeria and Echeverria of Mexico, among others, called for structural reforms in the international economic system. Their governments' initiative resulted in the adoption of such major U.N. resolutions as those of the Sixth and Seventh Special Session, and the Charter of Economic Rights and Duties of States. These in turn provided the impetus for a long series of declarations, resolutions, position papers and studies on various NIEO issues by the United Nations system and the international community at large.

The coming together of these historical factors was not purely coincidental. The wave of decolonization was the culmination of a long-term historical process of democratization, and the rise of the concept of universal rights for individuals and societies. It led, in turn, to a mounting desire for rapid industrialization by the newly independent countries. This met with major frustrations. But as economic interdependence intensified, as trade and markets expanded, and access to energy and raw materials became crucial to the developed world's giant economic machinery, the concentration of economic power itself was modified. It was no longer wielded by a few powerful governments but also fell into the hands of oil exporting nations and transnational corporations.

The historical process which gave birth to a host of independent nation-states placed into sharp relief the inequities of the previous economic system, and provided some of the developing countries with fresh degrees of economic leverage. Since they not only control the supply of a number of important fuels and raw materials but also absorb about 25 percent of the developed world's exports, their demands can no longer be ignored. And they insist that a healthy growth in the world economy cannot be brought about within the framework of the existing economic system.

When the General Assembly, in December, 1977 called for another Special Session in 1980 to assess progress in the establishment of the NIEO, it took a decisive step in bringing the North-South debate to the Organization, where it belongs. It created an ongoing forum for discussions and negotiation in the interim through the Committee of the Whole, which during 1978 managed to define its role and function despite earlier disagreements. Together with the work of the bodies charged with the preparation of the International Development Strategy for the Third United Nations Development Decade, the Organization created the fora for substantive progress in the area of restructuring the economic relations of developed and developing countries. Faced with mounting pressures on national economics in all parts of the world, the international community now finds itself facing a watershed decision: to make use of these fora, or to continue to use mainly bilateral and sectoral corrective measures to mitigate tensions while entrusting the resolution of problems to the mechanisms of the free market.

This decision is intimately linked to an entire array of basic questions. Among them:

The question of cost and benefit. Who will have to bear the burden of instituting NIEO and will the results be worth the sacrifices? Will benefits really accrue to the poor people to help fulfill their basic needs and will developing countries be made truly more self-reliant -- or will the main beneficiaries be the already rich elites? Will the developed countries also benefit from NIEO (a positive-sum game) or will it mainly mean the redistribution of the current stock of wealth from them to the developing countries (a zero-sum game)?

The question of legitimacy. Is the free market the basic mechanism of world trade and the best vehicle of development, or is it merely a convenient fiction to cover up the current unjust manipulations of the major economic groups?

The question of morality. Do the rich countries have a moral obligation to help the poor, and especially the poorest? Does this responsibility extend to those countries who had no historical part in the creation of poverty in the third world?

The question of political feasibility. How strongly will different organized groups in society support or oppose governmental policies aimed at the achievement of the NIEO --and how much solidarity exists in these domains internationally, among the developing and the developed countries themselves?

It is unrealistic to expect that real progress will be made on specific NIEO issues (such as official development aid, technical assistance, debt renegotiation, removal of tariff barriers, technical cooperation among developing countries, the link between SDRs and development, voting power in the World Bank and IMF, transfers of technology, regulation of transnational corporations, a system of consultations on industrialization, and restructuring the economic and social

sectors of the United Nations) so long as the basic issues are
not resolved and a consensus does not emerge concerning
them. The NIEO can be achieved if, and only if, it is perceived that its benefits are universal and can reach all seg-
ments of the world's population (especially the neediest); if it
is held that its costs do not exceed its benefits; if its regulatory mechanisms are seen to be legitimate; if some real
sense of moral responsibility exists among members of the
human community, and if sufficient political support is
available nationally as well as internationally for the indicated
measures. If one or more of these preconditions are not met,
the NIEO will not be achieved; Member States will continue to
practice the existing, predominantly piecemeal, ad hoc and
mainly bilateral modes of adjusting to stresses and reaching
compromises.
      The basic purpose of the UNITAR-CEESTEM NIEO Library
is to provide an independent and objective assessment of these
issues, and to report its findings in time for the historic
events of 1980: the Special Session of the General Assembly
devoted to the assessment of progress toward the NIEO, and
the immediately following regular session, during which the
International Development Strategy for the 1980s and beyond
(the U.N.'s Third Development Decade) is to be debated and
adopted. It would clearly be an enormous waste of time and
effort to enter into these negotiations without forming a clear
idea of the issues that bear on their success. But reporting
on them is not a simple matter of using insight and intuition;
it requires painstaking and organized empirical research. The
requirement is to identify the forces that operate for or
against the NIEO in all parts of the world. Intuitive answers
concerning its cost and benefits, legitimacy, morality, and
political feasibility occur to all persons knowledgeable in these
areas, but such answers tend to vary and are thus not
sufficiently reliable. Expert research on the current obstacles
and opportunities associated with the NIEO in the different
regions of the world, and with respect to the diverse sectors
of the world economy, needs to be conducted. The results of
such research may shed some much needed light on the
chances of success in establishing a new international economic
order generally, and on the types of objectives and modes of
negotiations that, in the positive case, could lead to it
specifically. For although it is unlikely that a dominant
consensus already exists in the world concerning the cost and
benefit, legitimacy, morality, and political feasibility of the
NIEO (if it did exist, the international community would
probably not be experiencing the sense of frustration it has
today), the precise estimation of costs versus benefits,
legitimacy versus illegitimacy, morality versus indifference,
and political feasibility versus futility by different societal

groups could reveal highly differentiated potentials for achieving a dominant consensus in the future. Today's chaotic welter of opinions and pressures concerning the NIEO need not remain such, but could crystallize into a decisive mood favoring or opposing it. To those who object to such analysis on the grounds that economic theory, rather than wide-ranging socio-political considerations, must serve to decide the fate of NIEO, we may reply that economic theory, while relevant, is in itself over generous: it can often prove both sides of conflicting positions. Since both sides in a dispute can marshal some variety of economic theory in their defense, and no common criteria exist for assessing the relative merits of all theories, economic rationality as conveyed by economic theories becomes marginal in the negotiating process. We need to go one step deeper, inquiring into the reasons particular theories are summoned to defend particular points of view, as well as measuring the intensity of commitment to these viewpoints and the negotiating power of the parties subscribing to them.

Thus, the focus of the UNITAR-CEESTEM Library is not a given economic theory, but the perceptions and opinions underlying the positions taken by diverse actors. The configuration and strength of these perceptions and opinions will ultimately determine whether negotiations in the area of the NIEO can be successful, and if so, which strategies will have optimum chances of success.

The Library contains volumes arranged in three different series. First, there is a series of overview studies. These provide background, context, and basic reference data. They include a volume defining and classifying the principal objectives of the NIEO as agreed or debated in the United Nations and other major international fora; a volume giving an overview and assessment of alternative viewpoints on the NIEO espoused by various nongovernmental groups and researchers and different parts of the world; a third defining the most critical obstacles confronting the establishment of the NIEO; a fourth dealing with the specific problems of food and agriculture as they are debated in the framework of the United Nations. A fifth volume suggests the basic strategies which appear indicated and appropriate to accelerate progress toward the NIEO; and a final volume communicates the results of the associated UNITAR-CEESTEM International Opinion Survey of Decision-Makers and Experts on the crucial questions of the NIEO.

The second series contains geographic studies. Volumes in this series review the positions and postures of national governments and the attitudes of business, labor, the public media, and the opinion of the population at large in various nations and regions of the world. Individual volumes focus on the United States and Canada, on Western Europe, on Eastern Europe including the Soviet Union, on Asia including

Australia, on Latin America, and on Africa and the Middle East.

The third series of the NIEO Library is devoted to functional studies. Here experts give their views and assessments of such issues as the possible and the desirable structure of the world economy; of the patterns and problems of international trade and industrial development; of international financial matters, and of the associated political and institutional, as well as social and cultural problems and opportunities.

Among them, the seventeen volumes of the Library cover practically all the principal issues encountered in efforts to establish a New International Economic Order, through in-depth discussion by independent investigators, coming from different societies in different parts of the world.

The UNITAR-CEESTEM NIEO Library offers wide-ranging analyses, and sometimes divergent viewpoints, on a broad range of topics. It does not offer simplistic solutions, nor advocate one viewpoint indiscriminately over others. It seeks to illuminate the range and complexity of the issues, provide clarification of individual items, and to lend a sense of the vastness and significance of the NIEO as a whole.

It is the hope of all of us, researchers and consultants of the UNITAR-CEESTEM project on the NIEO, that our results, published as the NIEO Library, may render some service to the decisionmaker and negotiator who must cope with the problems of the international economic order, as well as to the student of international economic and world affairs, interested in further research on these topics. It is our view that the NIEO is a historically necessary, and humanly and politically appropriate attempt to create a world order that is sustainable for generations, equitable for all, and capable of meeting the most urgent needs and demands of the peoples and nations of the world community.

Ervin Laszlo
Project Director

Preface

As an opening remark to his article published in this volume, Albert Tevoedjre quotes the 1974 Cocoyoc Declaration to the effect that the ultimate goal of the economic process should be to develop human beings, not things. Recently, the United Nations General Assembly Special Session reassessed this essential truth:

> The development process must promote human dignity. The ultimate aim of development is the constant improvement of the well-being of the entire population on the basis of its full participation in the process of development and a fair distribution of the benefits therefrom.(1)

The need to proclaim the humanistic purpose of the New International Economic Order becomes urgent after the general conviction at the international forums in the sense that its basic objectives, designed in 1975, have not been achieved. Moreover the perspective for the 1980s does not leave much room for optimism about the ability of obtaining the developmental goals of Third World countries. It is time, then, to emphasize that the failure to implement the NIEO is a failure to design and realize a less unfair and exploitative society for hundreds of millions of human beings and not merely an unfulfilled technical or academic task.

The cultural and social issues involved in the establishment of the NIEO are multiple and complex. If economic progress is properly conceived, it cannot be thought of without due consideration of those human needs that if not satisfied prevent any civilized existence. Employment, education, and health issues are not lateral to economic growth but give it its real content. The arithmetic of gross national product data is relevant and significant only if, in its adduced averages, it implies the proper satisfaction of essential societal needs, both at the individual and at the collective levels. It is evident that the development strategies of even the most successful Third World countries have not fully replied to this urgent need. On the other hand the present international crisis leaves little negotiating space, at least in the short term.

The international crisis is today not only a historical phenomenon by which financial, trade, and energy issues are disputed at the conference table or on the battlefield. It is also the end of an era. Ervin Laszlo calls it the end of modern times, and he may be right. In essence, all models have lost their credibility. Nobody today advertises a national society as a spotless product to be imitated. Progress, that mysterious concept, is no longer the amicable god of Western society. The Western world has doubts. Power, domination, and superiority are challenged everywhere.

As a by-product of the crisis, there is a "systematic breakdown in existential relations between man and nature," to use Charles Jeanneret's words. Nature was never conquered, and ecological disaster threatens future generations. Many things will have to be retaught; there is much to be learned with a fresh start. Educational systems and conventional learning processes are not ready to face the challenges implied in the new conceptual revolutions, as becomes evident from reading both Porfirio Muñoz-Ledo's essay and the essay by Malitza and Sandi in this volume.

At this exceptional period of human history, mass communications media astonish everybody with their spectacular growth, even though there is general awareness of the primitive content of the information propagated by those same media, especially when volume is compared with quality. We seem to have the media and lack the message. The same appears to be true of the ability to produce new cities without a sense of proportion and balance. Glass towers next to paleolithic huts typify the landscape of Third World cities, and nobody seems to have global answers to this unacceptable contrast.

The challenge to the scientific notions of the past is probably nowhere better expressed than in the recent revival of traditional medicine, without which men and women of the Third World would not have survived. This rethinking of tradition is one of the creative signs of today's crisis, and so is the redefinition of the role of ethnic, cultural, or sex minorities in search of equity within diversity. In this sense the changing role of women remains prototypical.

The resolution of the most pressing questions of the era cannot be even properly approached without plural and democratic institutions that will share the burden of responsibility at both national and international levels. Political will for change is indispensable, and rhetorical proclamations, regardless of their ideological affiliation, are hardly a substitute. The ever-increasing expenditure on armaments is a dramatic manifestation of political will oriented in the opposite sense from creative responses to world basic challenges: the abolition of hunger, illness, and ignorance.

Only if the crisis is perceived in its global dimension will fresh and creative responses be imagined. Avoiding the philosophical and ethical implications of the crisis, expecting that mechanical and compartmentalized behavior will automatically find the way out will worsen the conflict and pave the road to a world conflagration. All responsible men and women know this. Often they despair; sometimes they feel isolated. But naked perception of facts and honesty of mind have been the trigger for many unexpected and wonderful solutions in the past. Let us keep working and hoping.

Jorge Lozoya
Haydee Birgin

NOTE

1) Assessment of the Progress Made in the Establishment of the NIEO and Appropriate Action for the Promotion of the Development of Developing Countries and International Economic Cooperation, A/ S-11/ AC.1 /1.2 (10 September 1980), p. 3.

1 Employment, Human Needs, and the NIEO
Albert Tévoédjrè

INTRODUCTION

> Our first concern is to redefine the whole purpose of
> development. This should not be to develop things
> but to develop man. Human beings have basic
> needs: food, shelter, clothing, health, education.
> Any process of growth that does not lead to their
> fulfillment is a travesty of the idea of development.

> Cocoyoc Declaration, October 1974.

The Cocoyoc Declaration represents one of the earlier indi-
cations of the growing dissatisfaction with the development
plans and strategies of the First and Second UN Development
Decades and of recognition of the need for the redefinition and
redirection of the entire concept of development to include
social factors.

Until the mid-1970s, development had been equated
entirely with economic growth, measured in monetary and
statistically quantifiable terms. In line with the economic
thinking of that time, the countries of the Third World had
fully accepted a rising gross national product (GNP) and a
healthy balance of payments as the hallmarks of success. A
basic premise of such thinking was that the widening gap
between the rich and poor engendered by the early stages of
industrial growth would decrease at its later stages as the
distribution of benefits automatically regulated itself.

By the mid-1970s, however, the whole idea of the effectiveness of economic growth as a strategy for the reduction
of poverty and inequality was being called into question. It
was noted too that the impressive 5 percent increase in GNP,

1

which in the 1960s characterized the developing countries as a
group, had done little to alleviate the growing problem of
poverty in the Third World. The question of who was bene-
fiting from this economic growth is now being asked in many
quarters. For example, statistics compiled by the International
Labor Organization (ILO) demonstrate that approximately 67
percent of the population of developing market economies can
be described as being seriously poor, that 37 percent of this
group is destitute, and that, in the majority of developing
countries, the richest 10 percent of households account for as
much as 40 percent of personal income, while the poorest 40
percent receive no more than 15 percent. In the words of the
World Bank, "Economic growth appears to have done very little
for the poor of the Third World's rapidly growing populations."(1)

In view of this poor record of the first and second
development decades with regard to the alleviation of poverty,
it must be acknowledged that equating development with
economic growth is insufficient unless that growth is accompanied by a simultaneous decrease in inequality, unemployment,
and poverty. The idea of growth as defined solely by GNP
increases is unacceptable because it neglects people and their
needs. The message for the 1980s is clear: There is a need
for a new development strategy designed and implemented to
give priority to the expression and satisfaction of fundamental
human values,(2) in short, a new international economic (and
social) order.

Ideologically speaking, it is essential to see any new
order in this light and to approach development not only from
the point of view of economic growth, but also from that of the
satisfaction of the human needs of all peoples through "a
selective attack on the worst forms of poverty."(3) It is only
by addressing itself to the needs of the masses that any new
order can find legitimation with them and can count on their
sustained support.

The common aim of the global community therefore should
be the improvement of the material welfare of all people and
especially the world's poorest people. Economic growth (which
is a necessary, but insufficient, condition for meeting these
objectives) must be complemented by the fullest utilization
of human resources, through productive employment, to ensure that the benefits deriving from development are equally
shared, for "It is no longer acceptable in human terms or
responsible in political terms to wait several generations for
the benefits of development to trickle down until they finally
reach the poorest groups."(4)

In its promotion of a basic needs strategy for development, the ILO has postulated that productive employment is
both a need in itself and a means by which other needs (a
reasonable standard of living, adequate income, food, shelter,

clothing, etc.) can be met. It has noted too that the crux of the employment problem, especially in the developing world, lies largely with the high proportion of the labor force earning inadequate incomes, that is, the underemployed. As can be seen from tables 1.1 and 1.2, there is a strong correlation between the numbers of the unemployed and those of the destitute, demonstrating that the problems of employment and poverty are inseparable. Thus it can be postulated that employment promotion is central to any strategy designed to alleviate poverty and to promote the satisfaction of human needs. A new international economic order will, therefore, require the restructuring of economic activity - especially industrial activity - on a global scale so as to allow for greater possibilities of industrialization in developing countries if employment promotion, the productive activity of the poor, and the improvement of their life situation are to be undertaken in an organized and responsible manner.

Table 1.1. Estimates of Unemployed and
Underemployed in Developing Countries by Region, 1975
(in millions)

Region	Unemployed(a)		Underemployed(b)		Total	
	Nos.	%	Nos.	%	Nos.	%
Asia(c)	18	3.9	168	36.4	186	40.3
Africa	10	7.1	53	37.9	63	45.0
Latin America	5	5.1	28	28.9	33	34.0

(a) Defined as "persons without a job and looking for work."

(b) Defined as "persons who are in employment of less than normal duration and who are seeking or would accept additional work" and "persons with a job yielding inadequate income."

(c) Excluding China and other Asian centrally planned economies.

Source: International Labor Office, Employment Growth and Basic Needs: A One World Problem (Geneva: ILO, 1976), p. 18.

Table 1.2.   Estimated Numbers of People in
Developing Market Economies Living in Poverty, 1972

Region	Total Population (millions)	Seriously Poor (millions)	%	Destitute (millions)	%
Asia	1,196	853	71	499	42
Africa	345	239	69	134	39
Latin America	274	118	43	73	27

Source: International Labor Office, Employment Growth and Basic Needs: A One World Problem (Geneva: ILO, 1976), p. 22.

The promotion of employment and the satisfaction of human needs through new, global strategies of industrialization require coherent and concerted international action in several areas.   On the international level these include:

1. modification of existing market structures in favor of the currently disadvantaged developing countries
2. elimination of trade barriers and protective tariff systems
3. promotion of Third World industrial development through the geographical redistribution of industries and the creation of new industrial facilities in the developing countries
4. establishment of mechanisms for the transfer of appropriate technology and for cooperation among Third World nations
5. promotion of the right of states to assume control of and benefit from the exploitation of their natural resources (including stricter regulation of the activities of multi-national corporations)

SPECIFIC STRATEGIES AND OBSTACLES FOR THEIR IMPLEMENTATION

Modification of Existing Market Structures

One of the major obstacles to the implementation of a new international economic order designed to promote employment and the satisfaction of human needs is the present international market structure which is undoubtedly biased in favor of the rich countries.

The increasing imbalance in the distribution of incomes, wealth, and control over world resources between the developed and developing countries has become an issue of major importance in the international arena. For example, it has been noted that in 1970-1974 the developing countries, with more than 70 percent of the world's population, received less than 4 percent of its international monetary reserves of US$131 billion - largely because the rich nations controlled its creation and distribution through the expansion of their own national reserves and through their control over the International Monetary Fund (IMF).(5)

If, therefore, a new international order is to be implemented, it is essential that there be some changes in international financial structures and institutions. Monetary reforms are essential in the context of a new order, and the working of the exchange rate system, the rules of the IMF, and the functioning of the private banking system should be improved so as to encourage the formulation and implementation of national policies seeking to promote employment creation and the satisfaction of basic needs. Reforms in the financial sphere would also need to include short-term debt relief, as well as long-term assistance to those developing countries which are making real attempts to implement sound, socially oriented development strategies. In this context it must be noted that the development plans of many Third World countries suffer from a lack of long-term, low-interest capital, access to capital markets often being determined by political affiliations rather than by economic necessity or worth.

One way in which the greater access of the developing countries to global financial resources could be enhanced is through their greater participation in international economic decision-making processes. A major obstacle to their effective participation in the context of the present system is their gross underrepresentation in the various key institutions. For example, their voting strength in the IMF is less than one-third of the total. Thus at present, when the developed countries meet to plan the economic future of the world, the advice of the developing countries on decisions which affect them is rarely solicited.

A second area in which steps must be taken to ameliorate the position of the Third World countries vis-à-vis the developed countries is that of international trade. The importance of equitable terms of trade for the developing countries cannot be overemphasized. By raising national incomes potentials, international trade could enable countries to achieve their income and growth objectives. In addition most of the developing countries need to earn the foreign exchange required to pay for imports and to service outstanding loans. They have two principle means of acquiring this exchange, through exports and through the import of foreign capital, both of which are dependant on their ability to gain access to world markets and on the terms of trade within these markets. The current terms of trade are invariably biased in favor of the developed market economies – the founders of the present order and the efforts of the developing countries to participate actively in international trade are hampered by various structural limitations which place them at a disadvantage in relation to the developed world. The developing countries have found that, simply because they are in too weak a position to exercise any meaningful control over the processing, shipping, and marketing of their primary products, they receive only a fraction of the final price of their products while paying heavily for the manufactured goods of the West. In addition, the combination of the global recession and the oil crisis has served to further reduce the terms of trade of the nonoil-producing developing countries. Thus, notwithstanding a continued increase in the actual volume of their exports, their terms of trade have been such that the import purchasing power of their export commodities has fallen markedly since the early 1970s, necessitating a corresponding cutback in essential imports. The obstacle that this trend represents to Third World economic development was noted by the Sixth Special Session of the United Nations in 1974, which emphasised the urgent need for measures that would "reverse the continued trend of stagnation or decline of the real price of several commodities exported by the developing countries, despite a general rise in commodity prices, resulting in a decline in the export earnings of these developing countries".

It is inevitable that such disadvantages caused by the biases in the international market system prevent the full and self-reliant development of national economies and affect adversely the poor countries' employment capacities, which depend to a large extent on their ability to industrialize. It is essential that the new international economic order address itself to the modification of those anomalies in the international system by instituting policies which would channel the benefits of trade more to the poorest nations by raising and stabilizing the prices of their commodities and manufactured and semi-manufactured goods.

Given the adverse impact of the recent global recession on the particularly vulnerable economies of the developing countries, an essential first step in this process would be the reflation of the world economy with the promotion of employment, as well as output, as its primary objectives. The restimulation of the economy must however be accompanied by further measures to ensure that the benefits of renewed economic growth are equitably shared by the global community.

Strategies for change in the existing market structures could include the elimination of a negative balance of payments by raising and stabilizing prices for Third World commodities, the institution of systems of preference in favor of these countries, the lowering of trade barriers against their products, and the encouragement of trading ties between them.

With regard to the modification of imbalances in the present market structures through the raising and stabilization of prices for Third World commodities, many of the most essential strategies have already been outlined and are currently being discussed or negotiated in international forums. In response to the Programme of Action's call for the "preparation of an overall integrated programme, setting out guidelines . . . for a comprehensive range of commodities of export interest to developing countries," negotiations are underway for the establishment of an Integrated Programme for Commodities (IPC) under the auspices of the United Nations Conference on Trade and Development (UNCTAD). The IPC, which constitutes a much needed safety mechanism to prevent extreme fluctuations in the price of raw materials, produced in the main by developing countries, is undoubtedly essential to the implementation of a new international economic order. The main task of the IPC will be to lessen the price-pushing effects of shortages and surfeits by setting up buffer stocks of 18 major commodities financed by a common fund. It is expected that such a program of arrangements and guidelines on commodities would improve market structures and lead to stable, remunerative, and equitable prices by cutting off the peaks and troughs which characterize the present market system to the benefit of all.

The potential performance of the IPC should be further strengthened in favor of the developing countries by a system of indexing which would assure an equitable relationship between the prices of their imports and exports by tying Third World exports to the price of the manufactured goods and capital exports of developed countries. In addition there is an urgent need for the institution of generalized systems of preferences which would increase the export earnings of developing countries, promote their industrialization, and accelerate their rates of economic growth through preferential tariff treatment for their manufactured and semimanufactured products, as well as their agricultural primary commodities. The Lomé Convention, which is currently being renegotiated, is an example of such a system which could usefully be extended. As the difficulties encountered in the course of past international negotiations in this sphere demonstrate, the main obstacle to the implementation of such strategies is less that of economic feasibility than that of the lack of political will, especially on the part of some of the developed market economies. However, the recent progress made by the UN Nego-

tiating Conference on a Common Fund (November 1978) indicates that the international political climate may be changing
in favor of the developing countries and that there will be
further possibilities for advancement in this field in the coming
year.
    One of the major obstacles to the implementation of
measures such as those discussed above is undoubtedly the
generally weak position of the developing countries relative to
their trading partners. The creation of producers' associations
and cartels along the lines of the highly successful Organization of Petroleum Exporting Countries (OPEC) should be
seriously considered as a possible strategy for changing the
structures of economic power and enhancing the bargaining
postion of the developing countries in the international market.
Both the Charter of Economic Rights and Duties of States
(1974) and the Lima Declaration (1975) suggest that such
organizations would contribute to a steady growth of the world
economy and the acceleration of the development of Third
World countries "by means of a continuous exchange of experience, harmonization of their activities and mobilization of
support for them in case of need."(6)
    A market area in which there is still considerable un-
exploited potential is that of trade links between Third World
countries themselves. At present only a small proportion
(approximately 20-25 percent) of the developing countries'
trade is with each other. Although past attempts to stimulate
this trade through trade liberalization agreements and schemes
for regional integration have had only very limited success,
there should be more scope for these trade links and less
reliance on trade with developed countries if the proposed
changes in production patterns and the geographical distribution of industries are implemented. Together with more
active credit and transport policies and with joint industrial
planning, these changes may well act to bring about closer
Third World cooperation leading to gains in income and
facilitating collective self-reliance.

Elimination of Trade Barriers and
Protective Tariff Systems

Together with the fluctuating and generally unfavorable terms
of trade discussed above, restricted access to the markets of
developed countries has seriously constrained economic growth
and employment promotion in developing countries. A major
source of restraint on the export earnings of the Third World
- and particularly the nonoil-producing developing countries -
and for the implementation of a new economic order has been
the proliferation of trade barriers including quotas and tariff
and nontariff barriers which the major developed countries

have had recourse to supposedly in order to protect their labor-intensive industries from import competition. If, as is generally agreed, international trade policies are linked with policies for the creation of employment and the satisfaction of human needs and if the developing countries are to earn sufficient foreign exchange to enable them to pursue independent development strategies, trade liberalization through a substantial reduction of tariff and nontariff barriers is an essential prerequisite.

As a first step towards this goal, international action will be necessary to eliminate existing loopholes in the present tariff and nontariff agreements, including those which permit departures from the agreed "standstill" and clauses such as Article 19 of the General Agreement on Tariffs and Trade (GATT) which allow "emergency action" on imports that are seen as a threat to domestic industry. In addition, it will be necessary for the international community to formulate, through negotiation, a flexible system of agreed limits to the use of import restriction and set up adequate machinery for the surveillance of such restrictions and of related adjustment performance. The inevitable fiscal constraints to such liberalization can and should be eased by the creation of an international reconversion fund for the purpose of financing adjustment assistance programmes. It must, however, be noted that if all developed economies share the burden of trade liberalization in favor of the developing world, the effects of such a policy on employment are unlikely to be very grave.

In any event, it can be argued that trade liberalization policies which favor the developing countries can, in the long run, have a beneficial effect on the economies of the developed countries as well and that trade barriers are as much self-defeating as they are an obstacle to the implementation of a new world order.

It has been estimated that the developing countries as a group could earn an added US$24 billion a year if all existing tariff and nontariff barriers were removed.(7) In addition, increased trade with the Third World would help the industrialized countries both through the creation of jobs in export industries and by reducing inflationary pressure by making lower-cost goods available to consumers. For example, for the United States alone it has been estimated that trade with the Third World at the same rates as those prevailing in the last decade would produce an additional US$27 billion worth of exports per year by 1985 - an increase which could represent approximately 2 million new jobs in American export industries.(8) Furthermore, a recent UNCTAD study concluded that a 3 percent growth rate in the nonoil-producing developing countries would result in an increase of 1 percent in the developed countries, representing an increase in GNP of US$45 billion per year.(9)

In general, therefore, trade in semimanufactured and manufactured goods, as well as in primary commodities, is an area of common interest to both the First and Third Worlds. In addition, as has been noted earlier, the expansion of trade links is essential if the developing countries are to earn sufficient foreign exchange to service their debts, the repayment of which must certainly benefit the industrialized donor countries.

Although opponents of trade liberalization argue that this policy would result in the reduction of employment in the developed countries - a very sensitive issue, especially given the present economic crisis - studies have been undertaken which demonstrate that this is largely a short-term drawback, specific to certain industries, and that, in the long run, increased trade with the Third World generally results in job creation in the export industries of the developed countries and in the lowering of consumer costs. For example, while it has been estimated that the volume of exports from developing countries rose from 6.8 percent in the First Development Decade to 7.7 percent in the early years of the Second Development Decade, and while the majority of these exports were to developed market economies, there is no real evidence that this has been in any way responsible for either the current trade deficit or the unemployment situation in these countries. Indeed, an UNCTAD study undertaken at that time estimated that the total number of jobs which might be lost, in the short run, in the major developed economies through the elimination of nontariff barriers and a 50 percent reduction in tariff barriers, would not exceed 10,000 jobs for the six original members of the EEC and the United States, the United Kingdom, and Japan. This would represent no more than 1/20 of 1 percent of the total labor force of these countries.(10) It must also be noted that, as the bulk of developed country trade is with other developed countries, only a very small proportion of job loss could be attributed to increased trade with the developing countries.

This is especially true of trade in manufactured goods. While the larger part of the developing countries' manufactures are indeed directed towards developed countries' markets, as table 1.3 demonstrates, they constitute a very small proportion of these countries' manufactured imports. Under these circumstances, it is unlikely that they will have a markedly detrimental effect on employment in all but a few industries in the developed countries, especially given the level of the latters' own exports to developing countries. A further UNCTAD study estimated that even in the industries most vulnerable to low-cost import competition, gross job displacement would be unlikely to affect as much as 2 percent of their total work force.(11)

Table 1.3. The Rich World's Trade in Manufactures with the Poor
(US $ billion)

	America			EEC			Japan		
	Exp.	Imp.*	Bal.	Exp.	Imp.	Bal.	Exp.	Imp.	Bal.
1972									
Oil LDCs	1.96	0.05	1.91	5.03	0.32	4.71	1.78	0.02	1.76
Nonoil LDCs	7.61	6.13	1.48	12.79	4.23	8.56	7.14	1.19	5.95
Total LDCs	9.57	6.18	3.39	17.82	4.55	13.27	8.92	1.21	7.71
1976									
Oil LDCs	9.95	0.14	9.81	22.28	0.62	22.66	9.01	0.08	3.93
Nonoil LDCs	18.47	14.82	3.65	25.70	11.05	14.65	16.38	3.52	12.86
Total LDCs	28.42	14.96	13.46	48.98	11.67	37.31	25.39	3.60	21.79

Source: GATT from UN figures, The Economist, December 1977.

The same is true of the agricultural sector, where developing countries currently face significant trade barriers, for example, for sugar, beef, vegetable oils, and various temperature-zone foodstuffs. Wide trade liberalization measures are imperative in this area, and the Food and Agriculture Organization (FAO) has estimated that reduction or elimination of trade barriers could result in the creation of job opportunities totaling 4-5 million man-years in the primary sector of the developing countries. The corresponding reduction in employment in this sector in the developed countries would amount to only about ½ million jobs for the whole of the 1970s, a relatively insignificant figure when compared with the annual reduction of 2 million already occurring in the agricultural labor force.(12) It is also probable that this loss would be offset as a result of the overall trade expansion.

The major obstacle to the implementation of policies of trade liberalization on the part of the governments of developed countries would appear to be the strong opposition from pressure groups composed of the workers, firms, and communities which would be most adversely affected by the adjustments which the proposed measures would necessitate. In general the industries most likely to be affected by low-cost import competition are those that employ a large number of semiskilled workers with lower mobility and fewer chances of reemployment. For the affected workers, firms, and communities, the long-term benefits of improved international trade relationships are eclipsed by immediate problems of unemployment and declining incomes and asset values. Together these groups constitute a powerful lobby in favor of protectionism.

It must be emphasized, however, that the structural changes demanded of the industrialized countries in response to trade liberalization policies are not of an immediate nature. The transitional period during which the developing countries would need to adjust their own production strategies to take advantage of the increased market access engendered by reduced trade barriers would allow the developed countries ample time to make the necessary adjustments in their own economies.

In any event, trade is one of the areas in which global interdependence is particularly strong. The developed countries are increasingly faced with the realization that the economic progress (or lack of it) of the developing countries can affect their employment creation programmes and economic well-being and that it is in their own self-interest to facilitate the development of the world's poorest countries. In sum,

developed countries should facilitate the development of new policies and strengthen existing policies that would encourage domestic factors of production to move progressively from lines of production which are less competitive internationally, especially where the long-term comparative advantage lies in favour of the developing countries, thus providing inter alia larger export possibilities for the developing countries and contributing to the attainment of their development objectives.(13)

Promotion of Third World Industrial Development

Together with changes in international market structures and policies of trade liberalization, the promotion of industrial development in the Third World through the creation of new industrial facilities and through the redeployment of some of the world's productive capacities from the developed to the developing countries is an important precondition and strategy for the generation of employment in these countries.

Noting that only 7 percent of industrial production is at present located in the developing countries (with far-reaching consequences for their employment capacities) the Second General Conference of the United Nations Industrial Development Organization (UNIDO) called for the redeployment of approximately 25 percent of global industrial production to the developing countries by the year 2000. The structural implications of a change of this magnitude have generated considerable concern and debate over the distribution of gains and the problems faced by the losers in the process, even while there is widespread agreement that, in the long run, the changes are both in the best interests of all countries and vital to the success of a new world order.

In recent years the comparative advantage of the developed countries in the field of industrial development has been somewhat eroded, at least in some industries, by the rising cost of labor, energy, and transportation, as well as by the societal costs of environmental pollution and urban congestion and its related problems. It is in the interests of developed countries, therefore, to transfer labor and other resources away from the declining industries to more productive industries that can adapt more easily to changing situations by becoming more capital- and skill-intensive and so keep their comparative advantage vis-a-vis the developing country industries. On the other hand, developing countries increasingly recognize the need to specialize in areas where their comparative advantage of human and natural resources can best be utilized, rather than to establish costly, capital-intensive industries that are in competition with the more advanced industries of the West and do not adequately meet their manpower needs. It is clear, therefore, that the expansion of international specialization through the geographical redistribution of industry is an area of common interest to both groups.

While the criteria for the redistribution of industries are not identical in all situations, certain industries are more likely to lend themselves to redeployment than others. As has been mentioned above, declining First World industries that are characterized by high levels of unskilled and semiskilled labor and are already in competition with Third World industries (e.g., textiles, clothing, leather, etc.) are the most likely candidates for geographical redistribution to the developing countries. This is especially true of industries based on raw materials imported from the developing countries themselves. A considerable potential also exists for the redeployment of some of the engineering and similar industries, such as the manufacture of spare parts, machine tools, and other capital goods. These are of particular interest to the developing countries both because of their high employment creation potential and because of the possible linkages with other national industries and small-scale production.

Past market performance demonstrates that the process of redeployment is unlikely to come about as a result of market forces alone. Rather than be treated as an ad hoc activity on the part of entrepreneurs, redeployment in the developed countries must be considered a government policy aimed at phasing out certain industrial activity in favor of the developing countries. Conversely, in the developing countries, government policies will have to be directed towards the encouragement of investment in new, export-oriented industries through incentive schemes and direct assistance to firms. In addition, as financial problems, import restrictions in developing countries, lack of skilled workers, and unstable sociopolitical conditions are seen as obstacles to future redeployment activities, developing countries must take steps to create a more suitable industrial climate. Further, as major buyers and sellers of goods, and suppliers of technology, and because of their knowledge and control of relevant markets, the multinational enterprises can act as vehicles for the restructuring of global industrial production. It must be noted that these enterprises have already generated some change in the structure of manufactured exports of the developing countries.

However, it is inevitable that policies for the restructuring of global industrial production will meet with great resistance in the developed countries where employment problems do indeed exist and where the interest groups opposing a more equitable international division of labor are both well organized and powerful. Such resistance constitutes a major obstacle to the implementation of policies for the promotion of world industrialization and, by implication, to the new international economic order.

The short-term costs of the adjustment assistance programmes that such policies would necessitate could well constitute a further obstacle to their implementation. Although it is undoubtedly in the long-term interest of the developed countries to transfer labor and other resources from low to high productive activities, trade adjustment programmes are not necessarily cheap in terms of budget implications. It has been estimated that in the United States alone it would cost approximately US$400 million annually to finance such a program.(14)

Nevertheless, the ease with which the process of adjustment to changed trading patterns is made is of fundamental importance to the export prospects of developing countries, and well-planned and implemented adjustment assistance programmes are essential if the present efforts to redistribute industrial development are to succeed. It is imperative, therefore, that the governments of the developed countries institute policies that not only would stimulate and support innovative progression in sectors that can readily adapt to changing comparative advantages but also ease the transfer of resources (including manpower) from sectors that cannot easily make this transition. It is equally important that those measures be undertaken before the problems caused by developing country competition become acute enough to harden resistance to change in the developed countries. The Japanese "industrial structure policy" and the Dutch "anticipatory restructuring policy" are examples of such measures.

Given both the long-term advantages of the global redistribution of industries and the inevitable resistance to change on the part of the "losers" in the process, it is essential that the new pattern of international specialization not be imposed on the basis of theoretical calculations but that it be reached progressively through a process of negotiation. A system of consultation should be established at global, regional, and sectoral levels to facilitate the formulation and achievement of goals in this field. In short, what is needed is a series of negotiated global policies with focus on the progress of the Third World, both as a goal in itself and as a way of ensuring the future progress of the developed countries.

Transferring Technology and Promoting Cooperation among Third World Nations

In considering strategies for the implementation of a new international economic order, it is impossible to overlook the potential role of technological progress in the augmentation of labor productivity and output and its influence on employment and incomes. If therefore the UNIDO target of the location of 25 percent of industrial production in the developing world is to be met by the year 2000, it is essential that the global community address itself to the question of technological development and its transfer to the developing countries.

The question of the role of technology in Third World development strategies has given rise to much controversy. On the one hand it is argued that, to avoid technological backwardness or stagnation, developing countries should adopt the most modern capital-intensive technologies, which permit economies of scale and which generate capital savings and larger surpluses for reinvestment. On the other hand, it is being increasingly recognised that technology cannot be separated from the socioeconomic environment in which it operates and must therefore be based on the resource endowments and needs of the country concerned, thereby facilitating its self-reliant development and reducing its vulnerability to international economic events.

While it is certainly valid that developing countries should have recourse to capital-intensive technologies where appropriate, in general the satisfaction of human needs, including the right to employment, necessitates the adoption of technologies that have the greatest potential for improving the welfare, employment, and incomes of the poorest groups. Simple, inexpensive technologies of a labor-intensive rather than a capital-intensive nature should be the keynote of the future industrialization programmes of the developing countries.

The major obstacle to the adoption of appropriate technologies on the part of the Third World countries is undoubtedly their present reliance on imported concepts and patterns of development. In many of these countries, continued adherence to structures of production and patterns of trade, consumption, and distribution of wealth that originated under alien regimes whose main concern was the advancement of the metropolis rather than the colony, has resulted in patterns of growth and choices of technology ill suited to either local needs or resources. This is reflected in the poor allocation of investment resources, the underutilization of land and labor, and the increasing concentration of income in a few areas of the economy.

This asymmetrical pattern of growth that favors the urban centers and a small portion of the population is in fact one of the major causes of unemployment and poverty in the Third World. In economies where income and power are biased in favor of the urban elites, the local market inevitably reflects their needs and tastes. The types of goods and services usually provided are, therefore, neither appropriate to the needs of the poor nor accessible to them. Furthermore, as they usually require capital-intensive rather than labor-intensive production techniques, they generate low rates of employment and income growth.

Considerations of national pride and prestige constitute a further - and related - obstacle to the choice of appropriate technology. Unfortunately, there is a tendency on the part of the political leadership of some developing countries to opt for the most advanced technology, without adequate reference to its suitability. Many of the products associated with such technologies are inappropriate for the majority of the Third World nations, not only because their high cost precludes their purchase by low-income consumers but also because the scientific nature of their production techniques are often unsuitable for the conditions prevailing in these countries.

While it is certainly true, therefore, that the developing world can use existing technologies and should have access to new developments in this field, the adoption of technology originating in the developed world should be selective and should be based on the resource needs and endowments of the country concerned. Development strategies to create employment and eliminate poverty will not be provided by simply transferring the experience of the highly industrialized countries to the developed world.

In any event, although the Charter of Economic Rights and Duties of States reiterated the need for all states to facilitate the access of developing countries to the achievements of modern science and technology, including the transfer of technology, the developing countries still face considerable obstacles in this respect at the international level.

In the first instance, given the fact that most advanced technologies have originated in high-income, high-growth countries, and the fact that its transfer is subjected to restrictive business practices, usually on the part of multinational corporations (MNCs), the cost of the transfer of technology to the Third World is prohibitive. In addition, and again given the role of the MNCs in the process, the developing countries generally have insufficient control over the use of technologies in national situations. In fact, technological transfers offered to them as broad "packages" inhibit both their choice of technology and cost reduction. Lack of information about the availability of alternative technologies also allows for inappropriate purchases.

Action needs to be taken on several fronts to facilitate Third World access to technological developments. In the first place, the experience of some regional groups such as the Andean Pact countries has demonstrated that it is possible to negotiate and regulate cost control, use and adaptation of technology, and its "unpackaging" to permit the acquisition of only those aspects appropriate to national or regional conditions. In addition, the governments of the developed countries that initiate such technology could facilitate its transfer to the Third World both by guiding the policies of MNCs based in their countries and by encouraging their public sector enterprises to assist the developing countries in this area. On the international level, it has been suggested that the setting up of an industrial technological informational bank with regional and sectoral branches could also facilitate the transfer of technology.(15)

However, it is the developing countries themselves that have the most important role to play in the transfer or development of appropriate technologies. If these countries are to concentrate on meeting the employment needs of the masses, it is essential that they reorient their development strategies in ways that would permit the choice of technologies that are capital-saving and generate adequate levels of employment. The ultimate objective of such technology should be to close the gap that exists in most developing countries between the rich and the poor by raising incomes and employment and laying the foundations for a more endogenous technological development characterized by labor-intensive, capital-saving, intermediate technologies designed for small-scale urban and rural production. Complemented by the expansion of research and training facilities and the provision of credit facilities and other inputs, these measures will facilitate the rapid expansion of both the industrial and the agricultural sectors in these countries.

Insofar as the creation of new industrial facilities in the developing countries is concerned, it is in their interest to foster a close coordination between industrialization and rural development. In most of these countries, nonagricultural rural activities have tended to be neglected, although the expansion and improvement of small-scale processing and manufacturing can be of great importance to both employment creation programmes and the development of indigenous technologies, as can similar urban-based activities. Undertaken largely on the subcontracting basis that characterized early Japanese industrial development, this kind of activity can be a valuable input into the industrial facilities of the developing countries. In addition, the expansion of rural activities per se through programmes of integrated rural development not only constitute a way of meeting the material and nonmaterial needs of the rural populations but also have an impact on the pace of industrialization through increases in demand generated by income increases and through more agro-industrial inputs resulting from this expansion.

While small-scale industries do not have an intrinsic advantage over large-scale ones in all circumstances, the generally weak economic situation of many of the nonoil-producing developing countries means that it is clearly more advantageous that they adopt production techniques that do not call for a heavy investment in capital equipment and infrastructures, whenever possible. While it would certainly not be appropriate to suggest that these countries avoid completely the utilization of large-scale (and capital-intensive) industries and production techniques, it must nevertheless be

noted that, besides comparing favorably with regard to efficiency, skill formation, and innovativeness, small-scale
industries also make more intensive use of the cheap and
abundant labor that characterize most developing countries. It
is, therefore, in the interests of countries with development
strategies oriented towards employment creation and the
satisfaction of human needs to encourage the creation of such
industries by facilitating their access to raw materials and
credit, by protecting them from unfair foreign competition,
and by enhancing skills through appropriate training programmes.

The pursuit of policies of self-reliance on the part of

Another way individual developing countries can take
action to encourage and facilitate the growth of industry and
technological development is by expanding domestic market
opportunities for locally produced goods and services. Encouragement of identification with local goods and materials
through advertising and through the demonstration effect of
the elite and government purchasing policies and fiscal in-
centives will encourage more investment in local production and
facilitate the vigorous growth of small- and medium-scale
enterprises geared to meeting local consumption needs.

By encouraging a policy of self-reliance in the fields of
research and training, the developing countries can also
facilitate the adaptation of technologies that are appropriate to
their development needs and make the fullest use of local
resources, including labor. Insofar as training is concerned,
the main emphasis should be on technical training and extension services for the small-scale producers geared more to
the improvement and adaptation of existing skills than on the
introduction of new, highly advanced technical know-how that
would benefit only a small minority of the population in the
urbanized industrial sector. With regard to research, the
Third World countries should set up national and regional
research institutions oriented not only towards research on
appropriate technologies but also on their practical application.
Their main objective should be the development or adaptation
of technology in support of their employment creation programmes in ways that would make the fullest possible use of
local skills and creativity and their cultural and national
heritage.

The pursuit of policies of self-reliance on the part of
individual developing countries does not in any way imply
isolationism or autarchy and certainly should not preclude the
fostering of economic and technological cooperation among them.
Indeed, technology is a very fruitful field for the development
of regional interaction and collective self-reliance. Although
the Working Group on Technological Cooperation Among Developing Countries noted that these countries were cooperating
increasingly among themselves, their capacities and potential
for technological cooperation have yet to be fully realized.(16)

There are still several fields in which they can build up technological exchanges through bilateral and multilateral arrangements, especially with regard to research and training. In addition to the joint preparation, financing, and execution of research projects among developing countries with similar needs and resources, the setting up of regional centers for the development and transfer of technology and the exchange of experts, advisory services, and trainees can contribute to the creation of a common resource pool. Developing countries in the same region can also take advantage of geographical proximity to formulate joint technological programmes based on collective self-reliance, so as to benefit from economies of scale and to utilize common installations and facilities to promote the best possible use of their resources.

Finally, as such collective self-reliance and joint action can foster the development of Third World solidarity in relation to the First World and the MNCs, planners of a new order should seriously consider the strengthening of technical co-operation among developing countries as a strategy for correcting imbalances and inequalities in the technological field.

Controlling and Benefiting from the Exploitation of Natural Resources

If the Third World nations are to fully develop their employment potential so as to satisfy the human needs of their people, they must asume the fullest possible sovereignity and control over the exploitation of their natural resources. National ownership of resources accompanied by increased local processing and more local control over the market price of commodities would give countries a greater degree of self-reliance - which is itself a basic element in any international strategy of development. The main obstacle to the implementation of such a policy appears to be the fact that "a high and increasing proportion of international transfers in goods, services, capital, and expertise takes place under the auspices or through the mediation of the multinational corporations."(17) This places the MNCs in a highly advantageous bargaining position in relation to the developing countries that are largely dependent on them both for their access to international markets and international technological developments and for the exploitation of their national resources. MNCs are, therefore, often able to impose their own terms on these countries, effectively reducing their practical sovereignty over these resources and even running counter to their national development plans and objectives. Given their weak position relative to the MNCs, individual developing countries are rarely in a position to counter such policies or to take effective action against such restrictive business practices as the prohibition of the market allocation of Third World exports, the domination of the key sectors of their economies, abuse of industrial property rights, discriminatory pricing, boycott arrangements, and tied purchasing and selling arrangements. The generally low levels of technological development and industrialization that characterize most developing countries also make it difficult for these countries to initiate or encourage local competition to MNCs.

In general terms, therefore, the present relationship between the MNCs and the developing countries is characterized by an unequal sharing of benefits to the detriment of the host country and by high levels of tension between them. Related actions on several fronts are necessary if this position is to be changed and the obstacles posed by MNCs to Third World sovereignty over local resources are to be overcome.

In the first place, there is a need for legislation on the national and international levels that would control and oversee the activities of MNCs. Such legislation could effectively be formulated on the basis of existing voluntary agreements such as the OECD Guidelines of 1976 and the Tripartite Declaration on Multinational Corporations adopted by the ILO in 1977. Such legislation could usefully address itself to issues like the regulation of the business activities of MNCs, the enforcement of conformity of the activities of these enterprises with national development plans and objectives, the regulation of profit transfers out of host countries, the promotion of reinvestment of profits in host countries, etc.

Legislative measures should be reinforced by bilateral and multilateral industrial cooperation agreements between the governments of developed and developing countries that would reduce the MNCs control over international trade and the transfer of technology by bypassing them in favor of more direct cooperation in both these areas, based on considerations of solidarity.

Developing countries themselves must take steps to improve their bargaining position in regard to the MNCs through the pursuit of policies of collective self-reliance based on Third World solidarity. There is considerable potential for building up a credible confrontation deterrent through the development of a common Third World front (or trade union) in three areas (i.e., in their respective capacities as exporters, importers, and hosts of MNCs). Joint policies in all three areas would enable developing countries to take a firm stand with regard to their access to international markets and technological developments and would improve their bargaining power vis-à-vis the MNCs and so improve their control over the exploitation of their national resources.

In addition, economic and technological cooperation among the developing countries themselves will facilitate the development of indigenous appropriate technologies and open up new markets for Third World products. This in turn will enable them to build up flexible and innovative industrial enterprises that can compete with the MNCs on the local markets, especially where development strategies are oriented towards the creation of employment and the satisfaction of basic needs.

However, the positive role the MNCs could play in the economic development of developing countries and the promotion of their employment creation policies cannot be overlooked. In all fairness, it must be noted that at least some of these enterprises are willing to operate under strict controls, as long as the rules that govern their behavior remain stable. It is, therefore, in the interests of the developing countries to provide these companies with a stable legal framework in which they can operate.

For their part, MNCs must take steps to reduce the tensions that presently exist between them and their host countries by subjecting their short-term profit maximization to the long-term development needs of the host countries. This would include fitting their own activities into the development plans of the Third World countries by contributing to the development of national and scientific technologies, by increasing employment opportunities and standards in these countries in consultation with national unions and employers' organizations, by promoting local processing of raw materials, by policies of subcontracting for intermediate goods and services, by the use of labor-intensive technologies where possible, and by the adoption of skill formation and vocational guidance programmes for local personnel at all levels.

In sum, if the MNCs can be brought to see that such policies of good citizenship are to their own long-term advantage, there is considerable potential for the pursuit of complementary activities on their own part and on that of the developing countries.

A POSSIBLE PLAN OF ACTION

In general terms a realistic approach to the implementation of action in all these areas in the context of the new order must recognize the existence of very real problems of adjustments to changes, especially in the developed countries. In a situation of redistribution of international assets, it is inevitable that certain sections of the population are disadvantaged and are likely to resist such changes. The fact that these groups are usually well organized and powerful elites and pressure groups constitutes a major obstacle to the generation of the international political will necessary for the implementation of international action to promote a new order.

However, given the fact that problems (such as those of employment and income security) do exist in the developed, as well as the developing world, the situation of the sectors and the people who will, in the short run, be adversely affected by the implementation of a new order cannot be ignored any more than the common, long-term benefits to all people can be subordinated to their short-term interests. Policies for the implementation of the new order must be so conceived as to allow for the short-term adjustment of these sectoral problems, as well as for the long-term amelioration of the situation of the world's poorest peoples.

In practice the reconciliation of the conflicting interests of the various groups of people affected by the implementation of this strategy means that the new order should be based on a three-point plan of action:

1. concerted action by all nations based on the concept of world solidarity
2. the phased introduction of the new order
3. the active participation of the masses in development

Concerted Action Based on World Solidarity

The need to reconcile the conflicting interests of the parties involved in the implementation of a new order based on the more equitable distribution of economic opportunity, wealth, and power calls for the provision of an international framework for discussion and negotiation.

The present crisis in international political and economic relations has its roots in the colonial past of the majority of the Third World nations. Based on patterns of dependence, domination, and exploitation, colonialism and neocolonialism have led to the perpetuation of inequalities in the international arena. On the economic level these are manifested in an unequal distribution of economic activity and of the income derived from it, and on a political level in the exclusion of the developing countries from participating in most of the decisions that affect their economic future. A new international order that intends to rectify these inequalities must therefore address itself to changing present structures through "a process of give and take, an element of collective bargaining"(18) - in short, negotiation.

Equitable negotiations between the parties involved in the formulation and implementation of a new international economic order call for the global harmonization of international goals and policies and the fostering of a sense of solidarity among nations. The beginnings of such a sense of solidarity and harmony can already be perceived in the present dawning recognition of the fact that both the developed and the developing nations are being increasingly confronted by common problems that necessitate joint action in pursuit of shared goals. As has been noted earlier, equitable trade relationships, the development of appropriate market structures and mechanisms for the transfer of technology, the creation of employment, and the satisfaction of human needs are all fruitful fields for negotiation and common action based on the concept of global solidarity.

As a strategy for the implementation of a new order, such solidarity is at its most effective when it derives from a sense of mutual responsibility and the commitment, on the part of the negotiating parties, to a specified contractual obligation. The attraction of such contracts based on "active solidarity" is that they are "the results of equitable negotiations and do away with the distinction between helpers and helped since they imply participation, under conditions of legal equality, of the parties to the arrangement, on the basis of the sharing of a common task."(19)

Contracts of solidarity must therefore be seriously considered as a viable alternative in any attempt to find new forms through which to give international cooperation the new direction and content that would ensure that the prosperity of some countries are not achieved to the detriment of the others and that would foster the "awareness of belonging to one world . . . and sharing a common destiny."

The Phased Introduction of the New Order

Given the failure of previous development strategies to address themselves effectively to the questions of changing existing economic and political structures so as to ensure the more equitable distribution of international assets and resources, despite the apparent willingness of the international community to do so, the planners of a new order must obviously explore other ways of achieving this goal.

In this context it is essential to remember that support of resolutions in international forums does not necessarily constitute more than an ideological commitment to their general principles. Faced with the realities of political opposition from powerful lobbies of the groups most likely to be adversely affected by measures for the implementation of such principles, political leadership in developed - and developing - countries might well be constrained to avoid taking any decisive action on them. In many cases, too, the general nature of these resolutions renders them unworkable in their present form, thus reducing them to the status of slogans rather than desired and practically implementable goals.

An essential strategy for the implementation of a new international economic order is, therefore, the formulation of realistic and manageable subgoals that could be implemented one by one in order of priority until the desired global situation is ultimately achieved. In the field of trade, for example, wide-range demands for immediate and total access to developed country markets are much less likely to succeed than systematic negotiations on conditions of access.

In addition, such a step-by-step approach to the implementation of the goals of a new order would facilitate the swift identification and attenuation of the negative social effects of such action. For example, the gradual realization of the geographical redistribution of industries would allow the developed countries ample time to adjust their own economic policies accordingly and to institute programmes of adjustment assistance for those groups of their workers adversely affected by the changes this necessitates. Such an approach would be much less likely to generate strong opposition in the developed countries and would thus facilitate the final implementation of the various goals of a new order.

A step-by-step approach to international development would also allow for the orderly identification of objectives, the setting of priorities, and the preservation of a necessary degree of flexibility in relation to the choice of strategies. If developmental plans are to remain realistic and to achieve optimal success in all areas, the constant evaluation and revision of their goals and strategies are essential. Such a policy will pinpoint the shortcomings and unintended social consequences of chosen strategies and will facilitate their immediate correction, as well as the reformulation of priorities and subgoals to meet changing needs and situations.

In sum, the phased implementation of the new order, characterized by a high degree of flexibility, cooperation, and solidarity, will undoubtedly facilitate the negotiated implementation of a politically and economically feasible agenda of international action.

The Active Participation of the Masses
in Development

In 1973 the participants at the Algiers Conference noted that structural changes undertaken in the context of a new international economic order would call for the conscious, democratic participation of the popular masses as a decisive element in any effort to implement the dynamic, effective, and independent development of nations. At the international level, too, the participation of all nations on terms of equality is vital to the successful implementation of a new order.

At the national level, the participation of various social institutions and target populations in decision making at various levels and stages is crucial to the formulation and implementation of realistic goals and strategies oriented towards the creation of employment and the meeting of human needs.

The participation of interested social groups at the preparation stage of national (and indeed international) development plans and strategies is invaluable because it places a wealth of information at the disposal of the planners, enabling them to formulate realistic objectives more in tune with the needs and aspirations of the target groups. Such participation also makes for greater cooperation in the implementation of the provisions of development plans insofar as shared decisions are better understood and more easily identified with than unilateral ones. In addition, the inclusion of various groups with conflicting interests in the formulation of development plans and strategies will ensure that their final provisions comprise an aggregate of interests and make adequate provisions to ease the situation of the "losers" in the process - especially at the international level. This would both ensure the general acceptability of the various elements of development strategies and reduce the possibility of conflict at the implementation stage.

Again at the national level, participation is crucial to endogenous development because it ensures the mobilization of popular interest in development issues, the exploitation of the people's latent energies and creativity, and the best possible use of local resources, including manpower. People involved in the formulation of strategies clearly beneficial to themselves would certainly be more willing to involve themselves in the implementation of these strategies in a spirit of self-reliance and solidarity.

Participation in development must be facilitated by bringing decision-making centers closer to their popular bases. This can be done through the creation and encouragement of various responsible and representative institutions such as trade unions, employers' organizations, rural cooperatives, and peasant organizations to serve as mechanisms for active involvement and self-expression. The successful working of the ILO's tripartite structure is adequate proof of the viability of such processes at both the national and the international level.

Since the early years of the present decade, increasing numbers of people have been demanding the right to participate at both national and international levels in drawing up the rules that govern the global community. Consequently the future society being formed by the new international economic order will be based on the principles of collective negotiation and world solidarity.

CONCLUSIONS

To sum up, it is essential that political leaders recognize that a world in which every nation exercises its power to attain its own ends, even at the expense of other nations in the international community, is a world characterized by conflict. Given the increasing interdependence of nations and the long-term mutuality of their interests, it is a matter of common concern to all nations to formulate and implement a new international economic – and social – order.

Given the fact that the present crisis in international relations is caused by imbalances in the distribution of international resources, assets, and wealth, redressing these inequalities is a vital element in any new order. This can be achieved, at least in part, by changing existing market structures, trade links, and the international division of labor in favor of the developing countries, by revising the terms for the more adequate transfer of technology to them, and by establishing mechanisms for the promotion of cooperation among nations. The promotion of the economic and social development of the Third World nations is not merely an expression of international solidarity. It is also a vehicle for promoting growth in all countries and so ensuring global prosperity and the satisfaction of the fundamental needs of all people.

NOTES

(1) "Basic Needs: An Issues Paper" (Policy Planning and Programme Review Department, World Bank, March 12, 1977), quoted in John McHale and Magda Cordell McHale, Basic Human Needs: A Framework for Action (New Brunswick: Transaction Books, 1977), p. 9.

(2) Jan Tinbergen et al., Reshaping the International Order: A Report to the Club of Rome (New York: E.P. Dutton and Co., 1976), p. 63.

(3) Ibid., p. 63.

(4) International Labor Office, Employment, Growth and Basic Needs. A One World Problem (Geneva: ILO, 1976), pp. 21, 22.

(5) Mahbub ul Haq, "Into Phase Two: The Next Critical Step," International Development Review 2 (1978): 7.

(6) The Lima Declaration and Plan of Action on Industrial Development and Cooperation, March 1975.

(7) Mahbub ul Haq, p. 10.

(8) John W. Sewell, "Can the Rich Prosper Without the Progress of the Poor?" International Development Review 2 (1978): 18.

(9) Ibid., p. 17.

(10) ILO, p. 113.

(11) Ibid., p. 114.

(12) Ibid., P. 113.

(13) UNCTAD IV, Resolution on Adjustment Assistance Measures, May 1976.

(14) ILO, p. 120.

(15) Resolution on Development and Economic Cooperation, September, 1975 (A/RES/3362 (S-VII)).

(16) Working Group on Technical Cooperation Among Developing Countries (TCDC), Report on the Third Session, May 1974 (DP/69).

(17) ILO, p. 157.

(18) Tinbergen et al., p. 179.

(19) Eugene Chossudovsky, "The Concept of World Solidarity and its Role in the Restructuring of the International System," Labour and Society 3, Nos. 3-4 (July/October 1978): 289.

2 Education and the NIEO

Porfirio Muñoz-Ledo

Education is an area which very sharply reflects international inequality. Any kind of national or regional analysis of the figures and trends dealing with access to education, as well as the real expectations of social progress brought about by it, leads us to alarming conclusions.

In the short and medium term, there is practically no solution to the problem of the availability of educational resources to the less developed countries, resources that are indispensable to the expansion and improvement of the educational systems, and which are related to the needs arising from demographic growth, modernization, and aspirations towards general well-being.

Research reveals that in the low-income countries the educational systems are very poorly equipped to meet the objectives that justify their existence, that is, homogeneity and social equity, the creation of endogenous development models, the affirmation of national cultures, as well as the large-scale promotion of policies oriented towards individual and collective change.

The majority of the studies indicate the following principal problems: the intergenerational transmission of inequalities, submission to external cultural centers, and an indirect contribution to the concentration of wealth due to the influence exerted by the educational systems with respect to the prosperity of the productive enclaves and the availability of a cheap, semiliterate and poorly qualified labor force.

The United Nations Educational, Social, and Cultural Organization (UNESCO) has confirmed that, since the beginning of the 1970s, the expansion rate of schooling in the developing countries has lowered considerably. It is thus felt that if these present trends continue, educational inequalities will become quantitatively and qualitatively greater. We must not be deceived by the general advancements observed in schooling in previous decades, since the differences between the regions of greater and lesser development still remain and are even on the increase.

To understand the seriousness of such problems, it is sufficient to consider that in Latin America 25 percent of the population is without schools. In Asia the figure reaches 35 percent and in Africa 55 percent. These statistics do not include the very low schooling standards among the adult population of these regions, standards that have remained practically static.

The problem is evidently structural and is linked with the development process in its entirety. In spite of the fact that in the short space of 20 years, world education investment multiplied ninefold and the efforts of the least developed countries to direct growing amounts of public spending to that goal were considerable, at present, there still exist some 300 million children without schooling. For those who enjoy education in the Third World, only 9 percent of the global budget is alloted to that purpose.

While demographic growth and common fiscal narrow-mindedness hinder educational expansion in the developing countries, the standard of studies lowers for want of re-sources. At present, a student from the underdeveloped area receives – on average and in monetary terms – ten times less than one from an industrial society.

Educational backwardness accumulated in the less developed countries will have a strong bearing on the shape of their labor forces until the end of the century at least. The prospects for the present and future young population are no more gratifying. It is estimated that during the next decade in the poor countries the age group between 15 and 20 will increase in number to approximately 250 million persons. On the other hand, in the industrialized countries, the population of that same age group will gradually decrease during the same period.

Even if the resources allocated to educational demand were to be maintained at the present volume inequality between the developing world and industrial society nonetheless would still increase. Furthermore, it is unlikely that budget in-creases for education in the less developed countries will exceed the percentage of public expenditure already allocated to this sector. The relation between public expenditure and the gross national product is thus modified very slowly.

On the other hand, private educational investments are clearly oriented towards the middle- and high-income sectors, while the dominant groups implement the media to generally strengthen the modern sectors, their ideology, and the pro-duction and consumption models most favored by them.

Beyond this we can observe the educational differences between countries reproduced on a large scale and in varying forms within the less developed countries. The transformations carried out in the first stages of industrialization and correlative urban growth have encouraged the demands of the emerging classes and thus the expansion of secondary and higher education.

In addition, the need for high specialization which generally comes from imitative technological transfer, determines the allocation of a significant portion of available public and private resources to the education of the higher income groups.

In this way, a social structure based on inequality tends towards a strengthening of its position, in which a minority enjoys modern information and training systems - national and foreign - while the great majority begin work at a premature age and suffer further marginality. Finally, a sharp dichotomy is established between the cultural forms and substances pertaining to each level as well as between the values divulged through the media and those sustained precariously and at times heroically in the school.

It would seem that an insurmountable obstacle impedes the carrying out of values which have inspired the extension of the educational process since its secularization. For more than two centuries, we have believed that the progress of the human spirit, through the diffusion of knowledge, would lead to equality and widespread advancement. The legitimacy of the democratic regimes was founded on the capacity of their educational systems to integrate the national states and form civil societies of large-scale participation.

On another level, it also seems that the period of influence begun 25 years ago has reached exhaustion point. This period sought to set up links between education and development. During these years, eager efforts were made to revalue the importance of educational investment within the national programmes so as to generate global strategies which would change the priorities characteristic of "developmentism," the fundamental ideas of these strategies being the policies of employment and the expansion of human resources.

Contrary to these theses, present trends show that progress continues to be based on material growth and not on the development of the creative possibilities of the population. This has accentuated rather than alleviated income concentration, unemployment, and economic dependence.

It is clear that the main obstacle to the expansion and improvement of the educational systems is financial. A simple explanation arises from the analysis of the low per capita incomes if we take into consideration that only a small percentage of the national income corresponding to each individual comes back in the form of educational services through public spending.

Thus considered, the problem is insoluble within the traditional frameworks of market societies at least in the first stages of capital accumulation. Due to the poor development of economic forces and economic growth models that have favored the most modern sectors for a long time, a broad-based democratic educational process does not seem attainable.

The aggravation of inequalities fomented by this phenomenon prevents, in its turn, a substantial rise in productive capacities and participation aptitude, factors that would make the acceleration of progress or the change of model possible. A clear example of the vicious circle of underdevelopment is thus established.

For this reason, the educational question is essentially ideological. Any educational project expresses a political decision and corresponds to a development model adopted implicitly or explicitly by society. The importance given to education does not, strictly speaking, come from its financial or operative viability. Rather, the opposite is true.

The industrialized and socialist countries postulate - from different approaches - a highly participatory society. This involves widespread productivity, the absorption of marginal sectors, and a considerable degree of social cohesion and scientific and technological creativity.

Unfortunately, in most less developed countries, the emphasis on social participation does not seem to enter the logic of the prevailing systems. We should, of course, acknowledge some limited efforts - at important moments - be they induced from the outside during the final phases of decolonization or generated from within the most intense stages of political change.

The so-called theory of concentric circles, according to which development implies a gradual diffusion of property and a progressive incorporation of the social levels into the benefits of modernization, inevitably reduces the task of education to a secondary plane.

Contrary to the fundamental theoretical principles of education that come to us from learned thought, civil society, within this framework, is the result not of integration but of exclusion. More exactly, civil society and its ambitions of real and formal freedoms are restricted to the sectors effectively participating in modernity. The prosperity of these sectors in turn relies on the existence of a dual society and processes that are commonly summed up in the expression "internal colonialism" and which imply the abundance of a poorly paid labor force and the political demobilization of dependent social groups.

The global development model preponderantly determines the scale of social priorities and the role actually played by education as a factor of immobility or change. The problem, however, is less simple. Even with the acknowledgement of education's reproductive role with respect to the existing social structure, it is undoubtable that every system brings with it evolutionary ferments that contribute to its self-preservation, as well as trends toward radical transformation that dialectically oppose such a preservation.

A dual society is not, in effect, an express proposal of the system. It is, rather, a structural reality that prevents the attainment of the objectives proposed, at least formally, by that system. What is more, it would be impossible to keep the set of social relations static, even through highly repressive political methods.

Demographic expansion, the expectations of the rising social classes, the influence of the mass media, the transfer of the rural population to the city, and the exigencies of the modern sector generate demands such that if on the one hand they overflow into the educational systems, they also oblige them to grow and be modified.

It is paradoxical that the educational systems in the developing countries are generally more complicated than those in the more advanced and integrated countries. We frequently encounter an intricate web of institutions and educational mechanisms that reflect, even to the point of caricature, the juxtaposition of forms, the diversity of demands, and the coexistence of social levels and historical ages that characterize the Third World.

This dispersion of efforts, almost always unfinished and poorly efficient, increases the scarcity of resources and unmasks the depth of the problem: the impossibility of a reasonably homogeneous educational system that would bring about the formation of a model citizen, when structural limitations impede the adaptation of formal education to a heterogeneous society.

Such adaptation processes unfortunately do not imply the acknowledgement of the values that the cultural plurality contains. The underestimation of autochthonous cultures is frequent as is the clear predominance of the methods that tend towards a superficial incorporation into the dominant culture. This culture's sole contribution is to strengthen exploitation mechanisms. Also well known is the growing division between different popular cultural forms and the formal schemes diffused by schooling.

All this deepens functional illiteracy and cancels the possibility of finding endogenous solutions to social problems since it converts the marginal sectors - to which most students belong - into mere receivers of cultural instruments. It also annuls, rather than promotes, the development of their creative potentials. The existence of only one scholastic language hides the subsistence of diverse real languages, which, since they cannot be fully expressed nor articulated one with the other, leads to frustration.

A more subtle although no less important phenomenon, appreciated within our educational systems, is the contradiction persisting between the values sustained by education and those society actually lives: the antimony between the democratic discourse divulged and the real inequality and marginality experienced.

While the reiteration of traditional scholastic messages is no substitute for the development of social conscience and the will to change, the dichotomy of languages will continue to sharpen. In this way, formal education will fatally strengthen the dual structure of societies in which some diffuse what they scarcely believe and others passively receive what they know is not true. This essential lack of credibility annuls the integrating purpose of education at its foundations.

On another plane, our educational systems usually become distorted by the imperatives of demand. The authentic needs of the people are thus forgotten. In spite of their apparent dynamism or their eventual quantitative growth, these systems sharpen their reproductive character and diminish their contribution to social change.

It is enough to point out the disordered growth of higher education, the concentration of resources in urban zones, and the high rate of school absenteeism, for us to confirm that the educational processes are more obedient to the contradictions of an unequal society than to the rational projects of individual and collective liberation.

The apparently reformist procedures that attempt to put education at the service of development frequently result in its adaptation to the reality of underdevelopment. For example, the excessive stress put on the premature specialization of students, in detriment to certain formative aspects; increases rather than bridges the gap between the worlds of education and employment. This limits the occupational mobility intended by progress and the scientific and technological advances this progress ought to foment.

In the same way, priority efforts are directed to favoring general elementary education, in countries where the initial development stages have already been surpassed. Thus goals that are actually retrogressive are put forward as being ambitious. To pretend that an educational system is substantially democratized so as to offer all students five or six years of schooling and then send them out into the social world poorly prepared – at the end of childhood or on the threshold of adolescence – is the same as dangerously prolonging the actual suppositions on which underdevelopment is based.

The weakness of most educational efforts, as well as the obstacles faced by the most enthusiastic strategies of recent decades, contribute to a climate of frustration. The general impotence with respect to the objectives to be attained has given rise to a regressive literature that questions education's influence on development.

We insist that educational expansion does not necessarily mean its democratization, since different factors - among which the cultural environment and the economic status are prominent - are determinant inasmuch as the improvement within the schooling system notably favors the upper classes, even in the most advanced countries.

To this we may add the weakening of the role that the schooling standard plays in social reclassification. According to numerous analyses, the family origin of students continues to be a preferential factor with respect to their future employment. This phenomenon contributes to so-called educational stagflation (expansion of schooling facilities and the diminution of employment possibilities) and to the negative effects it has, particularly on the lower income sectors. It also provokes a strangling effect in the tertiary sector, whose expansion no longer stems from the industrialization process but from excess in the supply of the urban labor force.

Other studies underline the insufficiency of the educational systems to promote the change of social behavior and cultural patterns. In conclusion, they state that it is difficult for education to go beyond a servile function with respect to the existing systems. It has thus failed in its essential purpose: to encourage the evolution of the mentalities and forms of social life.

In the final analysis, this current trend reveals the insufficiency of traditional schooling and the urgent need for more innovative attitudes with respect to the educational process. The historical influence obtained by the accumulation and diffusion of knowledge cannot be denied. On the levels of productivity and scientific advancement attained by the industrialized societies, such progress would be unthinkable without the previous substantial development achieved by education.

What is also suggested - except in periods of crisis or revolutionary transformation - is the fact that the capacity for a global and energetic educational action to increase capabilities and transform behavioral guidelines has hardly been put to the test. It is not even possible to conceive of a desirable social structure that has not been preceded and accompanied by a liberation effort in the spheres of knowledge and moral awareness.

In education, what is actually at work is the desired social model and its viability. To affirm that the serious educational insufficiencies of most peoples are none other than the reflection of their degree of development, or one of its components, is to avoid the problem. In fact, world and national attitudes with regard to the impulse that should be given to education and employment delimit the frontier between a development-oriented policy and one that prolongs domination and inequality.

The solutions put forward are many and complementary. Nevertheless, their grade of efficiency depends on the extent to which they are committed to the transformation of other social spheres. The action of the educational authorities and the teaching profession alone are reduced almost to impotence due to the disproportion between the resources at their disposal and the challenge they face.

To summarize the different proposals made on a theoretical and practical level to reform education implies the consideration of different degrees of political commitment that the proposals entail. Such proposals range from those that mainly have confidence in the traditional role of schooling to others that involve the radical transformation of society.

First, we find the so-called progressive schemes, stemming from the most prestigious theses of the previous decades, above all those made fashionable by educational economy. According to these schemes, efforts should be made to give education a higher priority among the state's policies. These schemes maintain that only through the expansion and improvement of public schooling can differences be lessened. The defense of their programmes is based on the undeniable influence obtained by the formation of human capital in economic development. They propose the most rapid and balanced possible growth for the educational systems, from the pre-school level to higher education.

Their ideals are classical: homogeneity and social ascent through education. Their strategies are new: They put the stress on pedagogical innovation and administrative efficiency. To gain the state's confidence, they carry out productivity projects that are often sophisticated. Evaluation, experimentation, administration through objectives, rational budgeting, and vigilance of schooling yields are all predominant themes due to the objective need to optimally benefit from limited resources and because of the argumentative value of these themes when confronted with those who define the priorities of public spending.

In their ambitious hypotheses, these projects require greater attention to education as a whole and to each of its specific areas. Nevertheless, on certain educational levels, they frequently accept a reduction in their plans or the adoption of transitory campaigns that weaken the general purpose of schooling. Thus the approach is not only limited in its original scope but often yields to the rigid policies of the national treasury motivated by political priorities.

A second, newer school of thought may be defined as globalist. Within this perspective the task of education cannot be reduced to the traditional role of schooling. The reasons are broad-based and categorical. It puts forward the mobilization of resources that could be used by society to complement and enrich schooling. The themes favored within this approach include open education, technical training, extrascholastic culture, community development, social services for the young, and intensive use of the mass media in the service of educational objectives.

When some of these methods are adopted so as to systematically substitute the imperative of extending schooling, then they become dangerous. They camouflage the purpose of reducing educational spending by using the pretext of modernity. What is gained in extension is lost in depth. The true globalist strategy presupposes the fulfillment of the above, and it seeks to multiply rather than supplant the influence of schooling. The strategy is not seen as an emergency solution, but rather as one of political congruency.

The principal advantage of this approach is the attempt to link the cultural environment of schools with that of society. It also tends to diminish the difference of languages through permanent education that takes place in everyone, before and after the periods and hours of schooling. What is more, it makes education, the responsibility not only of the teaching profession, but also of society as a whole.

All in all, carrying out the global programmes has been very poor in relation to its possibilities. These programmes require a political will, a level of political awareness, and an articulation of social commitment that do not appear to be coincidental with the scale of priorities and the play of predominant interests within the developing world.

Third, there is talk of structuralist solutions. All these solutions start from the following hypothesis: Education, aside from other social transformations, faces irreparable limitations for the carrying out of its goals. Instead of contributing to improving income distribution, it usually furthers existing inequality.

There are different forms of structuralist theory, according to the levels of social change sought after. The most modern proponents - called functionalists - do not speak of the modification of the economic system, but rather of its adjustment. Their theses have been partially applied in some relatively less developed countries and have frequently found inspiration in ILO studies, from which methods have arisen to link production systems, employment policies, and education models.

In addition to these essays, in our days there is an abundance of progressive literature - theoretical and party oriented - that uncovers the inability of the present systems to promote a democratic educational system. According to this literature, the values implicit in the task of education demand a revolutionary action that would substantially modify class relations. Education is thus at the service of a more ambitious project of an eminently political nature. This project will bring about the fulfillment of the goals of education.

With similar suppositions in mind, yet involving different methodological approaches, the radical theories of education have won recent renown. Their common denominator is a critical and often destructive attitude towards schooling itself and toward traditional education procedures.

The differences between political and economic regimes are no longer clearly defined. In one way or another, all are seen as insufficient for total liberation. Thus the educational action promoted by these radical theories is alienating since it is oriented towards strengthening a structure of power and oppression.

While some voice the advantages of educational processes void of school curricula, in which the individual is educated through work and community life, others defend the benefits to be had from the direct transmission of knowledge and the different forms of liberating education carried on outside of and even in opposition to the school system.

The pedagogical discoveries contained in these theses are frequently valuable. However, they are obviously inapplicable in their totality unless a radical change in society takes place. Otherwise, they would lead to a polarization between new methods and old institutions. This could foment possible revolutions yet would be of little service in integrating educational projects to take in the action of the public powers and social agencies still existing in most countries.

No matter what innovative methods are adopted, the need to grant the highest possible priority to the equality of opportunities in schooling promotion is beyond question. In the same way, there exists the need to obtain the decisive participation of the community in the educational task, as well as to establish methods and subject matter that promote change, and to relate these processes to reforms introduced in other areas of economic life and social organization.

Any important solution implies an objective of general transformation. It implies the cancellation of strategies according to which access to well-being is a derivative and gradual process, since such a process has already revealed evident signs of stagnation and even backwardness. Any important solution demands the search for new development alternatives.

If the prevailing models are to continue indefinitely, there is the risk that acute national and international differences will become greater during future decades. Dual societies characteristic of underdevelopment will be reaffirmed, with elitist groups linked to foreign power centers and the presence of large marginalized masses. This would perhaps inevitably lead to the generalization of authoritarian political systems.

If within every country, education at the service of development implies important modifications in ideological conceptions and in the correlation of forces, on the world level exactly the same phenomenon occurs. Education understood as a promoter of equality and a permanent guarantee of peace today demands a revision of the true political objectives of contemporary society. It is thus intimately related to the new international order.

On the one hand, education suggests a considerable broadening of different areas of international cooperation that until now have been frankly precarious. It would be convenient to reexamine, for example, old proposals related to the transfer of resources directed to armament and to consider the economic and human development of the less developed countries.

This was one of the preferential themes during the first years of UNESCO, when it was outlined that two clearly different alternatives faced humanity: postwar surpluses directed either to the arms race or to the educational transformation of countries. The result can be seen in the statistics. In spite of educational expansion in recent decades, the global amount of public resources allocated to such expansion still does not surpass world armament expenditure.

This question is also closely linked to scientific and technological cooperation. The conditions for such cooperation require the priority participation of the educational institutions, thus bringing about the effective contribution of this cooperation to development, and not solely strengthening the position of the nuclei that make up the transnational economy. Such participation implies the development of high-level research and teaching centers and the support offered by education in the formation and diffusion tasks directed to the whole of society. The scientific evolution of countries is inseparable from their ability to reform education.

Similarly, the exchange and adaptation on a large scale of educational experiences and instruments must be encouraged. The field is vast and has hardly been explored. It is enough to consider the existing quantity of audiovisual equipment and printed material and the possibility of reproducing and distributing it worldwide through financing systems based on equitable cooperation.

Exchanges among countries with similar development levels would also be highly beneficial, countries to which specific international aid could be allocated. In the long term, this would also be a suitable way to strengthen their solidarity.

Furthermore, the fortune of education is indissolubly linked with the new order, since only through carrying out its principles is such an order viable. It is impossible to conceive of substantial progress in democratization without important modifications in the present structure of international relations.

While present trends continue, the concentration of resources in the poles of greater wealth will be accentuated,

and this on a national and international plane. Thus, the
stability of the dominant models will demand, as a counterpart,
the permanence of social imbalances and the preservation of
dependent relations.

The enormous change facing education - on which the
society of the future depends - is thus conditioned by a series
of political wills. If the present correlation of forces does not
bring about a reasonable attainment of the objectives of education, then other roads will have to be looked to for its
realization, roads that are far from entering into these discussions.

3 The NIEO and the Learning Processes of Society

Mircea Malitza
Ana Maria Sandi

THE HUMAN FACTOR IN THE NIEO DEBATE

In recent years, the New International Economic Order (NIEO) has come to stand for a vast program aimed at developing profound changes in the contemporary world. A gradual widening of the range of issues dealt with in the frame of the NIEO debate can be noticed.

The core demands of the developing countries were initially oriented towards economic measures aiming mainly at correcting the inequitable terms of trade that were constantly disadvantageous for the producers of raw materials and commodities, playing to the advantage of the producers of processed goods.

The Declaration and the Program of Action adopted at the Sixth Special Session of the UN General Assembly (April 9-May 2, 1974, in New York) aimed at achieving profound changes in international economic relations; for example, a

> just and equitable relationship between the price of . . . goods exported by developing countries and the prices of . . . [goods] imported by them with the aim of bringing about sustained improvement in their unsatisfactory terms of trade and the expansion of the world economy.(1)

At UNCTAD, debates are under way to find ways to encourage development that would lead to narrowing and abolishing the anachronistic and intolerable existing economic gaps.

However, in a broader sense, it has been admitted that NIEO also requires the restructuring of political relations

41

among states based on the principles stated by international
law, the first among them being independence, sovereignty,
equal rights, noninterference in domestic affairs, and nonuse
of force or threat with force.

Romania has adopted in unequivocal terms the stand of
thorough acknowledgement and implementation of the principles
of international relations.   In the words of Romanian President
Nicolae Ceauşescu,

> Along with the other nations, with the progressive
> forces in the world, Romania is strongly supporting
> the establishment of a new international economic
> order, based on full equality and equity, which
> would favor a more rapid progress of the states,
> especially of those lagging behind and enable the
> large and unrestricted access to the latest achieve-
> ments of modern science and technology, of the
> contemporary civilization.(2)

Besides its political dimension, NIEO reveals also a social
one.   Developing countries have important tasks in achieving a
more equitable distribution of the national income.   "To neglect
equity and welfare ultimately damages efficiency and development."(3)

As stated in the developing countries' declaration from
Mexico (1975), "Reforms of the international order will be
meaningless and even impossible without corresponding reforms
in the frame of the domestic order."

Emphasizing the orientation towards the satisfaction of
basic needs, the Reshaping the International Order (R.I.O.)
report says that

> we must be concerned with identifying minimal needs
> capable of guaranteeing a meaningful existence and,
> after defining them, to become sure that they become
> the right of hundreds of millions of people living at
> present below the level of these needs.(4)

Thus the new order emerges as a restructuring of existing institutions, both at the international and at the domestic level, and of existing relations, leading to new norms,
values, and attitudes.

Several important debates organized by UNESCO have
explored yet another dimension of NIEO; the cultural one.   As
stated during the Round Table on Cultural and Intellectual
Cooperation and NIEO (UNESCO, June 23-25, 1977), "Culture
is the key factor for the identity of a nation, asserting the
personality in the cultural field being of the same value as
declaring the independence and sovereignty in the political
field."

It is worth noting that the cultural components of NIEO cover a much wider range than the common subjects of training, access to new technologies, and provision of scientific centers for developing countries - subjects already included in many investigations.

Culture reveals itself as the very laboratory where values, essential for decision making and for choosing an individual path, are set up. The way of living and thinking bears the stamp of various value scales. Their variety is not an alarming reason but on the contrary, a precious resource for solving global problems. Respect for cultural identity, diversity and personality, and dialogue and communication are necessary conditions of a constructive climate in which each people builds its development strategy according to its own conditions, history, and aspirations.

Recently, the UN General Assembly adopted by consensus three resolutions concerning the new informational world order in the interest of peace and mutual understanding. One of the resolutions expresses

> the necessity of establishing a new world order in the field of international information and communications in order to consolidate peace and international understanding; the new world order should be based on free circulation and broader and more balanced diffusion of informations.

Thus NIEO, which had started from material considerations, by including at the beginning the external factors of life, is now acquiring a wider scope and a more accurate and complete picture by dealing with human and cultural factors.

In fact these factors are not included with a view to describing different phenomena - an economic one, a political, a social, a cultural one - but rather for asserting different approaches to the same widespread contemporary process. And with each step, the tendency for a broader involvement of the human factor is ever more conspicuous.

The same evolution is to be seen in another field belonging to nongovernmental research. No longer than a decade ago, an unusual kind of research began to develop: global modeling. By using analytical and systematic methods, these models helped the debate upon the main trends in economy and social life.

Global modeling was not left completely outside the NIEO problematique. Some evidence is given by the discussion of six global models(5) at the UN General Assembly in 1977(6) and the elaboration, at the UN initiative, of the Leontief economic model.

Moreover, two global models, RIO and the Latin American model, started from the assumption of setting up a new international economic order. It is worth emphasizing that in the development of those models, the same orientation can be found as in the evolution of the NIEO concept, namely, including the human factor in an equation that already covered natural resources, population, industrialization, energy, food, ecology, and urbanization.

The same tendency appears in the selection of topics for debate for the UN global conferences. The list includes along with development, food, oceans, habitat, and industrialization, the discussion of several social problems: women (1975), employment (1976), and children (1979). Therefore, the guideline of the present paper is the human perspective on the major problems facing mankind.

THE HUMAN FACTOR AND THE LEARNING PROCESSES

Alternative Modalities for Including the Human Factor

There are several trends of investigation in which the human element is included in the debate of the global problématique, in search of viable and realistic solutions. A great deal of research starts from the basic human needs. The Latin American world model is based on the premise that "in the new society the production system has the satisfaction of basic human needs as its main objective." Looking for the major problems facing society, the authors state that the main obstacles are not physical but sociopolitical.

Another trend of thinking investigates values and ways of life, considering values the clue to understanding and solving the problems facing mankind. The World Order Models Project (WOMP/USA) specifies a preferred world in the light of four specific and explicit values:

1. the minimization of large-scale collective violence
2. the maximization of social and economic well-being
3. the realization of fundamental human rights and conditions of political justice
4. the rehabilitation and maintenance of environmental quality, including the conservation of resources(7)

An important trend is to consider the goals of different societies as starting points, due to the fact that the existence of a goal is an essential human characteristic. In the report to the Club of Rome, "Goals for Mankind," an assessment is made of a variety of global goals, in search of those most appropriate for the present situation of mankind.(8)

The international project "Goals, processes and indicators for development," sponsored by UNU has also started its research both from goals and from basic needs. Other proposals suggested the use of the human rights concept for including the human factor in the NIEO debate.

The present investigation starts from the assumption that another useful approach for including the human factor in the debate of the world problématique would be the introduction of processes specific both to individuals and societies - namely, the learning processes.(9)

Why Learning Processes?

There are seven strong reasons that favor the learning approach to the key NIEO issues:

1. Learning is a characteristic phenomenon of the human universe, a process with respect to which all people assert their equality, thus pointing to the fundamental statement on which NIEO is based.

2. By defining learning as the development of competence for action in new situations, NIEO emerges as essentially a learning process of unprecedented proportions. The very nature of the new order is the acquisition and development of a new set of answers for dealing with new economic, political, social, and cultural situations. Thus the emphasis is mainly on action based on competence and not on performances. All the key issues of NIEO rely ultimately on human competence, on the capacity of people to deal with problems. This capacity is only partly assured by formal education. Schooling, with all its extension, is too narrow a frame for the discussion of learning processes which are lifelong.

3. All the previous approaches that start from needs, goals, values, and rights are implied by the present one. As we learn to recognize basic needs, we learn to assimilate and change values and to define and extend goals.

4. Learning processes are characteristic for both individuals and societies. We may speak about societal learning in the same way we speak about societal development, but whereas development usually implies that latent structures or activities develop as soon as favorable conditions are met, learning expresses a more dynamic mechanism. New answers are being prepared for probable situations in order to cope with an increasing complexity, in a time of rapid change. Learning is a prerequisite for development, for solving problems, for avoiding catastrophes, for survival in an uncertain, hostile, and unsafe environment, in short for coming to terms with nature and mankind:

Development must be seen as a societal learning
process, the growing ability of a community or a
nation at first to project goals which conform to a
set of accepted values - some variant on the theme
of equal opportunity for each person to fulfill his or
her own potentialities, extended beyond the present
to future generations - and then, to work towards
these goals while keeping within the external constraints imposed by nature and inherited from history.(10)

5.   As NIEO implies profound changes, the underlying
learning processes must be not of the incremental, but of the
restructuring type.   It is not a question of adjusting the old
order, but of restructuring it.   Trial-and-error strategies for
correcting the existing situation are failing to provide satisfactory procedures.
6.   As NIEO implies the acknowledgement of an order
based on common admitted norms, a readjustment of value sets
is needed.   This again implies learning.   No social situation
involving choices is, or can be, value free.   The arena of real
world problem-solving makes for inevitable trade-offs, both in
general among the values and specifically within a single value
frame.   More than one voice has been heard in recent years
asking for a change of life styles in the rich nations.   This
change calls for new values and attitudes:

The new style will make less demands on the material
resources of the globe, but more on our moral
resources.   This is not likely to happen unless
considerable changes are made in our educational
system, with a change in the whole cultural climate;
all this would tend to stress internal more than
external human satisfactions.(11)

7.   As NIEO implies a better management of the earth's
natural capacities and resources, learning is once more
present.   The already started process must lead to the declaration of common heritages of mankind in many areas.   The
example of the seabed and ocean floor (objective 19)(12) must
be learned and applied to the atmosphere, the cultural monu-
ments, etc.

LEARNING PROCESSES RELEVANT TO SOCIETY

What is Not Relevant?

In discussing learning processes, we shall first review several main schools belonging to different disciplines which have investigated this subject. In doing so, the guiding principle shall be the relevance of the considered concepts to societal learning. As usually happens in scientific research, a direct transfer of a concept from biology, cybernetics, or other fields to society is not feasible.

The mechanism that taught the species to find new answers when faced with new situations - adaptation - is well known. Despite the evidence of man's specific behavior and unique cultural universe, which enable him to share and transmit to future generations the results of learning, the idea still persists that human learning processes are similar to those of the species adaptation, the difference being only in time scales: a lifetime as compared to the millions of years of the species life.

But, as is clear from a social perspective, in the first place, human actions are deliberate and conscious. It is the privilege of man to examine and construct alternatives, to choose among them, to change the environment in a preferential direction, and to prevent untoward events from happening.

Secondly, adaptation implies a harmonious adjustment to a fixed environment after some changes occurred in it, and men have no such immutable niche available.

Learning mechanisms pertaining to cybernetics have also failed to give the needed answer. Their main concern is with self-regulating systems, with maintenance realized by correcting deviations from a preestablished target. Processes engendering change and innovation are thus neglected.

Despite the immense contribution that the cybernetic approach and the concept of information have brought to the social sciences, there is a threshold the information theory could not overcome: the meaning, the understanding, and the values that are deeply imbedded in the information processed by humans.

Interesting analogies were found between learning in animals and men. Ethology asserts the existence in animals as well as in man of certain innate, fatalistic drives. Thus behaviors like aggression are innate and not learned, the role of learning being merely that of a controller or tanner. Certainly, when moving to the sphere of acute social phenomena, the emphasis must be on those differences between man and animals that account for more affective, rapid, and less expensive solutions than the procedures that have made

the history of the animal world look like a huge cemetery of
failures and disasters.

What is Revelant?

The value of the previous types of learning cannot be denied,
especially when dealing with automatic behavior, habits, and
answers to current, repetitive situations. However, if we wish
to use learning in societal processes, we must rely on processes that entail restructuring and changes affecting not only
the abstract learner, but his values, tools, images, associations, and language as well. In fact, these are exactly the
instruments by means of which any action essentially mediated
by them is carried out - learning included.

It is important to consider all the components of this set
at the same level. If some types of culture lay an emphasis on
symbols, concepts, rational models, and languages, others
draw attention to images. In spite of their greater spon-
taneity, images can be learned, thus providing powerful means
of reasoning and creation. They pertain not only to the
individual's inner life, but also to the social knowledge.
Restructuring due to learning at the societal level is encoded
also in what K. Boulding calls "public image" and not only in
the official documents and institutions.(13)

Despite their essential role for decisions and ultimately
for action, values are usually neglected by learning processes.
But without taking them into account, the articulation of
culture into systems of action cannot be grasped and decision-
making gets blocked. From the very outset, we have placed
ourselves in the sphere of the processes of learning with
understanding, in which emphasis is laid upon information
capable of bringing about a restructuring process. However,
what is learned turns into an action instrument only when it is
value laden.

By including tools in this set, by which we mean machines as well as know-how and technologies, we stress the
fact that the intelligence is not confined to the conceptual
sphere, but regards the capacity of handling tools as well.
Skills are not second-grade elements, of less importance than
knowledge. There is an intelligence of the hands practically
demonstrated in handicrafts and traditional arts, and this is a
tremendous asset for the skills required by the electronic web
of modern industries and fine mechanics.

Finally, it is through associations that people interact.
The capacity to enter into group relationships, to participate
simultaneously in several associations, is crucial for learning.

It is not enough to require that people interact in order
to learn and to see the relations or associations at the root of
the learning process. In a vertical or unequal association, we

found that teaching is at most coming from the top to the bottom. The association we have in mind is horizontal and symmetrical.

All the individual sets through which learning is accomplished have something in common: They have a social existence that precedes and succeeds the individual one. Culture is but a huge pool of sets, potentially available to all the people. The components, as products of societal learning, become integral parts of the individual's behavior and after being exercised and enriched in the learning process, are returned, shared, transmitted, and reproduced as a collective asset.

The individual does not communicate directly with the common pool; the hierarchical subsystems act as intermediaries. The remoter the subsystems are from one another, the more elaborate are the instruments by which interaction is mediated.

The man-machine interrelationship is served by a simpler system of words, images, and values than the society-industry interaction.

Existence within family and society makes use of relatively simple instruments as compared to those required by the interaction of individuals belonging to remote geographical and cultural systems.

From a careful analysis carried out during the elaboration of the Learning Project it was found that two requirements are essential for the efficiency of societal learning: participation and anticipation.(14) Participation describes the number and the quality of interactions the learner has established. It is conceived as a conscious, transformation-oriented social action, divested of any current sense of passivity.

Important trends of thought have pleaded against the learners' passivity in schools. The adults, who nowadays are involved in a huge one-way transmission operation due to mass media, are also deprived of real interaction. The available technical, audiovisual and computerized means have caused a growing passivity and have reduced participatory situations. Discriminations as well as existing power relationships also increase the difficulties of participation. Of course, all these factors that condemn people to play marginal, passive, and incomplete roles should be removed.

Nevertheless, the participatory aspiration ought to be completed with adequate instruments so that it should by no means remain only a desideratum, never to be fulfilled.

In a world in which the objective structures take the form of complex networks, denying a mere intuitive approach, participation makes it imperative to get trained if the new order is to be achieved.

Anticipation, the other essential for societal learning, is given by the exploration of the future and the use of the derived possible conjectures in simulation models. Anticipatory learning prevents direct experiences that may prove in the social realm extremely painful.

For individuals as well as for societies, both participatory and anticipatory learning translate themselves into the form of an increased autonomy and integration.

OBSTACLES IN THE LIGHT OF LEARNING

We have already stated that establishing NIEO is a learning process. What perspective is gained through this statement for the better understanding of the obstacles impeding, and the opportunities accelerating the process?

For a couple of years now, a large debate has pointed out new concepts. New ideas gained ground, as for instance that the free market is unfair, that behind inequalities are inequitable mechanisms, that NIEO implies restructuring at the international as well as at the regional and national level:

> The changes in attitudes, institutions and lifestyles required in our global lily pond amount to nothing less than a social transformation. The prospective changes in consumption and reproductive patterns are without precedent.(15)

It is now evident that the new order cannot be reduced to merely applying recipes or a design elaborated by using simple technocratic practices; that the economic type of reasoning, cleared of any social or cultural elements, is insufficient; that a new harmony with nature and a new attitude towards resources is highly required. NIEO should aim at satisfying the basic human needs, it must start from decisions arrived at through an endogeneous process, assisted by appropriate institutions. This debate cannot ignore the existing power structures, but at the same time, must rely on the broadest participation, national and collective self-reliance being essential factors.

A most valuable lesson is that NIEO requires a global approach, by tackling most of its objectives in a parallel and not in a sequential manner. Thus at least two of its tasks should be thought about and realized together: economic development and equitable distribution.

Growth deserves the criticism of the opponents of economic reductionism only when it is pursued by completely neglecting social and human factors. Otherwise, it is an essential process in a world devastated by poverty, which is starving not only from the lack of food, but also from the lack of energy, of adequate technologies, of healthy, skilled, productive people, and of sufficient working places. Thus, NIEO is not simply and solely redistribution.

There are lots of examples of pursuing each objective separately, to the detriment of the other one. Some societies experiencing rapid growth have also undergone extreme polarization into abundance and poverty. On the other hand, honest attempts at a just redistribution have failed in some cases due to the lack of concern for increasing correspondingly the production of goods.

All these conceptual steps forward are evidence of a learning process in the sense of an increased competence for dealing with the new situations that will emerge in full acuteness by the end of the century.

However, summing up, we don't get a satisfactory result. Widening gaps, alarming figures of the world population living below the level of the satisfaction of basic human needs, and of resources being diverted to destructive purposes instead of being directed towards productive ones are conspicuous evidence for the existence of serious obstacles. The fact that a large part of the public fails to respond to what should become a worldwide compaign, alongside of the great number of failures registered by the attempts at negotiating efficient and urgent measures prove that the learning process is hampered in fulfilling expectations.

The main factors blocking learning processes in the view of NIEO are as follows:

Immobilizing Resources in the Frantic Arms Race

The astronomic figures of arms race expenditures, reaching as much as $1 billion per day, are well known. Their effects on economic and social life were the subject of a UN report which deserves full attention.(16)

Unfortunately, the wastage and blockage of human resources involved in this process are still insufficiently emphasized. Out of the 22 million people kept by the military forces, a lot are young people in military service at the age of their highest productivity, being trained for arms professions, and unlearning the requirements of social life, which are suspended in barracks. The few cases of involving the army in public works are but exceptions to the rule and not a general practice. The human intelligence and creativity necessary for NIEO purposes are used for producing more and more precise, sophisticated, and destructive weapons.

We may state that currently no invention used for civilian purposes incorporates such quantities of knowledge, imagination, and mental resources as an up-to-date weapon requires. In the sense of incorporating results from pattern recognition, automatization, accuracy, and the ability to transform its own programme rocket is a far more intelligent machine than any machinery used in industry, farming, administration, or health protection.

The level of involvement of science in military purposes
(25 percent of all living scientists are somehow involved in
army research) confirms the general trend of mankind, which
is actually engaged in a learning process directed toward
insecurity and self-destruction, a process taking away the best
resources and means from the civilian learning processes.

Keeping the NIEO Process Only
at the Conceptual Level

The main centers of the debate on NIEO are still the official
meetings of governmental representative and the nongovernmental meetings of specialists, despite the antielitist and
antitechnocratic content of the new order, which in fact
identified elitism and technocracy as main features of the old
order.

Actually, some formerly omitted groups, either belonging
to the social and human sciences, or to trade unions, and
women's and youth movements, are more and more involved.
But as the societal learning process is necessarily participatory, it must be expressed at the grass-roots, personal level.
Thus an effort is needed to overcome the dry language of
official documents and resolutions together with the too specialized language, full of technical expressions, in order to
provide the broad distribution of texts intended to reach the
grass-roots level.

NIEO is not only an exercise in general and abstract
concepts, however correct and beneficial they are, but also a
long list of meaningful stories: Petroleum and bananas increasing tenfold in price from the production to the distribution
place; the ton of rice that can buy fewer and fewer tractors;
the discussions around natural and chemical fertilizers; the
history of technologies and of learning them - all may be
displayed through images in pictures or through other mass-
media means.

The real headquarters of NIEO must be in the field. The
most important feature of learning is that it can be shared and
transmitted.   But information does not always flow from
country to country, from one continent to another in order to
provide the sharing of new experiences, be it the establishment of a cooperative farm, or of an industry producing a
great social impact, or a successful negotiation between foreign
partners, or the conclusions reached by a national energetic
project or a literary program, or a reevaluation of local
resources.

Let us be clearly understood. Stressing the value of
case studies does not mean running away from abstractions.
A lot of studies and even mathematical models are necessary to discover the hidden vices of the invisible mechanisms

that lie behind the financial phenomena and trade. But eventually, these too must also reach a stage of clear and simple explanations.

"Things" versus "Processes"

The initial propensity of mind, helped by several centuries of analytical thought, is oriented toward seeing around us ready-made "things," liable to manipulation, maintenance, and even growth. An additional effort is required in order to grasp their inner dynamics and to understand them as processes of change. The NIEO is an unprecedented attempt to apprehend and cope with new phenomena as far as their vastness and complexity is involved. To face such a challenge, a new intellectual methodology based on systems and processes including values and contexts is required.

If we conceive technology as a thing, then we can move it unchanged from one place to another. The notion of transfer reflects indeed this conception. If we conceive technology as a process, then we must ask ourselves some questions: In what contexts and with what purposes was the technology elaborated? How should it be changed in order to satisfy another context and different expectations?

If we think in the framework of things, knowledge will become objects too. A good textbook should be useful everywhere. Moreover, educational systems could be transferred or reproduced together with their curricula, teachers, and apparatus. This has been done more than once, with disastrous results. But if we deal with processes, then education is only a part of the cultural movement of society, having its own history (past and future), integrating itself with the processes of change of the whole society.

In the conception of "things," objectives, needs, and values are finite, fixed things. What we have to do is state them as goals and try to attend them.

From the viewpoint of processes, objectives, needs, and values change during the same learning process that changes techniques, knowledge, images, and the structures of society.

The worst outcome of living in a world of "things" is to assign people to this category as well. This leads to the idea that they can be manipulated, sponsored, and improved, or that they can be involved in processes irrespective of their agreement or participation.

Only things are processed through external decisions. Neither political and social institutions, economic and cultural models, nor management schemes concerning society are things, and thus they cannot be transferred and dislocated from one place to another.

There is the maintenance type of learning of use for all things with stabilized functioning that does not change context. This type is concerned with performances.

Since we live in a rapidly changing world, another type of learning is needed - one that increases competence, the ability to tackle new elements, and the ability to anticipate, grasp, and tame them.

Persistent Fallacies

Despite the fact that the NIEO debate brought about firm ideas and a better vision of the phenomena developing in today's society, vagueness continues to persist at several sensitive points. They concern essentially the attitudes toward work, authority, structures (administrative), science, and technology.

The high wave of criticism in the Western world has justly asserted the alienation of labor, the abuse and repression by authorities, the rigidity of structures, the orientation of science and technology towards provable ends. But it also left in some circles the impression (caused by a well-known logical error) that it is not the system engendering those phenomena that should be blamed, but all forms of work, authorities, structures, science, and technology. These attitudes obscure the efforts for NIEO. From the viewpoint of learning processes, they are quickly identified as errors.

Work continues to be the main link between all the learning elements (language, images, values, associations, and tools), the essential element for achieving an autonomous personality, capable of integration and social responsibility.

It is misleading to talk about a "civilization of holidays," about the leisure period. Any learning process presupposes effort, concentration, work, an ability to tenaciously follow long-term objectives.

Paradoxically enough, the developing countries are asked on the one hand to apply a self-reliance policy which implies strengthening the public sector, controlling resources, taking a firm position in international negotiations, and following the delinkage of dependency relations; on the other hand, hypotheses are suggested about weakening the power of the central authority and even about the disappearance of the state.

The continuous necessary reinforcement of units, places, communities, and regions cannot be achieved to the detriment of a central authority, without which any policy of development and pursuit of NIEO would be useless.

The same thing applies to the justified criticism of bureaucracy and rigidity that some people think should lead to the suppression of records, statistics, forms, and accounts, which are in fact vital for managing complex systems. A school of "new philosophers" denounces any structure, even society, as if individuals themselves would not be the creations of those structures.

The struggle for cultural personality is part and parcel of the struggle for economic independence, self-reliance, and progress. However, we cannot overlook some dangers looming large because of the erroneous consequences of fallacious reasoning. Some upholders of the theory of cultural personality went as far as to reject modernization, industrialization, urbanization, the growth of production potentials, the assimilation of high-grade technical production forces. It is on behalf of humanism that some authors disregard technology in favor of originality vindicating poverty. There are numerous statements whereby progress would trigger the disintegration of the solidarity and spirituality of primitive rural communities. (17)

The Attitude Towards Science

Because of the effects of some of their creations, science and technology must not be questioned on the huge and decisive capacity they have for contributing to the establishment of NIEO. Metaphorically, it can be said that science and technologies are the lever of the big projects of the new order. "No real economical development can be conceived without a minimum investment in scientifical research."(18) But in 1976 the R & D expenditures of the Third World were about $2 per inhabitant, with variations in the Arab countries from $0.10 per inhabitant to $53.25 per inhabitant (Kuwait).

Underlining the incompatibility between the scientific mentality and the values of a traditional rural culture, an Indian scientist stated that the traditional Indian culture, consisting of all the religions, creeds, myths, and the structure of family, has long resisted all the Western attacks of science and culture, because it is well defended and self-contained. (19)

But the humanistic assertion of values, the preservation of original cultures, and even the fight against the domination of foreign cultures should not be taken for resistance to progress and to the advance of technique, implying the rejection of modern production means. As pointed out by President Nicolae Ceaușescu, "equality in poverty is no equality."(20) The fulfillment of the ideals for an independent and civilized life and the preservation of the traditional culture cannot be conceived outside a powerful economic emancipation, higher living standards, assimilation of the latest techniques, and sound foundations for a national modern production.

A number of works are ultimately meant to discourage the developing countries from trying to gain access to an advanced technique. There was even a tendency to lend these countries out-of-date technologies and means belonging to the non-profitable category of the developed countries or producing great pollution.

One of the most debated themes is that of technology transfer and intermediary technology. The merits of the latter should be well weighed. The role of technology is to provide the goods required by an ever larger humanity; there are not so many procedures for the production of steel, sugar, or synthetic fibers. Schumacher speaks highly of the "small thing," but he overlooks the fact that the greatest outcome of miniature production, the walkie-talkie, is the result of the most advanced technologies.(21)

Undoubtedly, the tendency points to a civilization based on the energy of the sun and mastering the biological cell. However, to learn the mysteries of the conversion of the energy of the sun into organic matter requires the gigantic installations of chemistry, and implies most refined mathematical solutions. Moreover, it is unjust to look upon the traditional communities of the developing countries as unable to adjust themselves to technicality.

Referring to the capitalization of the wet tropical forests, a scientist stressed that the native population had thorough knowledge of the environment, which is simply ignored by modern ecologists.(22) The tradition of collective work, the feeling of natural solidarity, collective organization - these are the elements proper to the old structures of the developing countries whereby their receptivity to the socialist formula is considerably increased. To their mind, socialism has experienced technical development without the social differentiation entailed by capitalism.

A leading African economist said:

> I do not think we should question the machine proper, but social relations, which under various forms of social organization, labor division, etc., impose a certain use of the machine and a certain subjection to the machine; it is not technique itself which must be called into question, but the social relations within which the techniques are used.(23)

Cutting the Links

The prevailing process of growing systemization described by some authors as "an accretion toward increased complexity and greater interdependence in an advancing differentiation"(24) is irreversible. Any attempt at ignoring it by isolationist measures is shortsighted and self-defeating.

Another hasty conclusion drawn by some of the theorists of cultural authenticity is the rejection of cultural contacts and the closing of frontiers. History testifies to the fact that only those cultures that accepted the dialogue and its highest form – cooperation – have found it's easier to innovate, enrich, and advance. The example of Japan, which stayed closed for 200 years only to discover later that it was surrounded by powerful states with all metal steamships, is often quoted to illustrate the consequences of the above-mentioned alternative of isolation and stagnation.

Today, cooperation is imperative in a world that has become small and limited by the large number of technical means that can bring closer two places, however remote from each other, and by an ever deeper state of interdependence. Isolation is practically impossible since the great number of new means of communication and events pursued collectively make an effective connection among people.

The best way to assure economic growth is to rely on national forces and master national resources, but the latter is enhanced by international cooperation and by assistance between the developing countries, which have turned mutual assistance into a principle.

HINTS TO EDUCATIONAL AND TRAINING SYSTEMS

From the viewpoint of individuals, learning is a process that goes beyond education and instruction and shouldn't be limited to them. Some people consider schooling a stage during which the "storehouse" is going to be filled up for all the rest of one's life. Others consider, on the contrary, that school lessons are irrelevant and superfluous, the only appreciated lessons being, despite their high cost, those of life (a name usually given to failures). Evidently, both approaches rely on the dichotomy between school and life. However, learning processes are with us from birth to death.

In recent years, efforts to create and expand educational structures have been supported by large-scale international cooperation. An important study published by UNESCO(25) suggests a large number of activities for stimulating learning: educational exchanges, mobility of teachers and students, equivalence of diplomas, exchanges of experts, programmes of international understanding, limitation of the brain drain, and the strengthening of international institutions, beginning with UNESCO. The study also lists sources and modes of assistance, including technical and financial assistance, educational credits, the equitable distribution of resources, correlation with the overall development strategy, new types of action, etc. It recommends an "international educational innovation programme" to provide scientific, technical, and financial support to all states wishing to explore new openings in this field. Even if such a programme had not been launched, the present structures in any case contribute to a universal dialogue and to operational activities in favor of the countries in greatest need of rapid development of their educational structure.

The Latin American model(26) takes into account all forms of education: school and postschool, initial, on-the-job, formal, nonformal, and informal, institutionalized and independent, direct and indirect.

An interesting innovation is the criterion of autonomy, a concept that has been recently introduced for the purpose of evaluating the results. According to the authors of the model, the level of educational autonomy is reached at the point when decisions concerning one's own education and its planning and control can begin (point of departure for self-education). The objectives to be reached are concerned with indispensable minimum levels for the satisfaction of individual and social needs. Basic education begins at the age of 6 and continues until the time when the point of autonomy is reached 8 to 12 years later; it is followed by middle-level and higher education, directed towards the training of a suitable number of supervisors. In connection with lifelong education, another innovation appears: the guarantee of the right of all adults between the ages of 20 and 50 to personal upgrading and development for one-tenth of the time - i.e., three years divided into 30 modules. Another category, compensatory education, gives the members of the population who have not passed through the phases mentioned above the opportunity to attain targets recognized as valid for the whole society.

Without exhausting all the forms for societal learning, the structure of the educational system, its state and efficiency, are decisive for the process of development.

One of the three criteria that led the UN Committee for Development Planning to include, in 1971, 25 countries in the group of developing countries was that of literacy (the other two being per capita income and the weight of the processing industry in the global industrial production). As over one-fifth of the world's population is still deprived today of the right to communicate through the written word, a most urgent worldwide action is the undertaking of a literacy programme, as a redistributive and transformative measure that should not be assessed in terms of immediate economic returns although it will, no doubt, turn out to be the most valuable investment in the long run.

Specific modalities for launching such a programme should be carried out as, for example, its inclusion within the framework of the "integrated rural development" so as to have a direct impact on the satisfaction of other basic needs.

Up to the age of educational autonomy, young people generally follow the trajectory of school.

Further on, some conclusions for this period are presented (in connection with the NIEO objective 21):(27)

1. Designing curricula oriented towards processes and problems, not towards things and disciplines. Reassessing instruments neglected by the traditional school by attaching the same weight to the development of attitudes (values), teamwork (associations), and skills (tools) as one does to obtaining knowledge. Applications and practical activities should prevail rather than the expository lesson; induction should be cultivated together with deduction; sciences should be presented not only in the logical, but also in the historical, way.

2. Constant organization of complete and real interactions, such as that provided by work. Drawing young people into school management, assigning them specific roles. Creating situations that allow for participation in community life, such as the apprenticeship stages in institutions, shops, plants. Creating situations that imply decision making. Enabling discussions and debates on such experiences.

3. Developing anticipation capabilities through prospective investigations concerning the future of individuals, communities, regions, countries, mankind.

4. Promoting solidarity and responsibility in relation to global problems. Initiating international activities such as radio amateurs, correspondence, fraternal schools etc.

The second period beings at the age of educational autonomy, when youngsters may adopt their own learning programmes.

The principles of such a programme are the following:

1. open alternatives for all possible combinations such as first, profession; second, school; third, other vocations; sandwich solutions for alternating them; day and evening classes; parallel activities
2. periodical consultations with guidance factors, equally acquainted with the subjects of school and qualifications, and with the exigencies of professional life
3. the choice and carrying out of civic activities; inclusion of such activities as parts of the program
4. raising social and political awareness; the approach in depth of social structures and institutions
5. developing the understanding of large systems and global problems

The education of cooperation must constitute one of the prime objectives of both periods. Cooperation makes a rather poor showing compared with the spirit of competition or even aggressiveness. Literature and all the mass media are full of situations of conflict, mostly due to their sensational nature. History is presented as a series of confrontations and wars, and the future is predicted in terms of possible antagonisms. Aggressiveness, war, and violence are more assiduously publicized than peace, cooperation, and understanding.

Apart from the objective reasons for this situation, we must recognize that conflict is easier to understand, while cooperation is more complex, requiring greater efforts for representing and achieving it in practice.

If the contribution of games to the development of team spirit is undeniable, it must be noticed that their effect is often nullified by the fact than one party must win and the other lose.   But in cooperation, both parties win or lose together.

It is work that lies closer to an apprenticeship in cooperation:

> It presupposes an increase in communication through the intermediary of cognitive patterns and rules, it permits savings in experience, whereas the latter is usually wasted in games; it requires effort and offers higher rewards than those offered by games (discharge of energy and catharsis).(28)

OPPORTUNITIES IN THE LIGHT OF LEARNING

Simultaneously with the NIEO debate, conferences are held under the aegis of the United Nations, on those vital problems that by their nature come out of the sphere of action of individual countries and require international cooperation. They end up with declarations, calls to mankind, and plans of action.   We must note that they are not well correlated and that their conclusions do not bear influence on one another. Never was felt a greater need of synthesis.   NIEO represents an organic link of these problems.

A tighter and more convincing form of simultaneous treatment of the main problems of existence (food, water, energy, cosmos, science and technology, habitat, desertification, oceans, etc.) as well as of the social and human problems and those of elaborating the NIEO strategy is highly needed.   In fact, they are all together a plea for NIEO as they become unmanageable, reaching the crisis level in the frame of the old order.

Global problems ask for anticipation, which itself is a condition for societal learning.   More scenarios, conjectures, hypotheses - more models are necessary for meeting the future.   A better cooperation with the scientific world modeling movement, which had a big impact on public opinion and scholars, would be welcome.

The force with which the group of 77 countries acted during the 23rd General Assembly Session (1978) justifies the belief that the process of establishing NIEO will score new progress during 1979 and 1980 and will strongly mark the thoughts and action of the coming decade, which is a new decade of development.

Thus, UNCTAD V (Manila, 1979), the nonaligned summit (Havana, 1979), UNCSTD (Vienna, 1979), and the special session of the UN General Assembly devoted to the new order (1980) will constitute as many instances for synthesizing the huge accumulated experience. They will provide a magnificent opportunity for including human beings and their learning potentialities in the NIEO processes.

The learning approach to NIEO points out the necessity to renew the concepts, methods, and intellectual instruments that were the latent assets of the old order in treating its problems. Thus the progress of NIEO asks for more elaborated studies and additional efforts in the following directions:

1. Including values as well as cultural contexts in reasoning, both when elaborating the NIEO principles and when the latter are applied. Identifying a core of universal values (survival, basic needs, peace and security, development, human rights, equity and equality, etc.) and using them consistently in order to avoid the concrete and specific traps that come out all throughout the NIEO literature as a temptation of denying any common basis.

Recognizing the fact that various values take the shape of conflicting interests and the need to improve the means for rational and peaceful resolution of litigation, avoiding traumatic experiences, high social costs, and sacrifices of human lives.

The NIEO is characterized by a heterogeneity of goals. Developed countries are primarily interested in the balance of international power and ecological protection. World Order thus means an answer to the questions, "How can the likelihood of international violence be significantly reduced? and How can tolerable and ecological stability be created."(29)

For developing countries, the goals with the highest priority are those related to development, industrialization, and disimpoverishment.

It is only through a process of explicit formulation, rational trade-offs of values, and dialogues, and cooperation that agreement can be reached in the most urgent problems mankind is facing.

Another aspect of the problem arises from the intrinsic dynamics of the values. If the needed actualization is not made in time, we will still try to solve the threats of nuclear bombs through application of prenuclear beliefs and values and to put an end to the pollution crisis by means of preecological assumptions.

The propensity for societal development should not be identified with the inevitability of progress. We must learn to make this process desirable, progressive, and beneficial. This requires the learning of new values leading to new attitudes that will make possible the elaboration of new norms for international relations. It is necessary to

> improve the norms of international laws, to adopt new norms and principles in international relations corresponding to the requirements of people wishing to live together on the basis of equality and mutual respect, of securing the progress of each nation in agreement with its legitimate aspirations and desires, of building up a justified, lasting, and durable peace on our planet.(30)

The new norms must become active factors for changing the international life according to the imperatives of building a new order.

2. Realistic strategies and plans should be drawn up only by a study of the context. This implies an inventory of resources and means, the analysis of the existing skills and practices of the traditional technologies.

Specific contexts give the possibility of assessing the economic, social, and environmental impacts of all the actions.

Information received in the learning process has meaning only when confronted with accumulated knowledge (which implies a certain record of history) and with existing structures (which are given by a context) and further on when subjected to inferences (which leads to bridging the gaps).

For NIEO, learning the contexts requires the careful study of each measure in the appropriate frame: local, regional, or national. In the industrialization process, for example, this approach leads to social and ecological assessment. The selection of an industrial location becomes a process of comparative analysis based not only on economical but also on social costs.

The case of the green revolution in certain developing countries reveals the dangers of ignoring the regional contexts. The tensions and conflicts generated by the advanced technologies of using selected seeds, chemical fertilizers, and pesticides can be explained only in specific socioeconomic contexts. "The green revolution, even in the many cases where it can bring undeniable advantages to all social categories, risks creating even worse frustrations among poor people."(31) It surely will fit some cooperative forms of rural development where it will not bring about a cleavage in the population.

At the global level, NIEO itself has a meaning only if it creates a universally accepted context of shared values and prevailing common interests, if it will bring to the fore new approaches, new concepts, and new procedures.

3. An important principle is modularity. Learning for acquiring competence, for being able to act in different situations, settings, and times implies using only modules of prefabricated solutions, which further on can be recombined and enriched, in a restructuring process.

A good example is provided by the experience of learning from the technological transfer. Usually, the learning capacity, sometimes called capacity to adapt, is considered a key component of the management process related to transferring technologies. But, as is more and more obvious, such a capacity cannot be created by the transfer of products, or "turnkey" plants, even if they are provided with the necessary know-how for operation, repair, and maintenance. Also needed is a certain

> level of knowledge about the basic scientific concepts on which technology is founded . . . of motivation required to keep abreast of the evolution of that knowledge . . . of attitudes which make this motivation possible.(32)

Even the much talked about intermediate or appropriate technologies are, from the learning viewpoint, disappointing in their results.

If the conclusion is that "the only truly suitable technology is one that is self-generated and self-generating,"(33) the lesson is obvious: imports of selected modules of foreign technologies and also of foreign experts, followed by gradual substitution for both by national products. The case of Japan is relevant in the sense that any "transfer" means mainly a recreation of the transferred products.

4. Scientific forecasting, initiated mainly by developed countries, was considered for some time to be an activity adequate only to their possibilities. However, due to its importance for learning processes, the anticipatory attitude is more and more connected to the developing prospects of less developed countries. A more concentrated effort is needed for increasing the number of forecasting projects, debates, and adequate institutes.

Setting both short-term and long-term national objectives should be based on careful analysis of alternative scenarios and of the results of forecasting models.

The transition from trends to a normative conception in future exploration, taking into account the core of universal ideas set forth by NIEO and asserting the methodological priority of forecasting, is badly needed.

5. The type of social relations that favors learning is the same as the one required by NIEO in international life.

Contrary to the vertical relationship of teaching, the horizontal, symmetrical relationship of equality, reciprocity, and mutual respect is the key to a participatory society and world, for equitable mechanisms.

Vertical relations supported domination, oppression, and exploitation. They are based on dogmatic inequality and superiority (of race, belief, sex, culture, intelligence, nationality).

Even when abolished through declarations, these preconceived ideas persist through the predominantly vertical way of organizing the society, which places decision on the top and execution at the bottom in the simplest and most circulated version of efficiency.

NIEO is the international process of learning and acquiring new relations. The global community must learn to deal with international relations since "the sphere of international relations is simply not composed of the same kinds of interactions or not even of similar kinds of interactions as a national macrostructure."(34) However, the above mentioned horizontal structures are pertinent to the characterization of the striving of NIEO.

Many authors are nowadays concerned with the fact that policies associated with NIEO may aggravate the situation existing in developing countries. The main expressed doubts are "whether the redistribution of world resources towards the poor countries will ultimately also benefit poor people from those countries,"(35) whether the present strategies are nót leading towards "development without disimpoverishment."(36) Recommendations go either for establishing urban settings with a population structure not too different from what is found in rich countries or, on the contrary, to avoid the urban bias by ensuring first an accelerated rural development.

Without denying the importance of both attitudes, it must be stressed that only through imparting a dynamic characterized by maximum involvement and commitment of people can the problems related to development be overcome. Conditions must be created, through campaigns and specific actions, for ensuring the largest participation.

Learning processes take place at the society level only if full participation is provided. Despite this evidence, most development models have a strong tendency to ignore or underutilize the only abundant resource each nation has - people.

Women and young people, together with all groups discriminated against on the basis of race, language, or beliefs, represent important categories for the contemporary learning processes.

The task is not only to state the principle of participation in official declarations, but to ensure it by setting up adequate institutions, organizations, etc., enabling the most diverse and large participation in the discussions and decisions concerning all the problems facing the nation. "Participation in systems is a learning process as a result of which actors learn how to redefine their objectives in order to make them rational."(37)

6. The institutions to which NIEO resorts are liable not only to adaptation as a result of past events, but to restructure, following the perception of new, future challenges. But the majority of the existing institutions are rigid ones. Even at the international level they proliferate because the new tasks or structures do not find in the existing institutions elastic frameworks prepared to meet them.

The learning institutions should have mobile walls. The theory and practice of these institutions should avoid an anarchic growth of new institutions, which by conflicts due to competition and vain rivalry could harm the NIEO.

A more strenuous effort is necessary for developing a learning capacity at the UN system. To date,

> the adaptation has been directed to the manifold changes which occur within the international system but on which, except in a few cases, the UN system has had a limited influence. The UN system has to date been much more faithful in reflecting some of these changes than it has been in initiating them.(38)

7. If learning will be regarded as a key element for NIEO, more concern for the human factor and its qualification will result. No economic or social dossier should fail to point out the implications concerning the learning processes, the increase of people's competence for dealing with new situations generated by industrialization, urbanization, or rural development, new agricultural techniques, reevaluating local resources or the use of new technologies, and even protection against natural disasters (drought, earthquakes, floods).

The greatest need for developing skills and capabilities for productive work is felt by the vast proportion of people undergoing the process of change from the traditional rural life to the modern technical one.

Including the human factor and learning must, from now on, be a rule. Thus the UN, the United Nations Development Program (UNDP), UNIDO, and FAO could adopt as a rule the inclusion in any investment made in developing countries of a compulsory subproject on learning (LP), consisting of a unit for extending people's qualification. This unit should also be used for adults' compensatory learning, having a larger scope than that of simple training for the productive unit, but affecting the development of the whole community or region.

Of no little importance must be the effort of learning to restructure the "tools" we use at present. By the kinds of energy they are using, by the organizational and management modalities they imply, by the excessively hard, expensive, and centralized technologies, based on the enormous consumption patterns they use, the present tools are not suited for a new order.

8. The learning approach has the advantage of taking the NIEO from the level of national and international measures and organisms to the level of individuals and communities. It is only by a large-scale popularization campaign that the unwarranted effects and the negative consequences of man's action may be learned. The interdependences in today's world strongly ask for such an approach, as decisions based on partial views have dangerous consequences when viewed from a general standpoint.

The awareness of the problems concerning mankind must be obtained by organizing large national debates, with the help of the mass media, on such topics as food, environment, water, deteriorations (desertification, deforestation, soil erosion, and pollution), and health.

The fact is extremely significant that the learning features emphasized by the latest research on this topic - namely participation, anticipation, autonomy, and integration - coincide with the requirements for equality stated by NIEO - pursuit of long-term objectives, self-reliance, cooperation, and solidarity. It brings to the NIEO debate the mark of high optimism revealed by the long proven capacity of mankind to unlearn in time the old formulas, however much authority they would bear, at the very moment of the historical requirement for learning new structures.

The thirst for learning is immense in the countries that have recently obtained their independence or asserted their resolution not to accept economic and cultural subservience. More than half the population of those countries are young people. Assuming that big catastrophes will be avoided, their life as well as the existence of the societies they belong to will be dominated by two commandments: emancipation, pursued by NIEO, and learning.

There are reasons to believe that the two processes are in fact identical.

NOTES

(1) Declaration, point 4J.

(2) N. Ceaușescu, România pe drumul construirii societatii socialiste multilateral dezvoltate (Romania on the road of build-

ing up the socialist multisided developed society), vol. 14 (Bucarest, Ed. pol., 1977).

(3) Michael Lipton, Why Poor People Stay Poor (London: Temple Smith, 1977).

(4) Jan Tinbergen, R.I.O.: Reshaping the International Order (New York: E.P. Dutton, 1976).

(5) D.H. Meadows et al., The Limits to Growth (New York: Universe Books, 1972); M. Mesarovic, E. Pestel, Mankind at the Turning Point (New York: E.P. Dutton, 1974); H. Kahn et al., The Next 200 Years (New York: William Morrow, 1976); J. Tinbergen, RIO: Reshaping the International Order (New York: E.P. Dutton, 1976); W. Leontief et al., The Future of the World Economy (New York: Oxford University Press, 1977). A. Herrera et al., Catastrophe or New Society? A Latin American World Model (Ottawa: IDRC, 1976).

(6) UN Economic and Social Council, Review of recent global long-term projections (E/5937/Add.4/30 March 1977).

(7) Richard Falk, A Study of Future Worlds (New York: The Free Press, 1975).

(8) Ervin Laszlo, Goals for Mankind (New York: E.P. Dutton, 1977).

(9) The conceptual framework used henceforward on learning processes, was elaborated while contributing to the next report to the Club of Rome, On Learning, coordinated by Mircea Malitza, James Botkin, and Mahdi Elmandjra, to be published Spring 1979.

(10) Ignacy Sachs, Crises of Maldevelopment in the North: A Way Out (IFDA Dossier 2, November 1978).

(11) Gunar Adler-Karlsson, New Way of Life in Developed Countries: Report: Symposium on a NIEO (The Hague: 1975).

(12) Ervin Laszlo et al., The Objectives of the NIEO (New York: Pergamon Press, 1978).

(13) Kenneth Boulding, The Image (Ann Arbor: University of Michigan Press, 1956).

(14) Botkin, No Limits to Learning (New York: Pergamon Press, 1980).

(15) Lester Brown, The Twenty-Ninth Day (New York: W.W. Norton & Co., 1978).

(16) Economic and Social Consequences of the Armaments Race and its Extremely Harmful Effects on World Peace and Security, Report of the Secretary General (New York: U.N., 1977).

(17) The phenomenon is examined by Boris Erassov in La personalité culturalle dans les idéologies du tiers monde (Cultural personality in third world ideologies, Diogend 78, 1972).

(18) Mahdi Elmandjra, Lente évolution de la recherche scientifique dans les pays du tiers monde (Slow evolution of scientific research in third world countries, Almaghrib, no. 392, Nov. 12, 1978).

(19) O.P. Sharma, La science et la technique et les changements socio-culturels dans l'Inde rurale (Science and technology and socio-cultural changes in rural India), La science et la diversité des cultures (Paris: UNESCO, 1974).

(20) Nicolae Ceauşescu, Cuvintare la marea adunare populara de la Oradea (Speech made at the great people's meeting in Oradea), Scinteia, June 19, 1976).

(21) E.F. Schumacher, Small is Beautiful (New York: Harper, 1973).

(22) I. Sachs, Vers une nouvelle civilisation industrielle des tropiques, (Towards a new industrial civilisation of the tropics), 2000, Tiers monde et Ressources, no. 34).

(23) Samir Amin, Le tiers monde et le nouvel ordre économique international (The third world and the NIEO, Cultures, III, no. 4).

(24) Szymon Chodak, Societal Development (New York: Oxford University Press, 1973).

(25) Learning to Be: The World of Education Today and Tomorrow (Paris: UNESCO, 1977).

(26) A. Herrera et al., Catastrophe or new society?

(27) Laszlo et al., The Objectives of the NIEO.

(28) Mircea Malitza, "Solidarity and social learning processes" Labour and Society 3, no. 3-4 (July, October 1978).

(29) M. Washburn, L. Metcalf, and S. Mendlovitz, "The Crisis of Global Transformation, Interdependence, and the Schools" (draft for discussion 1977).

(30) Romanian Communist Party Programme (Bucharest: Ed. Pol., 1975).

(31) Kalpana and Pranab Bardhen, "Green Revolution and socio-economic tensions: the case of India," Revue Intern. des Sci. Soc. 35, no. 3 (1973).

(32) A. Benazzouz and A. Baez, "Knowledge transfer in North Africa: the case of electronics," Impact 28, no. 4 (October-December 1978).

(33) J. Clayson, "Self-sufficiency Through Local Innovation," Impact 28, no. 4 (October-December 1978).

(34) Chodak, <u>Societal Development</u>.

(35) Johan Galtung, <u>Poor Countries vs. Rich; Poor People vs. Rich. Whom will NIEO benefit?</u> (University of Oslo, Paper No. 63, 1977).

(36) Lipton, Why Poor People Stay Poor.

(37) Chodak, <u>Societal development</u>.

(38) Mahdi Elmandjra, <u>The United Nations System: An Analysis</u> (New York: Faber and Faber, 1973).

4 Mass Media in the Third World and the NIEO

Juan Somavia
Fernando Reyes-Matta

The New International Information Order seeks to provide a response in the field of communication and culture to the efforts being made on a wider scale to establish a New International Economic Order.(1) The emergence on the political scene of the new Afro-Asian countries during the post-World War II period and the agreement reached by a number of Third World countries on the need to defend their right to autonomous economic development by controlling their own basic resources have inevitably led to the understanding that establishment of a New International Economic Order can only be achieved to the extent that ideological instruments, cultural systems, and the system employed in the day-to-day shaping of views and values are removed from the control of a dominating center of power to become paths for interaction and for the multidimensional and multidirectional flow of information.

At present, that centrally rooted value-shaping system is financed, organized, and programmed as to content by a transnational structure that benefits from it by using the cultural mechanisms as an instrument for furthering its expansion. It must therefore be remembered that when the need to create a new international economic order is proposed, what is being discussed in practice is a change in the transnational order that now exists. In the field of information, this implies detecting and changing the effects of that transnational domination on people's minds and on public opinion.

The problem of the relationship between development and the communication/cultural framework has been clearly revealed by most of the studies that have attempted to make an interpretive analysis of conditions that might make the establishment of a New International Economic Order possible.

"A near monopoly of international communications on the part of the transnational enterprises is a basic element in the

70

present-day hierarchic pattern of ideological and cultural domination by the center," states the Dag Hammarskjöld Report. The document notes that this situation also affects international communications among the countries of the Third World and is linked to the control exerted by the transnational enterprises over the majority of the communications media and to the influence they have over almost all of them.

Another of the effects that type of information system has on the framework of international understanding is its contribution to maintaining a partial, distorted, and frequently prejudiced knowledge of Third World realities. Just as the center is ill-informed as to the outlook and aspirations of the periphery, so too are the peripheral countries sometimes unaware of all the potential opportunities for dialogue that may exist among certain social sectors of both regions for joint action to create a new international order. In that sense, the RIO Report has also been most explicit:

> It must be recognized that the international dissemination of information has long been the object of discriminatory practices. The flow of information from the Third World to the industrialized countries is controlled by a handful of western news agencies; the information is bought and sold in a very oligopolistic market. Consequently, information is subject to manipulation and can be used and is used as an instrument for the perpetuation of preconceived ideas, ignorance, and apathy. It serves to maintain systems, not to change them.
>
> Public opinion in the industrialized countries will not have real access to full information on the Third World, on its demands, aspirations, and needs, as long as information and communication patterns fail to rid themselves of sales-oriented sensationalism and from their present characteristic presentation of news items, and to rid themselves conscientiously, as well, of ethnocentric prejudices. Expansion of the capacity to inform must be considered an essential component of attempts to create a new international order; consequently, monopolistic and discriminatory practices inherent in the present dissemination of international information must be considered one of the worst, albeit subtle, characteristics of the present system."*(2)

---

*Translator's note: Retranslation from Spanish version of original English.

All these facts have been touched upon in the debate over the establishment of a New International Economic Order, and constitute specific instances of what the Third World countries call neocolonial aspects of the relations between North and South.

The declaration concerning the establishment of a New International Economic Order approved by the Special Session of the General Assembly of the United Nations (Sixth Period), in 1974, recognizes the progress made in recent decades both on the level of political independence and on that of technological advances contributing to the general well-being of man. But it also takes note of existing difficulties:

> Nevertheless, the persistent vestiges of a foreign and colonial domination, of foreign occupation, of racial discrimination, apartheid and neocolonialism in all its forms continue to be among the great obstacles to the full emancipation and progress of the developing countries and their peoples.

To the extent that analysis succeeds in identifying all the forms of neocolonialism, evidence emerges of the role played by information as a neocolonial mechanism in today's society. That neocolonial aspect is in large measure sustained by the expanding power of transnational organizations.

The transnational communications system covers the entire field; it includes news agencies, advertising agencies, and data banks, as well as the provision of information-gathering services, radio and television programs, films, radiophotos, magazines, books, comic strips, and comic books that have international circulation. Its different components, most of them based in the industrialized countries, reinforce each other's action and together stimulate consumers' aspirations to forms of social organization and life styles imitating those of the industrialized capitalist countries, which experience has shown can only be reproduced in Third World countries on the basis of an increasingly high concentration of income in the hands of a minority and of unacceptable social inequalities. At the same time, information pressure coming from so many apparently different but actually related sources gradually eliminates the ability to react to the message, so that recipients are progressively transformed into a passive element, unable to exercise their own judgement. The process of communication, then, becomes for people a sort of theater for them to watch but take no share in. Under those conditions, the public is gradually convinced that the transnational pattern of consumption and development is historically inevitable. The communications system thus fulfills its main function - the cultural penetration of human beings for the purpose of conditioning them to accept the political, economic, and cultural values of the transnational power structure.

In that cultural context, the transmission of information has, in addition, become a real industry. A brief study of the process of observation, compilation, selection, evaluation, and transmission of international information shows that it forms an integral part of the modern industrialization process. Like industries that manufacture steel, petrochemical products, automobiles, or shoes, the communications industry manufactures a product of its own - information in all its different dimensions and forms.

THREE SIGNIFICANT FIELDS

The list given previously of the different components that make up the overall transnational communications system includes three fields that clearly demonstrate the significance of the present dominating structure to alternative development possibilities:

1. the news agencies, their transnational presence, and their evaluation of reality based on the criteria of the center
2. the advertising agencies and their transnational expansion in a direction opposite to that taken by development proposals based on national projects for change and on international development strategy
3. the growth of informatics, whose organization and data processing and retrieval systems appear to be increasingly determined by certain transnational corporations whose operations are affecting not only North-South, but even North-North relationships

Each of those fields is described below in considerable detail, in order to show the obstacles they present to the objectives of the New International Economic Order.

The World of Transnational News Agencies

Since the beginnings of this decade there has been a growing awareness of the fact that it cannot be accepted that only four transnational news agencies, all of them belonging to the industrialized world, have major control of the flow of information to and from the countries of the Third World; that it is equally impossible to go on accepting a juridical situation in which the news agencies are neither legally nor socially responsible for the errors and distortions they may commit in their selection, elaboration, transmission and presentation of the

news, and just as unacceptable to consider that the
function of information in a society is simply to
prolong the action of a particular government or of
private sectors which are unlikely to disregard their
own economic or political interests.

We are on the threshold of a real revolution in
the way of viewing and organizing the function of
informing. For too long, now, "freedom of information" has been synonymous with the freedom the
owners of communication media should enjoy to inform
others in the manner they deem most convenient.
The right to information has been considered solely
from the viewpoint of the "communicator," never
from that of the rights of the recipient. The concept of "free flow of information" has in practice
turned out to be just one more instrument for the
cultural penetration of underdeveloped societies,
without any real questioning of the implicit values
and interests represented and defended by the
massive international information channels.(3)

The predominance of certain information structures over
others is reflected in the growth of certain news agencies
since World War II. Table 4.1 notes the extent of that growth
in terms of offices and number of words transmitted per day:

Table 4.1. News Services - Size and Output

Agency	Offices Abroad	Words transmitted per day (in millions)
UPI	81	11 200 radiophotos
AP	62	17
AFP	108	3.4
REUTERS	105	1.5
TASS	40	---------------
ANSA	69	0.3
EFE	52	0.5
TANJUG	46	0.1
IPS	44	0.1

This situation in terms of power is confirmed by the lists of clients or subscribers of the transnational agencies. One finds a clear predominance of certain agencies that have imposed predetermined news values and have a scale of priorities for evaluating events in the peripheral countries that depends, to a great extent, on ongoing political and economic processes in the countries of the center, especially those in which the home offices of the dominant agencies are located (New York, London, Paris).

"Who would seriously deny," says Sean MacBride, chairman of the International Commission for the Study of Communication Problems called together by UNESCO,

> that a problem exists, when it is known that two-thirds of the daily production of news in the world comes directly or indirectly from New York? Or that almost two-thirds of the correspondents of the major news agencies are stationed in North America and Europe? Certain logistical considerations may make this situation very difficult to change, but it certainly implies a very special responsibility on the part of those who control the news agencies to ensure that information is balanced and that no distortions occur."

The situation MacBride describes would appear to be fully borne out by conditions in such areas as Latin America. Any study of the flow of information and its penetration in Latin American communication media will show the hegemony of the transnational news agencies - specifically UPI and AP - which together account for more than 60 percent of the items. When one inquires into the criteria the correspondents employ in selecting the news they report, and those applied, in turn, in selecting the items to be published in the mass media, one encounters a circular process of ratification contrary to the interests of society as a whole.

Local "gatekeepers" send their New York offices what they think the main bureau wants, and this office in turn retransmits to Latin America news items like those the newspapers there habitually consume. This series of presuppositions culminates in the ratifying attitude of the local media, which insist on providing their readers with the kind of news they are expecting to read. In this way a closed circle of ratifications is produced in which all the presuppositions are confirmed, on the accepted basis that demand is free. The liberal concept just mentioned was the origin of the present pattern of information: individuals, naturally and freely, select and demand what they want, without realizing that their wants are actually conditioned by the medium in which they live. The circle is thus closed. Viewed in terms of the task of the

major news agencies, the mechanics we have just reviewed can
be described as follows:

1. Reality is composed of a multiplicity of facts. Some
of these facts are selected as news material by reporters of
the national media, in accordance with the prevailing criteria
and values that have guided them in their profession.

2. The transnational news agencies obtain the information
from the national media and through their local agents, and
make their selection of what to transmit in accordance with
what is traditionally accepted by the regional or main bureau.
As an anonymous AP correspondent has put it,

> My attempts at trying to correct the criteria followed
> by those in charge of the New York bureau in
> selecting material have so far been minimal; I don't
> think they'd be interested, unless I put a little
> creativity into it. And even so, I still fall back on
> preconceived notions of what is wanted.

3. The main bureaus, like the one in New York, once
provided with the material preselected by their own representatives, send their ·clients the material they supposedly
want, which systematically coincides with what the media are
used to receiving, and which dovetails perfectly with the
prevailing values of journalism in the continent. Moreover,
the local media's receipt of the cabled information on events
they were the first to report marks the completion of the circle
of ratifications.

4. Finally, the public ratifies the prevailing journalistic
orientation of the news by consuming the kind of information
to which it has become accustomed.

The preceding leads us unavoidably to gauge the gravity
of the existing problem. It is one that far surpasses any
economic solution. And the answer, to be sure, does not lie
in the mere mechanical nationalization of the news media, their
feeder sources, and their programs, since the concept of news
value that prevails today is shaped by and impregnated with a
commercial and industrial concept of the news. As Mattelart
says,

> It is not by suppressing programs produced in other
> countries, particularly the United States, and by
> that means alone, that we will fully solve the prob-
> lem of cultural dependence. A program produced in
> Chile can reproduce the same ideological plot and
> therefore suffer from the same vice as the foreign
> material.

What is needed, then, is a prolonged and joint effort by those
in charge of information activities, at empirical and theoretical

levels, to obtain a new order in that information - an effort in which their critical perception of the inherent deformations in the sector enables them to propose feasible means of correcting them. This makes it legitimate to pose some very specific questions, such as the following:

- To what extent are those news values legitimate and capable of persisting within the context of the present-day sociopolitical reality of the Third World and the proposals for a new North-South relationship?
- In what measure are prevailing news values contrary to development processes undertaken for the benefit of the great neglected majorities of the Third World?
- If information is viewed as a growing process of alternative education, how can a concept of news that seeks the out-of-the-ordinary, the anecdotal, the negative, the abnormal, the "impacting" be accepted?
- To what degree is prevailing professional conduct a valid response to the needs of contemporary communication processes? Or, might it not simply be the expression of a pattern rooted in publicity formulas that continue to be accepted merely because of a sort of loss of the capacity to question them?

The World of the Transnational Advertising Agencies

Advertising has become a great world activity, making its presence felt in almost every country on earth and causing economic, political, and cultural effects of grave concern to an important sector of today's society. In 1974, the total amount spent on advertising in the world (except for the socialist countries) reached more than $49 billion, according to the report of the International Advertising Association published in 1976. Advance estimates for 1977 placed that total amount at more than $60 billion.

Advertising in today's world is part of the cultural landscape and exercises an increasingly larger influence over what is called "mass culture." That is why there are many who consider advertising a threat to the cultural identity of developing countries, viewing it as the bearer of foreign ethical values and, consequently, as something that can deform the customs and life styles of the countries and peoples it affects. This explains why the UNESCO MacBride Committee considers advertising one of the communication problems of modern society. Advertising is one of the principal sources of income for the mass communication media, and therefore influences all their activities and their orientation to a greater or lesser degree. It is combined with other communication content and can openly or underhandedly pervert the action of the mass communication media in such areas as politics, culture, and recreation. In many societies, advertising contributes effectively to creating demand and a mass market, but its influence on consumers and on the mass communication media can be decisive, as well as negative. It can contribute, everywhere, to raising the level of people's aspirations and can be an incitement to improve the quality of life, but it can also serve to augment frustrations and to promote consumption considered as an end in itself.

It must be remembered that advertising is one of the principal forces at work in the world today. It plays an increasingly important role on the international scene, since the very small number of countries that produce most of the advertising in the world can thus exercise a strong commercial and cultural influence over the immense majority of the rest. American advertising, which continues to grow at a regular pace, has a spectacular influence everywhere in the world. Around 1975, seven of the ten most important advertising agencies in the world were totally American, and Americans were majority owners of the other three as well. In 1977, the four most important advertising agencies were either American or Japanese; either directly or through their numerous subsidiaries throughout the world, they did a total volume of business amounting to about $1.4 billion (Dentsu), $1.2 billion (J. Walter Thompson), $1.1 billion (Young & Rubicam), and over $1 billion (McCann Erikson), according to Advertising Age, April 17, 1978.

In addition to the analysis of the effects advertising has, or can have, on communication media, one must also take into account the consequences it may have from a more far-reaching point of view on national and international development strategies. One may validly ask oneself the following questions: Does the pursuit of a New International Economic Order meet with a friend or an enemy in advertising and its effects? Do strategies aimed at more solidary international development and more self-dependent national development find support in advertising growth strategies? A comparative analysis based on the International Development Strategy (IDS) for this decade can help us find the answers.

Paragraph 84 of the IDS refers to the "mobilization of public opinion"; the communication media are basic instruments in that task. The goal in this case is to "help the public to understand the interdependent nature of development efforts during the decade . . . and the need to aid developing countries in the task of accelerating their economic and social development." As we have previously noted, the expansion of the communication media, and television in particular, during the decade has required the growing presence of advertising, which has developed convincing theories in favor of an individualistic consumer culture, thereby creating artificial needs. The effects of this pressure on the individual and on society as a whole create distortions in planned development and simultaneously rob the goal proposed by the IDS - achieving a more just and balanced society - of much of its validity. Some examples of the contradictions that exist between IDS proposals and the messages transmitted by transnational advertising will give a clearer view of the matter.

Arguments of the IDS	Arguments of transnational advertising
1. An attempt must be made to improve the quality of education, reduce illiteracy, and reorient educational programmes at all levels, so as to meet development needs.	1. Advertising is an alternative form of education, inasmuch as it promotes social values and develops methods that permit incorporation of illiterate members of the population into the consumer society.
2. Developing countries should formulate coherent programmes for the prevention and treatment of disease and for improving the general level of the population's health and well-being	2. It has been shown that advertising, as a tool of transnational pharmaceutical firms, is usually guided mainly by commercial interests rather than by any real interest in the health of the population in promoting their medical products.
3. Nutrition levels must be improved as regards average consumption of calories and proteins.	3. Evidence exists of strong links between transnational advertising and the promotion of foods and drinks with no nutritive value, which in some cases may even be harmful to people's health.
4. Special efforts must be made to promote private savings through lending institutions, postal savings, and other such systems.	4. The basic task of advertising is to promote spending on consumer goods, with a view to increasing and speeding up sales of client companies' products.
5. Developing countries must adopt national policies for promoting the participation of children and young people in the development process and for guaranteeing full attention to their needs.	5. Children and young people constitute a privileged market. Consequently, promotion of consumer society patterns that are both superfluous and foreign to the culture represented by their national development patterns is aimed at them, and particularly at youth.

Advertising strategies have identified certain areas to which advertising attention must be directed during the coming decade:

1. interaction between education and advertising, by defining tasks that are common to both processes with a view to improving the "quality of life"
2. growing standardization of consumer habits, promoted as part of the image of a world that affords the opportunity of achieving greater equality among countries
3. intensification of goods traffic between different geographical regions, as well as between the different social sectors, within a pattern of interdependence
4. understanding approach to cultural diversity, but a diversity viewed as part of the overall cultural unity that facilitates consumption

In view of the foregoing, one begins to see that development needs are viewed by transnational advertising agencies in terms of their own strategies. As one of their spokesmen has said:

> The main product of this new generation of agencies, as they have been called, will not be the filming of commercials, although it will still be necessary to design them and follow them up. Nor will it be designing trademarks, though they will have to do that too. Neither will it be the preparation of the pamphlets they may be asked to do. Their main product will be communication strategy, and the agency will increasingly provide the "outside" view so necessary to the future management of corporations.
>   The agency will have to operate within the difficult field of ideas, in which the currents of change are running ever faster and stronger. Clients will no longer pay them high prices for doing jobs that are routine for agencies today. They will, however, pay high prices for high-level counselling as to strategies.

The World of Informatics and Transnational Concentration

One of the main phenomena of postwar cultural industrial expansion has been the rapid growth of the systems used for compiling, processing, storaging, and retrieving data related to immediate and long-range human development.

Few human activities today are not linked in one way or another to electronic data-processing machines or influenced by them. Public opinion, however, is still largely unaware of their true importance. This world of data and catalogued information is what is known as "informatics," a world that is expanding so forcefully that certain specialists have taken it as the empirical basis for predicting an age of information in which every activity of society will be determined and controlled by computer-based communication.

Computer-based communication has been defined by Ithel de Sola Pool as

> any communication in which the message is stored at least one point in the memory of a computer and later processed and transmitted under computerized control. This definition includes communication between computers, as in the case of transmission networks; between man and the computer, or vice versa, as when a person works with a computer from a remote terminal; and communication between users through a computer that stores, processes and transmits messages, as in interconnected communication systems.

The impact of "informatics" on contemporary society is making it necessary to develop policies at the national level aimed at at least three different aspects:

1. protection as regards the flow of data from one country to others and its effects on national sovereignty
2. protection of individuals, social groups, and organized national society against the workings of an all-powerful informatics system
3. protection of equal access to technology that permits more efficient classification and use of data

These three lines of action resulted from the analysis of the situation made in August 1978 in Torremolinos, Spain at the Conference on Informatics called by the Intergovernmental Bureau of Informatics (IBI), an agency connected to the general programme of UNESCO. However, the problem confronting contemporary society as a result of the growth of informatics is not the existing power of informatics, but the identity of those who wield that power. The necessary equipment is manufactured by a limited number of private firms, and in the specific field of computers, IBM holds a wide lead over all others both within the United States and abroad, with more than half its income coming from sales in other countries. In 1975, 52.6 percent of the general computer market in Western Europe was in the hands of IBM, and it is considered that this share of the market will remain the same in coming years.

A recently occurring phenomenon in the field of the different branches of the electronics industry involved in activities that have to do with computers is the formation of consortiums that even further increase the notable power of monopolies in that field. IBM, the Comsat General Corporation (a consortium devoted to the commercial use of satellites) and the Aetna Life and Casualty Company combined in 1977 to form SBS - Satellite Business Systems - for the purpose of building data-transmission satellites to meet the growing needs of big transnational corporations. This situation, the economic potential it indicates, and the role that "informatics" can play in widening the gap between developed and underdeveloped countries necessarily call for a far-reaching analysis of the overall situation, since any gains that may have been made in fighting information dependence in the mass media area may be lost as a result of the action of those who control computing power. In that context, Herbert Schiller's recent thoughts on this subject seem pertinent, illustrative, and well worth quoting in full:

Great changes are being made, at a dizzying rate, in the organization and dissemination of information and in the specialized application of data to production and distribution processes in the market economies of the western world. This has been made evident by all public discussions of the subject, in which the most important topics have mainly had to do with technical questions of costs, translation and access to information.

No mention has been made, however, of the fundamental and priority questions involved. In other words, the question is whether the worldwide instantaneous information systems and networks now being installed and soon to be put in operation have the ability, the purpose or, where their proprieters are concerned, even the intention of helping peoples and nations to conquer cultural and economic poverty.

This is a matter of the greatest public interest. It requires and deserves full and open discussion, and the most careful consideration of the community as a whole, not just by "technical experts." If the possibilities now being developed are used for the same purposes and in the same way as the preceding communication services, a magnificent opportunity to correct a number of social and information imbalances will have been lost. Failure to seize that opportunity may well mean a greater deepening of the differences that now separate a handful of privileged nations from the far more numerous disadvantaged countries.

Optimistic valuations of the new computer-based communication system undoubtedly abound. "The advantages to mankind of progress in international communications" have been widely publicized. It is considered that they will:

1. Increase the utilization of economic resources at the world level;
2. Speed up general technical progress;
3. Satisfy the special information needs of the less-developed countries;
4. Facilitate and expand world trade, and
5. Aid the diversification of universal culture.

Those attractive prospects are mere eventualities, however, owing to conditions and considerations that make it far more probable that the benefits of the new technology will continue to be unevenly distributed and that the dependence of countries and their social classes will be heightened, rather than diminished. This negative, but perhaps more realistic, valoration takes into consideration the context of the market into which the new technology is being inserted. It also recognizes the fact that this framework entails continuation of the doctrine of the free flow of information, with all its defects, in the very same way that has prevailed throughout the years since the second World War.(4)

POLITICAL AWARENESS

Everything that has just been said goes to show that information forms an integral part of the industrialization process and therefore allows a series of conclusions to be drawn with respect to the role it plays in relations between the industrialized countries and the countries of the Third World. Just as they do in their international economic relations, our Third World countries sell raw materials and buy manufactured products in the field of information. Except that in this case, our raw material is not copper, petroleum or bauxite, but our own reality. When our mass media buy, for example, the services of the transnational news agencies, what we are actually acquiring is our own reality, our own facts, our own circumstances - in other words, our own raw material, selected, evaluated, characterized, or processed as manufactured goods by agencies that are alien to our environment.

Awareness of these problems has been increasing both within political movements, especially that of the Non-Aligned

Countries, and in a variety of nongovernmental organizations that have put their research abilities to work at defining the new concepts that will support the proposed New International Information Order and make it viable.

The findings of progressive academic sectors of the Third World and the developed world have shown that the entire program of concepts that emerged at the end of World War II as a result of the debates on the right to information, the free flow of information, and freedom of expression has only served to further the growth of a communications system that tends to benefit the development model promoted by the dominant capitalist system.

The complex of practices and principles that emerged during the postwar period and the regional and world organizations formed at that time with the approval of the relatively limited number of countries that made up what was then the international community provided the base of operations for a system in which the new Third World countries had to make a place for themselves on achieving their political independence. The system was already structured when the African and Asian countries joined the so-called international community. They found themselves faced with an order that was politically and economically favorable to the expansion of the powerful and that stifled the zeal for progressive change encouraged by the new leaders. What they found was a system rooted in the diverse forms of colonialism and exploitation that have historically characterized the relations between a dominant center and the countries of the periphery. That system has been gradually perfected and adjusted over the last 30 years until it has become a coherent whole that may legitimately be termed the transnational power structure. The latter makes itself known through functionally differentiated forms of operation that, taken together, represent a complex set of instruments to be used for the central purpose of consolidating and expanding its capacity for action and influence throughout the world. The credentials it offers are a set of values and aspirations that claim to represent political stability, economic efficiency, technological creativity, market "logic," the virtues of the consumer society, the defense of freedom, and so on.

Growing awareness of the very significant role such information problems play in increasing dependence has been aimed especially at the question of the flow of news and the action taken in that respect by certain transnational news agencies. There can be no doubt, however, that the problem is of much wider scope, although it is true that news reports are the key information on which individuals and societies base the attitudes they take toward current events and the challenging decisions that lie before them. It is therefore important to take due note of the different political statements made on the information problem in the Third World, and to realize that although these were motivated by the problem arising from the special characteristics of the information presented in the mass media, they are equally valid for identifying other and greater obstacles in the field of information that affect the establishment of a New International Economic Order.

The growing political awareness in governmental sectors of what this phenomenon implies began taking shape only four or five years ago. One of the first instances in which people's attention was called to the matter took place in Latin America. In 1972 the Andean Pact countries, in a joint declaration by their foreign ministers, noted their concern over the fact that "an increasing volume of the international information circulating in and among our countries is being processed outside the subregion." This was the first time that mention was made in a Latin American high-level joint political declaration of a phenomenon of dependence so important and so long ignored.

The birth and growth of that awareness, however, has undoubtedly been most impressive and persistent within the political framework of the nonaligned countries.

The declaration issued in Algeria by the heads of state of the Non-Aligned Countries in September 1973 stated that "developing countries must take concerted action in the field of communications" and set as one of the most significant goals of that action "the reorganization of present information channels, which are a legacy of a colonial past and which have hindered free, direct, and rapid communications among them." Those concepts were ratified by the meeting of foreign ministers of Non-Aligned Countries held in Lima, Peru, in August 1975.

In March 1976, in a symposium on information held in Tunis, the Non-Aligned Countries agreed on the nature of the task to be performed:

> The symposium found that the Non-Aligned Countries have an enormous task before them in the analysis and diagnosis of that situation of dependence in the field of information of developing countries, as well as in the formulation of effective mechanisms which, through active and efficient solidarity, will allow them to overcome that dependence and create the conditions that will make it possible for information to begin serving the real interests of their peoples and to become a powerful interest for achieving their effective liberation.

The heads of state of Non-Aligned Countries, meeting in August 1976 in Colombo, Sri Lanka, ratified the foregoing decision. At the highest level of political representation, they declared:

The Non-Aligned Countries noted with concern the vast and ever-increasing gap between communication facilities in Non-Aligned Countries and in developed countries, which is a legacy of their colonial past. This has created a situation of dependence and domination in which the majority of countries are forced to become passive recipients of slanted, inadequate and distorted information. The identification and affirmation of their national and cultural identity is leading them to rectify this serious imbalance and to take urgent steps to strengthen this new area of reciprocal cooperation.

OBSTACLES AND ACTION

The new awareness of the aforementioned realities makes the task of building a New International Information Order one of a far-reaching nature that reveals the need for more dynamic liberation, democratization, and social participation policies. In that context, we can identify certain very specific areas in which action must be taken to strengthen the development of the New International Information Order from the point of view we have described here.

Coordination of Political and Governmental Action

1. Specific tasks to be performed at this level include such things as the development of new legal principles for international information, since "to date, no real body of laws on international information exists that respects and protects the interests of all countries and, in particular, of those progressive countries which want to introduce substantial modifications in the unjust internal orders prevailing in a large part of the Third World."

2. Within that juridical framework, one priority question is the establishment of certain rules for regulating the operation of transnational agencies. Progress is now being made toward establishing a code of conduct - a limited instrument, but one which nonetheless marks a step forward in efforts to obtain a new economic order. It is particularly necessary where activities of the transnational news agencies are concerned, since these are not regulated in any way.

3. Equally necessary is mobilization to establish new communication policies, in the understanding that these form an integral part of development strategies. Consequently, there may be as many different communication policies and information models as there are development plans, all based

on lines that will give the majority sectors of each nation's population access to effective participation in the political life of the country.

4. Political and governmental action must have the parallel aim of creating action mechanisms for promoting international loan support for projects undertaken in the information field. This is particularly significant within the framework of the United Nations, and that organization must also be encouraged to put new concepts into practice in the field of information, especially as regards the news value placed on events occurring within the international organizations.

Development of New Technical-Professional Approaches

1. One of the essential questions to be resolved in shaping a New Information Order is the development of alternative media that will serve, on the one hand, to satisfy the information needs left unattended by the transnational system and, on the other, to generate in industrialized countries a similar need for approaches and interpretations other than those they now apply to contemporary reality.

2. This working goal calls for transfer among the countries of the Third World, among their progressive forces and among solidary professional institutions of organization techniques and methods of proven efficiency. It also requires an attitude that is sufficiently autonomous to refrain from trying to achieve the same pattern of technological development as the transnational communication media because it seems to represent the only possible solution, and to recognize instead the communication potential afforded by instruments that may appear precarious but exert a strong influence on the public.

3. In a parallel fashion, material drawn both from experiences of the people and from industrial action focused on change should be employed in putting into operation information systems that combine with the "professional efficiency" so favored by the transnational structure a vision enriched by their search for compromise solutions based on the awareness that information is a social benefit.

If industrialized technology has created such instruments as the videocassette, records, tape recordings, slides, etc., the important thing now is to develop a recovery consciousness that takes such tools and turns them into means of spreading new truths. Why isn't it possible to establish networks for exchanging among progressive-minded countries and peoples videotapes with a new sort of interviews, programs, and content? What stands in the way of increasing exchanges of recorded radio programs with new music, with the voices of people who view and interpret today's problems in a new and different way? There is a challenging field of action here whose failure so far to grow has been due not so much to lack of money, as to lack of determination or a proper understanding of the strength that can lie in alternative forms of information, even if the media employed to transmit its messages are different from those postulated by the transnational system.

Training for the Creation of Communication Patterns Affording Active Participation

1. As the New International Information Order promotes new and different principles for the action and presence of the communication media, the need will arise to recognize education for communication as a fundamental task. Broadly speaking, this means that political, professional, and communication sectors and social leaders and organizations must acquire an understanding of the new concepts and models suggested by the potential residing in new communication practices.

2. Although we have repeatedly insisted that access and participation of the different social sectors in the communication process is a basic necessity, we also believe that this calls for education systems in which every individual and social group is made aware of the powerful aid the communication system can provide in their dialogue with others. As those sectors of society come more and more to understand the real meaning of communication, a new and powerful voice will be raised in those countries that suffer the causes of dependence, demanding the presence of a New Information Order - in other words, a new type of content, news, access, and participation, far different from the one the ideology of the transnational power structure has postulated.

NOTES

(1) This paper summarizes opinions expressed in the following articles: Juan Somavía, "La Estructura Transnacional de Poder y la Información Internacional"; Somavía, "Participación del Tercer Mundo en las Comunicaciones Internacionales: Perspectivas después de Nairobi"; Fernando Reyes Matta, "Un modelo de comunicación con participación social activa" and Rafael Roncagliolo and Noreene Janus, "A Survey of the Transnational Structure of the Mass Media and Advertising."

(2) Jan Tingenberg, coordinator, Reshaping the International Order (New York: E.P. Dutton & Co., 1976).

(3)   Juan Somavía, "La Estructura Transnacional de Poder."

(4)   Herbert Schiller, "Informaciones por computadora.   ¿Por quienes y para qué?"   Boletin Comisión Nacional Cubana de la UNESCO, Nos. 75-76 (May-August 1978).

5 The Condition of Women and the Exercise of Political Power
Haydee Birgin

INTRODUCTION

The purpose of this paper is to demonstrate that any analysis of the condition of women must start from the understanding of some basic elements: the fact that the natural and necessary relationship between two human beings with biological differences is usually converted into a relationship of domination of the woman by the man, and that this historical process of differentiation brings in domination as a form of social organization.

It is important to understand that the marginalization of women is essentially different from that of other oppressed and marginalized groups, in the sense that women form half of the world and their oppression persists through different social formations.

In 1884 the Seneca Falls Declaration was passed in the United States. This event was significant in that it was the formal beginning of the feminist movement. The document condemned the multiple forms of women's oppression and total deprivation of rights.

It is important to stress that the feminist struggle concentrated initially on the right to vote. However, in 1869, with the emergence of a group led by Susan B. Anthony, the movement split. This group did not limit itself to the suffragette struggle, but considered the position of women in the world of work. Anthony argued that in all the pages of history where there exists a class with no civil rights, we must really see this as a degraded labor force. And so the struggle for equal pay for equal work was carried out along with the debate on divorce and prostitution.

However, as a historical paradox, everyone remembers the Martyrs of Chicago and the whole world pays homage to them on May Day; but the same does not happen for the women who were assassinated a few years later in New York. In 1908, 129 textile workers, on strike for better working conditions, were locked in the plant by their employers who proceeded to burn down the building. The women were burnt to ashes, and the date has not entered the collective memory of the international working class, although it was chosen, much later, as International Women's Day.

There are two possible interpretations of the history of women. One talks of constant discrimination, lack of civil rights, social subordination, and exploitation at work. The other talks of women's struggle and active participation in every social or revolutionary movement, without exception. Women took up arms in the two world wars and took part in liberation armies. We only need recall, for example, their participation in the Algerian and Vietnamese liberation struggles, the setting up of the national women's army and its leading role in the Great March of China, the thousands of women dead or tortured under regimes like those of Argentina, Chile, and Uruguay, those who continue the struggle for their families under arrest and kidnapped in these countries; the mad women of May Square, so called by the Argentine regime for their weekly meetings in the main square, or those on hunger strike in Santiago cathedral.

Where then is this inferiority on which domination is based? There is no doubt that an explanation of the historical oppression of women must go beyond biology and the concrete forms taken by the economic exploitation of man by man. An analysis of the women's problem must be in terms of power relations. Reductionist concepts, which aim to assimilate the domination of women into the class division of society, prevent adequate explanation of the nature of the problem. Man-woman power relations are not submerged in class relations. We must start from the assumption that not all power relations are class relations. The existence of relations of man-woman domination in class societies - although they are marked by class relations - is analytically distinguishable; that is, domination is based on different premises.

An analysis of each of the forms of domination will enable us to disentangle the specific features of each historical context. It is important to undertake the analysis in order to build a new concept of power. The analytical study of the theory of the state is the only element in the broad field of the exercise and functioning of power, since power is expressed in a multiplicity of power relations. Power cannot be examined only through the organizations of the state, it must also be considered from the point of view of the specific nature of domination in each and every one of the forms it takes; that is, from the workings of the apparatus of control, the institutions, the family, and the school.

This apparatus of power has not been sufficiently studied. The matter has been analyzed on the basis of the personality of those exercising power, on the basis of the history of the economic processes or infrastructure, but not on the basis of the strategies, apparatus, and techniques of control. An analysis of the type we have described may perhaps enable us to discover the relations of domination that underline the different forms of women's participation in society and how the natural difference between the sexes served as a basis for social differences.

TWO FOCI OF ANALYSIS

From a broad examination of the historical process, we can infer that women's struggle has taken place on two basic levels: for legal equality and for equality in employment. Consequently, two foci emerge for us to pursue in our analysis:

Legal-Formal Focus

If we analyze women's problems from a legal-formal perspective, everything suggests that the feminist ideals of the eighteenth century have been achieved. Equal rights are well included in the laws of nearly every state. Women first gained the right to vote in 1906 in Finland and in the United States in 1920. In 1929, Ecuador became the first Latin American country to grant the vote to women, and Paraguay brought the process to a close in 1961 by accepting that right.

The resolutions and studies of the Organization of American States - the first regional institution to take an interest in the political emancipation of women - were followed by similar documents from other organizations like the United Nations, the Economic and Social Council, and the UNCTAD Council. In June 1975, the ILO resolved to implement a plan of action with a view to promoting equal treatment and opportunities for working women.

Moreover, the labor laws of different countries have begun to establish specific regulations on equality for women, especially in relation to wages. We can also see evidence of regulations relating to maternity benefits and pensions for housewives.

However, much ground is still to be covered. The feminist aims, directed less towards formal equality guaranteed by legislation, and more towards the freedom of women to exercise such equality, are still under discussion in the parliaments of many advanced countries and have been successfully resolved in only a few. We are here making particular reference, among others, to rights over children, shared custody and control, the right to dispose freely of one's goods, and the right to abortion. We must recognize, however, that major legislative advances have been made in the formal recognition of equality between men and women.

This struggle for equality, for recognition as a human being, has only been one stage in the long march of women's liberation. At this very moment, we face another set of problems which can be neither analyzed nor solved in a legal-formal perspective because the differences between men and women, resolved within a legal framework, give only the impression that male domination has disappeared. This perspective prevents us from understanding completely, through the acceptance of formal equality, how the specific difference between man and woman manifests itself in domination.

Today, women are not fighting for formal equality; their struggle is based on diversity, on the establishment of their own identity in society as women. Unity in diversity can only be achieved on the basis of this identity. Diversity of functions does not explain the relations of domination-submission, expressed historically in power relations.

Economic Focus: Women at Work

There is a strong tendency nowadays to analyze the family as a productive unit and the woman as the key to this process. However, the participation of women in economic activity cannot be isolated from the process in which they are involved. In the case of the Third World, development, which is concentrated in certain regions and sectors, has favored only certain groups of people. Thus the participation of women takes on different aspects, depending on the stage of development in a region and whether it is urban or rural. It is clear that there is no such thing as "the Asian Woman" or "the Latin American Woman" as a global, abstract entity; what exists are different situations, with women in particular productive systems and different social classes. Once this is made clear, we can set out the general features manifested in different productive structures.

For some time now, a series of initiatives has been taking place to oppose discrimination and increase the participation of women in economic activity. There have been many such objectives, but all of them are based on a concept of economic development that needs women as a human resource.

The conferences on women and development held in 1975 were based on these premises. That is to say, women are considered an economic resource and the need for their incorporation into the productive process is paramount if resources available for development are to be fully utilized. As a variation on this theme, there is a demographic perspective too: This suggests that the increase in women's participation in productive activity will act as an effective instrument in reducing fertility rates. Thus the incorporation of women into production would have a positive impact within a more generalized policy of birth control by means of a change in their reproductive behavior.

On the basis of this concept of development, the incorporation of women into production would not necessarily imply a change of their subordinate role. On the contrary, present forms of exploitation of the female work force might be exaggerated.

This is why, when the need for female participation in development is put forward, it is necessary to be precise about the type of development involved and the way in which such participation will take effect.

A new type of collective self-reliance requires structural changes in social relations, both in the economic sphere and in the structure of power. Development considered as a whole redefines participation, which can only be democratic participation, participation in decision making.

When we recognize the importance of women's participation in the production process, what we see is the incorporation of a new perspective of development through participatory democracy. Only by integration into the process can the aims of equality at work be achieved; if this does not happen, inequality will widen. A focus that considers women only as a human resource will not modify the relations of domination on which their participation is based.

FORMS OF DOMINATION OF WOMEN AT WORK

Housework

We shall begin our analysis with housework - that is, the work women do for the family - since this is the type of work most women do.

In the origins of the family - in the domestic economy - the fact that some members begin to produce for exchange or sell their labor affects the family, since the woman's workload is increased. Some of the tasks formerly done by men - for example, fetching water and gathering wood - are now part of women's work. Thus the woman continues to produce for the family's own consumption, enabling the other members to sell their labor for less than the price of their own reproduction, since that is now guaranteed by the family system.

Work done in the home for domestic consumption is not considered a way of generating income, since as the quantity of service and consumer goods produced directly by women increases, so money income necessary to maintain the family consumption level decreases.

The question is at present at the center of a theoretical debate revolving round the value of domestic housework in the production process and the role of the family as key in women's oppression.(1) Unpaid work undertaken by women - the mechanism by which the transfer of housework to the capitalist sector is made - makes it possible to pay wages below the value of labor. Women's contribution is thus essential in the present production system, as a kind of underpaid and supplementary labor force that is, in effect, a reserve army of workers.

This theoretical debate in the women's movement is certainly not over. The richness of the debate stems from the fact that it is incorporated in a public debate on a question political economists would like to ignore. This is the recognition of women's work as housewives and the relation this work has to production.

Housework hides women's exploitation, particularly in the case of working-class and other employed women who, after a day's work in the factory or shop, have a second day's work at home. To de-hierarchise women's work, to take away their importance in the politicoeconomic field because they produce use-values not governed by prices and the market, is to hide the true nature of their contribution.

Urban Wage Labor

Women's participation in the urban labor market is not directly linked to the economic structure and industrialization process in the majority of Third World countries.

Industrialization policies have accentuated the inequality and deformation of the growth in our economies, with marked development in those branches and sectors of industry of interest to monopoly capital. The regime of low wages and growing inflation increased the concentration of income in a limited nucleus that in turn invests only in a small section of the economy. Industry uses labor-saving technology, preventing the growing work force from being absorbed. A relative population surplus has developed that is used in industries less likely to benefit from improvement in the productivity of labor. The jobs involved are unskilled or semiskilled and low paid. Another part of this work force does jobs that are not a necessary part of the productive process, although they are paid.

The consequences of this process are to be felt most crudely in African cities, where economic activity reflects the productive structure of the region: banks, commercial services, and import substitution industries. This type of economic activity is incapable of absorbing the increasing work force in the face of ever-growing migration levels from rural areas. We are dealing here with economies based on agricultural production and the exploitation of mines for export; industrial development is scarce and, in general, the participation of women at this level is very low. This type of industry offers few jobs, and those that exist are mainly reserved for men.

If we look at the present general economic situation of Third World countries, characterized by the ever-increasing poverty of the working masses, we can derive one very important fact about the female labor force: Increased participation of women at work over the last few years is a consequence of the worsening of the standard of living for a great part of the population. If women are compelled to enter the labor market – from necessity, without previous training and with levels of education lower than that of the male population – we can draw a significant conclusion: Whatever the productive activity of women, in terms of the labor force, they are always at a disadvantage to men.

We can point to specific differences in the sexual labor markets: The supply of female labor is derived from factors quite different from those governing the supply of male labor. The job opportunities the production system offers to men and women differ substantially from one another, this being reflected in the distribution patterns of the Economically Active Population Census (EAPC) on sex in different branches of activity.

In Latin America, for example, men are concentrated in industries connected with agriculture and product processing, and to a lesser extent in commerce and services. On the other hand, almost half of the female labor force is engaged in the tertiary sector, the only sector where the proportion of women is slightly higher than that of men. The manufacturing industry follows, with a lower percentage of the female labor force involved. (This characteristic of the female Economically Active Population is valid not only for Latin America, but also for the towns of Africa, despite differences in the structure of production relations.)

Varoius studies of the Latin American labor force have stressed this aspect of the labor market and the differences linked to the sexual division of labor. For men, at a productive age, work is a necessity. If productive work is not available, men look for occupations in services that may be totally useless from the point of view of production, but that enable them to survive. Men's decisions to enter the labor market are connected to factors affecting their own economic activity: the age structure of the population, the demand for labor, their education, whether they come from a rural or urban background, the legislation in force. Other factors are also involved, such as extent of their schooling, their marital status, the size and nature of the family group they belong to, the income levels of other members of the family, and the social habits of the group.

The distribution pattern of women according to age is quite different. In Latin America, female participation in the labor market is highest between the ages of 20 and 25. This fact is linked to marital status, since female participation tends to be higher in the years when women are single. As Kirsh points out, the involvement of single women in the Latin American labor market is a number of times higher than that of married women, and in the 20-25 age range this ratio reaches 5:1.(2) On the other hand, in industrialized countries, like France, Great Britain, Denmark, and West Germany, married women form two-thirds of the female labor force.

For women in the low-income sector, the situation is different from that of middle-income groups. For the first group, the decision to enter the labor market is linked to survival. Wages are necessary to support the woman herself, to support her children, or to supplement her husband's wage. This situation is the most akin to that of men, with respect to the factors operating on entry into the labor market.

For women in the middle or higher strata, the strategic variables are the number and age of any children, the woman's education, and the difference between the family's income and its expectations of consumption. An important variable in the decision to enter the labor market is the level of the woman's education. The most highly educated women are those with the biggest share in the labor market. If we consider that the educational level of the female population is lower than the male's, we see that, in order to obtain jobs where they compete with men, women must have a higher level of education than men. Although the majority of women do not compete in the same labor market as men, their market runs parallel and is characterized by activities that are an extension of their domestic functions.

In Africa, the education variable is a determining factor. Women who have had access to education are able to enter the labor market. In a study of 39 African countries, women formed 35 percent of the primary school population in 1969; in 1970-71 they formed 28 percent of the secondary school population; and in the same year, in higher education, the figure was 13 percent.(3) Professional training for women is determined by the job opportunities that justify such training. South of the Sahara, women who went to Western schools have a position of advantage: They get office, nursing, and midwifery jobs, and a small proportion even manage to become doctors or teachers.

In Third World countries, the demand for female labor is quite different from that for men. The male labor force is directly related to the structure of the production system, the type of development, and the use or nonuse of technology. Demand for female labor is influenced by social, cultural, or economic factors. Basically, the female labor force is limited to activities "suitable" for women, those considered to be an extension of their household tasks (clothing and food manufacturing). Their participation in industry is minimal; the majority are devoted to services and manufacturing. There are, however, industries that contract women especially for tasks requiring concentration and patience. Their part in the production process is generally in the later stages of the process (finishing, labelling, and packing), where the required level of responsibility is not decisive. This fact goes some way towards an explanation of the wage differentials between the sexes. However, the differences in qualifications are a result of a process that reproduces the inferior position of women in the labor market. On the other hand, when they are equally qualified, women tend to get lower wages and lower job mobility and prospects. Discrimination against women in the labor market is due to various factors. One explanation could be that employing women implies higher costs. Labor laws which protect women during pregnancy or in the first few months after the birth of their children, actually operate against women's entry into the labor market. Another cause can be found in the patterns of women's entry into and exit from the labor market, due to their marital status, fertility, and the role assigned by society to women in the family. In this way, the risks of training a woman are greater than those involved in training a man.

Women who work in industry in Africa are taken on as temporary workers and do not enjoy the maternity benefits conceded by law. The work they do is very similar to that of assembly operations prevalent in Latin America, which consist of illegal contracts, either on an individual or group basis. These workers are given a part of the process of production in exchange for an extremely low price per unit delivered. Using this kind of contract, as in the case of temporary or day-labor in African cities, labor legislation is circumvented; workers are completely unprotected and do not enjoy any of the benefits the law concedes to wage earners. This is the system generally used by large companies since it enables them to reduce costs and save on plant and machinery.

Although the nature of female involvement in the labor market is similar throughout the Third World, added to the problems of African women is their lack of training and the type of contracts that enable companies to pay any wages they

like. In general, they are complementary wages, since the
majority are migrants, who maintain links with the domestic
community they belong to. The fact that they do not join
trade unions contributes to their exclusion from legal protection.

The nature of the urban labor market cannot be considered in isolation from the rural sector. The phenomenon of
migration, which is the result of a particular model of development imposed on the agricultural sector, and which
produces a worsening of conditions for the rural population,
determines the conditions under which women enter the urban
labor market.

A study of the female labor force's part in commerce
suggests that one cannot consider this in isolation from domestic obligations. Commerce is an important activity of women
in African cities. In general, it is a matter of reselling, but
in some cases they sell their own produce. They are organized into associations that have very strong negotiating
powers. In Ghana, 80 percent of the traders are women, and
in Nigeria, half of all Yoruba women devote themselves to
trade and commerce. A similar situation exists in some parts
of Latin America, especially in predominantly agricultural
areas. Business women in Africa own shops, pharmacies, and
small industries. These women have been able to take advantage of the relations and social position of their husbands,
especially for obtaining credits.

In short, the characteristics of female participation in the
labor market are linked to the dependent nature of the structures of the production system. A type of development that
does not take into account the absorption of the work force or
the quality of jobs supplied will bring increased unemployment
and a permanent cheapening of the work force, which is only
to the advantage of employers, leaving both male and female
workers in a worse situation than before.

The conditions of women at work cannot be seen in isolation from the nature of development, and on the basis of
this, their increasing share in the labor market, as well as the
form that share takes, is conditioned by the alternative of
putting a new style of development into practice.

WOMEN IN THE RURAL ECONOMY

Rural women's work is a decisive factor in the productive
process. Their role is fundamental in policies aimed at the
rapid agricultural expansion needed to overcome food deficits
in countries of the Third World.

Capitalist development in agriculture, says Rodolfo
Stavenhagen, has increased social and economic differences

between social classes.(4) It has served to further concentrate wealth, power, and income in the hands of landowners and intermediaries, by taking the land away from the peasants and turning them into marginalized, landless laborers; it has substituted the idea of worth and use for the few for the idea of survival for the majority.

What characterizes underdeveloped countries is a polarization between a small land-holding elite and the growing mass of proletarianized rural workers. This process of rural development consists in the breaking up of the peasant subsistence economy, based on the use of family labor producing for local consumption on a small scale. As peasant agriculture breaks up, it is no longer able to satisfy the basic needs of the family unit; it is increasingly starved for capital due to its relative lack of resources, its primitive technology, and the effect of capitalist penetration in the country.

For Stavenhagen, the peasant economy fulfills a dual role: It serves to tie the peasant to the land and diminish the pressures on the nonagricultural economy at a time when there is a surplus of labor. It can reproduce labor much more cheaply for the global economy. The modern or capitalist sector is interested, to a certain extent, in maintaining and reproducing the peasant economy while it is subordinate to the modern sector. It functions, moreover, as a protective mechanism for millions of underemployed workers who would otherwise generate pressures on the social and political system.

An analysis of the agricultural sector helps one understand how women can be incorporated into the urban labor market and helps one see the migration phenomenon as a determining factor.(5)

The percentage of migration is influenced by trends in demographic growth. In the case of women, the phenomenon comes about because of unemployment in rural areas and the marginalization to which this kind of development condemns them. When they do enter the urban labor market, it is in nonproductive jobs, mainly in domestic service or prostitution.

The African case is different in terms of the causes of migration and confirms that the phenomenon is directly linked to the structure of production and capitalist expansion. Labor migration started at the beginning of the colonial period, and for purely economic reasons. Only men were involved; their families stayed in the tribal areas and the migrants returned periodically to their rural villages.

In referring to the features of women's participation in the cities of Africa, we indicated that the links that kept working women in touch with their communities enabled employers to pay very low wages, turning their labor into an activity which supplemented the family group's income.

A distinctive feature of African migration is its recurring pattern. In order to achieve the consolidation of wage labor, governments dictated measures to prevent peasants from being able to maintain themselves by means of subsistence agriculture. "Half" cultivation was forbidden, and high taxes were established in the rural regions. All this contributed to adult male migration to the cities. But at the same time, in order to avoid the political dangers of great concentrations of people in the cities, they prohibited migrants from establishing themselves permanently in the cities.

Meillassoux refers to the coercive measures used to drag peasant labor from the villages.(6) Among these measures, she underlines forced labor, recruitment, and indebtedness. Craft and related activities, such as building, hunting, and harvesting, were slowly abandoned for paid activity; in this way the domestic economy was turned into a supplier of indispensable commodities to the colonial sector.

Women in the Subsistence Economy

The role of rural women must be examined, according to what we have just described, from the starting point of the restrictions and alternatives inherent in the family unit. Changes in the organization and technology of production have an impact on the participation of rural women in production.

Technological progress has not caused any significant improvement in the conditions of women in the rural regions. On the contrary, they continue to use traditional tools and their own hands in their work. The division of labor is redefined in the heart of the family and in the domestic community.

In peasant economies, the basic unit is not the agricultural dimension, but the domestic unit. Productive labor in the fields is only one aspect of the multitude of alternatives pursued by the domestic unit in order to survive. If the man works outside the unit, his activity is added, as a contribution, to the combination of activities of the whole family group. Women devote themselves to the care and feeding of the family and so contribute in a decisive way, to the maintenance and reproduction of the labor force. They undertake a series of tasks which, although not considered specifically productive (clothes manufacture, fruit gathering) are a help for the whole unit; others are undertaken under company control (home assembly working), which is paid on a piece work basis.

Wage labor is combined with women's domestic activities. In the case of rural women, it is difficult to separate their activities in agricultural production from what might be considered specifically domestic. Their behavior is, therefore, determined by the needs of the unit.

In the lowest strata, women's activity is greater. Their domestic activity increases in order to cover the needs with less resources. In this sector we see the highest degree of proletarianization. The man enters wage labor before the woman, leaving her in charge of the agricultural work of the holding, along with what is specifically domestic labor. In this sector women also participate in the harvests as temporary laborers.

The decision to enter the labor market is based on economic needs. It is considered inconvenient and not socially acceptable for women to work outside the family unit. Ideological mechanisms show a marked tendency towards preventing women from working outside the home. Only the inability of the domestic unit to supply the family's needs determines the role of women in and outside the labor market. However, their choice of work is reduced, as much in the modern industrial sector as in the cities, when they join what are basically marginal occupations, such as domestic service or prostitution.

Women in the Modern Agricultural Sector

The wage labor market of the modern agricultural sector is predominantly male, although women participate to a great extent in the cultivation of coffee, vegetables, and fruit crops. Their highest share of the market comes at harvest time and whenever fruit is to be picked and packed. In modern agriculture, women are confined to secondary activities, to the final stages of the production process; their status is very low, and the work is eminently temporary.

The areas of participation of each of the sexes within the production process are defined. Female labor is restricted to labor-intensive activities. As tasks are mechanized and more skill is required, the number of women involved decreases. In tasks requiring intensive labor, the participation of women increases.

The use of tractors and other machinery does not require any special physical effort that would prevent women from using them; nevertheless, opportunities for women are limited in this field. This is not due to their inability to learn the skills, but to the lack of opportunities, conditioned as much by the male mentality as by the women themselves.

An interesting observation in this respect was made in a study of female labor in the tobacco industry. Both employees and employers have an interest in maintaining the present structure of the work force. Women tend not to extend the field of their work to those tasks considered to be men's prerogatives. One reason for this lies in the fact that women have to face prohibitions from their families, which limit their activity to the clothing industry and related activities. It is probable, the study suggests, that men do not accept the participation of women in those stages of the process in which female labor is unusual.(7) These prohibitions, exercised by men against their wives, are rooted in social and cultural prejudices. Women who work on the land take a lot of risks; they are considered to have no reputation to lose and are therefore devalued in their own surroundings.

The modern agricultural sector has a labor market with strong sexual discrimination. The greatest concentration of female labor is found in the manufacturing industry, in commerce, and in the service sector. The preferential use of female labor by companies linked to this sector is due to what has been called "special female aptitudes" or certain skills that make them ideal for tasks like picking and preparing bunches or cutting leaves. Behind this argument lies the main cause of their being employed: their weaker negotiating position, which makes them an easily exploitable work force.

We also see - to the disadvantage of women - differences in wage structures. These differences are explained by the position women occupy in the labor process, basically due to their lack of skills. What we have is indirect wage discrimination through discrimination in jobs.

Despite the differences from the previous case, women play the role of a reserve pool of cheap labor in both sectors. Their work is used to keep wage levels low, since their work at home and the amount of goods and services they produce enables the family unit to maintain a certain level of consumption, although income may be quite low. It is women's labor that is loaded in these situations. Their place in the modern labor market is characterized by strong sexual discrimination.

The Effects of Colonialization

In the case of Africa, it is clear that discriminatory policies in the passing of technology imported by the European colonialists created a breach in the productivity of female and male peasants. The change from traditional to modern methods of agriculture tends to increase the prestige of men and decrease that of women, who are relegated to a lower social status.

Senegal is a typical example of the result of increased agricultural productivity on the marginalization of women. Great efforts were made to introduce better techniques into rice production; men were trained to use these new methods, when really women had been responsible for agriculture up until then. Discrimination against women is directly linked to colonial domination and the introduction of technology carried out by the Europeans.

At the meeting held in Dakar,(8) some of the effects of colonialization were pointed out, relating to the kind of economy imposed:

- the imposition on peasants to produce only those products that traders offer to buy from them
- the substitution of imported industrial products for local craft products
- forced labor, compulsory crops, and the moving of populations to mining or plantation regions
- the granting of political support to the social classes with the authority to appropriate land
- the alliance with religious sectors who aimed to commercialize the taxes paid by peasants

African agriculture was predominantly female, with the exception of treefelling; women undertook all the tasks - removing and burning fallen trees, sowing and planting, harvesting, transporting the harvest - thus demystifying the physical weakness argument, the basis for the attitudes of sexual discrimination of which women are the object.

The worsening of living conditions for African women is directly related to the implementation of the colonial model and its forms of exploitation. Contrary to certain statements on the marginalization of women, it was they themselves who paid the cost of maintaining and reproducing the labor used for agricultural exports.

The consequence of the colonial model was the slow marginalization of women from the powers of decision making, from the modernization process, from the use of advanced technology, relegating them in this way to subsistence production.

The need to concentrate the whole labor force on crops for export redirects the sexual division of labor in accordance with the needs of capitalist production; women are integrated into the work force, in the case of horticultural production or where migration of the men is encouraged. This puts a heavier load on the women. Colonial policy organizes the productive capacity of the region in accordance with its own needs.

Rural women make up between 70 and 90 percent of the female population in African countries; they do 60 percent of the work in agriculture and cover 44 percent of the majority of tasks needed to feed the family.(9)

In areas where migration rates were very high, due to the demand for male labor by the mining industries or import substitution goods, women had to take on the traditional work of men and ensure their families' survival, adding the men's jobs to their own. The burdensome tasks of women in different regions are done in conditions of superexploitation.

The use of traditional techniques persists in order to avoid competition from imported manufactured goods.

Women were excluded from the new legal framework of land ownership; land is no longer a common good, and they are excluded from the laws on inheritance, since they have sufficient money to buy land.

An analysis of the participation of women in production - an analysis seen from an economic angle - shows the conditions of superexploitation they are subjected to.

"Invisible" work, that is, domestic work done in the heart of the family, involves women in great numbers of hours for which they are not paid, nor are these hours included in the national account. Although not socially recognized, this work is useful and necessary to the system as a whole. Reproduction is only a moment of production; the maintenance and reproduction of the labor force, therefore, is part of the production process itself that enables wage levels to be kept low and increases, through female labor in the manufacture of products necessary for food, the income level of the family group.

The labor market, as our analysis showed, is a sexually differentiated market, with deep-rooted inequalities. An analysis of this fact enables us to see more clearly the relations of domination, in a determined historical moment and a specific area of study. Despite the proliferation of legislation guaranteeing equality between men and women at work as well as protection for women - existing wage differentials, hidden indirectly by job discrimination, and the difficulties women have in gaining access to jobs that are not simply an extension of the type of work they do at home - are all expressions of the underlying relations of domination in legal resolutions.

The situation of women at work, their participation in conditions of equality, can only be changed by a new type of development. Women must be the agents of this process, of a participatory and egalitarian development whose democratic base allows their real incorporation into the social process as subjects with rights, and not only as human resources.

MAN-WOMAN RELATIONS AS POWER RELATIONS

A natural relationship between two human beings, differentiated by their bodies, serves as a basis for social differentiation, for a relation of domination-submission. Historical differentiation introduces domination as a form of organizing subjects.

To analyze the condition of women from a basis of power relations implies a consideration of power in a broader sense than the state apparatus.

Power is present in all relations; it is expressed and manifested in a multiplicity of ways. Where power exists, it is exercised. Our focus implies that power must be redefined and considered in the light of its dual aspects, in the use of coercion and punishment, and, in turn, the ways in which power uses satisfaction and pleasure to exercise its domination. Power relations are many and varied, they run through the whole of society, they are exercised throughout all our institutions: the family, the school, and even through our very bodies. As Foucalult says, the body is an object of power and the target of a mechanism that separates it from itself, puts it back together again, molds it, and makes it more flexible, more docile, more useful.

In man-woman relationships, women's submission is exercised not only through coercion, but through the system itself, which organizes satisfaction, produces desires, and allows the perpetuation of the model of domination through pleasure itself. The exclusive link that women establish with their children – a type of relation they usually deny to men – their indispensable role as the center of the family, by means of which they generate dependency, allows them an illusion of power, "as in the infantile world of our ancestors."

The importance of going beyond an economist's interpretation of power, consisting in attributing to the state apparatus a monopoly of the expression of power of one class over another, is fundamental if the analysis is to be deepened. We need to study power in its mechanisms, exercise, and techniques – techniques that have almost always been a response to the needs of a particular social juncture: the needs of industry, the overcoming of crisis. An example of this is the contradiction in the present nationalist movement in Iran, which suppresses many of the expressions of democracy. The thousands of women who demonstrated in the streets of Teheran in defence of their rights and against the use of the veil were violently repressed and attacked.

This does not mean that power is autonomous and that it can be analyzed without taking account of the economic process and production relations: Power relations are not exogenous but immanent in a different type of linkage and socioeconomic process. Power relations are found not only in the repressive functions of the superstructure, but also where they operate and where they have a productive role. Their effects are seen in many different forms; they are relations that run through, characterize, and form the total system, organizing us all. We are the carriers of power.

Reductionist concepts that focus their analysis on only one of the forms in which power is expressed – the economy – lead to the assumption that the replacement of one class by another in the leadership of the state apparatus will change relations of domination. However, it would appear that the problem of transforming the social relations of production is a necessary but insufficient condition; we must also transform the ideological superstructure that perpetuates sexual domination.

Another important aspect to consider is the power-knowledge link and how it operates in relation to man-woman domination. This would enable us to understand how from power have come the arguments with the aid of biology, psychology, and history that have served as a basis for all discriminatory legislation against women, legislation that restricts their liberty.

To analyze man-woman relations as power relations is to consider the complexity of their mechanisms, their specificity, and the forms they take in every social relation, relations that are not only the reproduction of the State. Man is not the representative of the State against woman, just as in the family the father is no longer the representative of the sovereign. The family does not reproduce society, and in turn, society does not imitate the family. What we must analyze is what mechanisms of power would enable the family to support policies of social control, what relations of domination, what techniques of subjection operate in the heart of the family and on which certain policies are inscribed. Finally we must disentangle the way in which the system appropriates for itself the mechanisms of power through which the nucleus of dominations is formed in support of the different ways it is expressed.

The nucleus of man-woman relations - domination-submission - has its own techniques and mechanisms: subjection, hierarchy, obedience. The system appropriates these mechanisms as long as they are useful and necessary to maintaining relations of domination in the factory, the school, and society as a whole.

The condition of women, as a relation of domination, can only be transformed through a new type of development, in which women, too, are agents in the process - a type of development that will change not only the economic structures, but the very structure of power itself. We need a new type of development, bearing in mind the utopias of this century, where alternatives are found to the present system of domination and exploitation between human beings. Only then will freedom be the basis of the man-woman relationship.

Table 5.1. Latin America: Participation of the Economically
Active Population as a Proportion of the Total Population
By Sex, 1970

Country	Year	Total	Men	Women
Argentina—**/	1970	38.5	57.9	19.4
Brazil—***/	1973	38.5	53.7	23.6
Columbia—***/	1970	29.5	44.0	15.4
Costa Rica	1973	31.3	50.3	12.1
Cuba—****/ */	1970	30.8	49.2	11.5
Chile—**/	1970	29.5	46.4	13.3
Dominica—**/	1970	31.0	46.1	15.9
Ecuador—*****/	1974	31.5	49.8	13.2
El Salvador	1971	37.0	52.8	21.5
Guatemala—**/	1973	29.9	51.4	8.2
Haiti—*/	1971	56.0	57.6	54.5 1/
Honduras—*/	1974	28.0	---	---
Mexico (8)	1974	27.4	43.0	11.6
Nicaragua—**/	1971	26.6	42.4	11.4
Panama	1970	34.2	50.2	17.8
Paraguay—**/	1972	32.1	50.8	13.6
Peru—*****/	1972	28.6	45.3	11.8
Uruguay	1963	39.0	58.9	19.3
Venezuela	1971	28.1	43.7	12.6

Source: ILO Yearbook of Labour Statistics
*/   Provisional

**/   Sample taken from national census

***/   Estimates based on home surveys

****/   Does not include domestic servants

*****/   Excludes indigenous jungle population

(*)   Official estimates

1/   These provisional data show obvious over-representa-
         tion.

Table 5.2.   Asia: Participation of the Economically
Active Population as a Proportion of the Total Population
By Sex

Country	Year	Total	Men	Women
India	1971	32.9	52.5	11.9
Indonesia*/	1971	33.9	46	22
Iran**/	1966	30.2	50.7	8.3
Israel***/	1974	32.9	44.4	21.4
Japan****/	1974	48.1	60.9	35.7

Source: TLO Yearbook of Labour Statistics

*/   Figures based on tables from samples of national
          census.

**/   Excludes   population   without   permanent   address.

***/   1974.   PEA figures are based on a sample survey on
          the work force.

****/   1974.   Estimates based on results of sample surveys
          on the work force.

Table 5.3.　Africa: Participation of the Economically Active
Population as a Proportion of the Total
Population by Sex

Country	Year	Total	Men	Women
Algeria*/	1966	21.7	42.2	1.8
Egypt**/	1973	26.4	49.3	3.1
Ethiopia***/	1973	24	35	12.6
Nigeria	1963	32.9	49.4	16
South Africa****/	1970	37.3	50.9	24.1
Tanzania**/	1967	46.6	50	43.5

Source:　ILO Yearbook of Labour Statistics 1975

*/　　　The EAP figure does not include some 1,200,000 women working mainly in agriculture.

**/　　Estimated based on a sample survey on the work force

***/　　Estimates based on results of sample survey

****/　70 figures based on tables from national census samples

Table 5.4. Europe: Participation of the Economically
Active Population as a Proportion of the
Population by Sex

Country	Year	Total	Men	Women
Spain*/	1970	35	57.5	13.4
France**/	1975	42.6	55.1	30.5
Italy***/	1975	35.4	52.2	19.4
Sweden	1970	42.3	54.7	29.9
United Kingdom****/	1971	46.3	60.6	32.9
East Germany	1971	48.1	56.1	41.3
West Germany	1974	43.9	57.9	31.1
Czechoslovakia*****/	1970	48.7	55.4	42.3
Romania	1966	54.2	60.7	48.1
USSR	1970	48.7	51.1	46.6
SSR Bielorussia	1970	48.7	51.1	46.6
SSR Ukraine	1970	50.5	54.4	47.3

*/ The 1974 EAP is 37.8. 1970 figure based on tables
from official census bulletin samples.

**/ Official estimates.

***/ (Italy) Estimates based on results of sample surveys
on work force.

****/ Figures based on tables of 10% samples from census
bulletins.

*****/ 1974 estimates based on results of sample survey on
work force.

******/ EAP figure does not include unsalaried family
workers.

Table 5.5. Occupational Categories of Female
Economically Active Population

Country	Self-employed & workers	Shop & factory workers	Family workers	Other & Unspecified categories
Argentina '70	14.1	76.91	77,050	128,150
Brazil '70	19.3	69.7	11	0.01
Costa Rica '73	5.3	91.1	1.3	2.1
Chile '70	49.8	98	1	6.3
Dominican Rep. '70	6.4	3.7	5.5	40
Guatemala '73	27.3	66		6
Mexico '75	26.2	66.6	7.2	
Nicaragua '71	25.2	63.6	3.6	7.4
Panama '70	14.3	73	5	7.6
Paraguay '72	38	5	8.5	3.5
Peru '72	32	71	88	
Uruguay '72	54	71	1	6.4

NOTES

(1) The main works on the question are Juliet Mitchell, La Condicion de la Mujer (Mexico: Extemporaneos, 1974); Margaret Benston, "The Political Economy of Women's Liberation," Monthly Review 21 (September 4, 1969): 13-27; Isabel Larguía, and John Dumoulin, Hacia una Ciencia de la Liberacion de la Mujer (Caracas: Central University of Venezuela, 1975); "Contra el Trabajo Invisibile," in Liberacion del La Mujer Ano Cero (Barcelona: Granica Editor, 1977); Peggy Morton, "A Woman's Work is Never Done," in From Feminism to Liberation, edited by Edith Hishino Albach (Cambridge: Schenkman Books, 1971); Maria-Jose Dalla Costa and Selma James, El Poder de la Mujer y la Subversion de la Comunidad (Mexico: Siglo 21, 1975); Ira Gerstein, "Domestic Work and Capitalism," Radical America, nos. 4-5 (1973): 101-128; John Harrison, "Economia Politica del Trabajo Domestico," in El Ama de Casa Bajo el Capitalismo (Barcelona: Anagrama, 1975); Wally Seccombe, "El Trabajo Domestico," in El Ama de Casa Bajo el Capitalismo (Barcelona: Anagrama, 1975): Jean Gardiner, "El Papel del Trabajo Domestico," in El Ama de Casa Bajo el Capitalismo (Barcelona: Anagrama, 1975); Sheila Rowbotham, Women's Consciousness, Man's World (Middlesex: Penguin, 1973); Marie Langer, "La Mujer: Sus Limitaciones y Potencialidades," Cuestionamos 2 (Buenos Aires, Granica Editor, 1973); Veronika Bennholder-Thomsen, "Reproduccion de Subsistencia y Reproduccion Ampliada, Alugunas Reflexiones," (Paper presented at the Conference on Underdevelopment and the Reproduction of Subsistence in Latin America, Bielefeld Universitat, July 20-23, 1978); Liliana De Riz, "El Problema Condicion Femenina en America Latina: La Participacion de la Mujer en los Mercados de Trabajo: El Caso de Mexico," in CEPAL Mujeres en America Latina (Mexico: Fondo de Cultura Economica, 1975); Claude Meillassoux, Mujeres, Graneros y Capital (Mexico: Siglo 21, 1977). One of the first essays, Juliet Mitchell's, points out the importance of analyzing the family not as a monolithic unit, but on the basis of its own internal structure: production, reproduction, sexuality, and the socialization of children. With Margaret Benton, we enter the debate through an economic framework. In their attention to the Third World (Samir Amin, Andres Gunder Frank, Claude Meillassoux) they consider housework as an essential contribution to primary accummulation in the capital accummulation process, to the extent that it is a matter of production and reproduction uncompensated by capital, of labor undertaken within the family.

(2) Henry Kirsch, "La Participacion de la Mujer en los Mercados Laborales Latinoamericanos" in ECLA, Mujeres en America

<u>Latina</u> (Mexico: Fondo de Cultura Economica, 1975), pp. 175-198.

(3) Marie A. Savane, Paper presented to the first Conference on Africa and the problems of the future (Dakar: UNITAR-IDEP, July 1977).

(4) Rodolfo Stavenhagen, "Campesinado, Necesidades Basicas y las Estrategias de Desarollo Rural" in <u>Hacia Otro Desarollo.</u> <u>Enfoques y Estrategias</u>, edited by Marc Nerfin (Mexico: Siglo 21, 1978).

(5) Lourdes Arizpe, "Migracion, Etnicismo y Cambio Economico (a study on migrant peasants in the city of Mexico)" (Mexico College, 1978). Lourdes Arizpe has undertaken research into migration, the family labor force, and employment character-istics. An important observation in her study on the causes of migration (linked to the very research method) is her assurance that the flow of migration has increased due to the combination of a series of factors based on links between the rural and urban sectors.

(6) Claude Meillassoux, pp. 156-166.

(7) Gabriel Maldonado Lee, La Mujer Asalariada en el Sector Agricola: Considerations on the work force in the tobacco industry (Mexico: CENIET, Serie Avances de Investigacion, 1977).

(8) See Note 3, above.

(9) Economic Commission for Africa, 1976.

6 Sexism as an Obstacle to Development

Irma Garcia-Chafardet

Human society stands at the threshold of a major historic change, the nature of which is largely a matter of choice. On the one hand, interdisciplinary research increasingly supports predictions of an unprecedented crisis, on the other, alternative trends towards a major leap into "human community" are stronger than ever before. In spite of its limitations, the New International Economic Order continues to be perhaps the most promising of these alternatives.

Recent events have made it clearer than ever that all the nations of the world are interrelated and interdependent, that any major crisis will affect all countries, regardless of differing political systems, and that all people are integrally dependent parts of a whole as passengers of our spaceship earth. What is not apparent yet, because of inadequate research, is the effects that sexism (defined, p. 116) has on progress towards the establishment of the New International Economic Order, and the influence of current sexist policies on the quality of all possible futures.

The purpose of this paper is (1) to offer an operational definition of sexism that will be useful for the development of a theory that identifies sexism as a key obstacle to the establishment of the New International Economic Order; (2) to test the hypothesis that sexism helps to perpetuate underdevelopment; and (3) to suggest the equitable sharing of resources at all levels as an achievable objective of the New International Economic Order through the utilization of the potential that efforts to eradicate sexism have to help overcome obstacles and enhance opportunities for the establishment of the New International Economic Order.

ELEMENTS OF A DEFINITION OF SEXISM

I define sexism as <u>deeply rooted attitudes, values, beliefs, customs, and practices that foster the denial of the authentic female principle and the growth of the distorted male principle among both women and men, limiting the development of human potential by socializing children to conform to the straitjackets of female or male sex-role stereotypes.</u> As a consequence of sexism, women are perceived to be inferior to men because they are born with different physiological, psychological, and spiritual characteristics, that lead them to perform work considered marginal to the process of production, since it is not remunerated and it is carried out in isolation in the inferior private sphere of the home.

Distortion of Femaleness and Maleness in Individual Human Beings

The energy that shapes human character develops four different sets of traits in all women and men: an authentic male principle or force (which manifests itself, in activation, assertiveness, and the rationality inherent in Logos); a distorted male principle (compulsion to control others and violence); an authentic female principle (letting be, conciliation, nurturance, and the intuition inherent in Eros); and a distorted female principle (dependency and victimization). The character of all women and men is a combination of all four. A healthy man or woman is one who has achieved a balance between the authentic female and male principles - even though these manifest themselves differently among women and men - and has overcome the negative consequences of her or his behavior prompted by the distorted female or male principles.

The Inferior "Feminine" Private Sphere of the Home

For centuries, attitudes have been rooted in women's and men's psyches as well as all institutions of society, through a socialization process whereby girls are brought up to render care and comfort to men and children in the private sphere of the home, with domestic work as a supplementary element, and boys are brought up to be decision makers, defenders, and providers for women and children in the public sphere of the polity and the economy. This division of labor may have been the natural consequence of the biological differences between women and men and their functions, such as the acts of childbirth and breastfeeding. Yet the functions performed in both the public and private spheres are creative human social productive activity. Both offer possibilities for happiness and fulfillment. Caring for home and children could be a road to self-realization for any human being, just like becoming a physician or a lawyer. The problem is that age-old attitudes that have become basic to modern civilization give much more power and prestige to remunerated production, defense, and decision making than to reproduction and the care of home and children. Society confers power and prestige on the biological function of motherhood. The social functions of care for men, children, and the home, however, are perceived as inferior to the functions performed in the public sphere because the prevalent attitudes in modern society tend to assign value only to what is exchanged for money. Since, ultimately, human beings are one with their environment, women who have been performing the social functions of the private sphere tend to feel inferior to people who are identified with the functions performed in the public sphere. As Paulo Freyre, the Brazilian educator, states, "The oppressed internalize the image that the oppressor has of them."(1)

Female and Male Sex-Role Stereotypes

The prevailing socialization process has conditioned human beings to a greater or lesser degree to feel superior or inferior to each individual with whom they relate. It seems that the more we fear and resent higher authority the more we tend to oppress those we perceive as inferior. This general phenomenon is most obvious in the most basic human relationship, that between women and men, perhaps because of the great physical strength men had in prehistoric times when physicality may have been the sole expression, and men tended to assume a general aura of superiority over all who were weaker. Yet relating to others in terms of superior-inferior hinders the development of human potential and militates against the attainment of human fulfillment through greater understanding of ourselves and others, greater communication, trust, and love. Depending on the degree of "success" of this socialization process, infant females and males are fitted and fit themselves to a greater or lesser extent into the strait-jackets of a "feminine" or a "masculine" sex role stereotype. Maybe both women and men are equally capable of performing both public and private functions. Whatever differences exist between them and the nature of the work they have been performing, however, does not make one better or more developed than the other. Women have the same intelligence, resourcefulness, creativity, psychic strength, and productive self-expression in life as men. But there is a part within women that has invited our enslavement. To the degree that women expect men to do for us what we are not prepared to do ourselves, we resent and blame male authority and play a game of victimization. This distorted female force is also present to a greater or lesser degree, among men.

The socialization process has allowed human characteristics to be branded as exclusively masculine or feminine. Each sex is burdened by the other's expectations based on the stereotypes. Like any other ideal type, the pure female and male sex-role stereotypes do not exist. Still this notion helps us assess the degree to which women and men are more or less limited by a stronger or weaker socialization process that molded their feelings and behavior. The stereotypes are like straitjackets that develop out of exaggerated distortions of culturally created differences between women and men, limiting their human potential to a greater or lesser degree depending on the extent to which their capacity to relate to and love others has been affected by the socialization process. The culturally created differences between women and men are perpetuated by the separation of the functions women and men are expected to perform in the private sphere of the home and the public sphere of the polity and the economy, and by a set of values that imposes notions of how to feel, think, and act in order to be female or male. These preconceived stereotypes are transmitted by the family, the school, the work place, and the media. The stereotypes become like straitjackets because they form rigid, unconscious facades and defenses. Female and male fears of abandonment and rejection, of death and destruction, desires for happiness and fulfillment, and needs for closeness, relatedness, support, affection, and love, but also for self-awareness, centeredness, assertion, preservation, and creativity, are basically the same.

The rigidity of the stereotypes leaves very little room for women and men to choose and create their own experience. They limit men's opportunities to exercise familial functions and women's opportunities to exercise the functions of decision maker, worker or artist. It is through the exercise of the power to choose, however, that people grow and develop their human potential. The rigidity of the stereotypes is unjust. They do not allow activity and passivity to be interchangeable. The imposition of the hierarchical ways in which people have been ranked in the public sphere to the private sphere, has produced devastating effects in family and personal relationships.

Let me give an example of how the sex role stereotypes decrease the human capacity to relate to the other sex in pleasurable, loving ways: Self-assertion is a human need of both women and men. If it is considered a characteristic inherent to "masculinity," while emotional behavior is discouraged as being "feminine," it tends to burden men with feeling solely responsible for wife and children, with the need to be in control of every situation, to be strong, reassured, calm, successful, with no margin for error, weakness, or need for support, and ready to perform sexually whenever the woman wants. Over-assertiveness may result in authoritarianism, destructiveness, or aggressiveness and not necessarily in self-centeredness. The more men have been effectively socialized in their masculine role, the more they will deny pain because "big boys don't cry." The tend to deny feeling frightened or unsure as being "unmasculine." Some deny early signals of disease and discomfort because being ill may mean being helpless, passive, and dependent. Sometimes the need for affection and love is also denied. The demands of "masculinity" have weighed men down with responsibilities and pressures to repress emotions that have often led to serious physical and psychological disturbances. In the Western world, men have had higher incidence rates of ulcers, heart disease, suicide, crime, and alcoholism than women.

By the same token, at different points in their lives, both women and men feel a need to take care and be taken care of, in spite of the fact that ultimately each person is her or his own responsibility. If nurturance, for example, is considered a characteristic of women only, men are pressured with fears of being considered "unmasculine" if they try to satisfy this human need, and women are encouraged to develop nurturance at the expense of self-centeredness.(2) If girls are brought up to expect to find men who will be responsible for them, a sort of self-center substitute, their nurturance tends to turn into frustration and self-denial. A woman whose "center" she identifies as being outside of her, does not develop a sense of self, of her dignity and worth as a human being. Excessive nurturance may make her develop into a self-denying "martyr mother," constantly sacrificing herself for the sake of her family without giving herself the opportunity to find out who she is or what she wants out of life. She is usually unaware of her own and her family's needs. People have very little to give if they do not develop their capacity to receive.

Neither self-assertion nor nurturance should be developed in human beings at the expense of the other. A balance between these two human characteristics within each person may be necessary for the growth of an authentic self within an authentic relationship.

The former Prime Minister of Sweden, Olof Palme, has emphasized that any society that shortens men's lives with ulcers and heart attacks and at the same time prevents women by the thousands from performing paid labor clearly needs to be changed.(3)

Women's Inferiority to Men

For thousands of years, the "nature" of the human species seemed to dictate that some people were superior and should be masters and other people were inferior and should be slaves. Only about 150 years ago elements of the elites began to suspect that slavery was not "natural," and that the servile and culturally undeveloped character of slaves could be explained by the very fact that these people were enslaved and brought up to be slaves - instead of proving that they deserved to be slaves. Support for the emancipation of women stands today approximately where support for the emancipation of slaves stood about two centuries ago.

Thus sexism is discrimination based on gender - prejudice against the female sex. Its consequences, however, are harmful to women, men, children, and the development process, defining "development" as the process of all countries and peoples towards the achievement of social justice, economic well-being, availability of opportunities for all women and men to participate in all public and private activity, ecological balance, and peace.

Paragraph 16 of the Declaration of Mexico of the equality of women and the contribution to development and peace (1975) states:

The ultimate end of development is to achieve a better quality of life for all, which means not only the development of economic and other material resources, but also the physical, moral, intellectual and cultural growth of the human person.(4)

How does sexism, however, constitute an obstacle to the establishment of the New International Economic Order? It is my contention that sexism helps to perpetuate underdevelopment.

HOW SEXISM HELPS PERPETUATE UNDERDEVELOPMENT

The more sexism is eradicated from the human psyche and from all institutions of society, the greater the possibilities of overcoming underdevelopment.

If sexism helps to perpetuate underdevelopment, then the more the integration of women into the stream of national, economic, social, political, and cultural life is made an integral part of all development planning and projects, including negotiations on restructuring the world economic order, the greater the likelihood of a New International Economic Order overcoming underdevelopment in the world.

Current Economic Structures and Processes

The world economy today may be compared with a serpent whose head is made up of the so-called developed nations and whose tail consists of some resource-poor countries still attempting to follow the head and imitate the "development model," hoping thereby to be able to satisfy the basic human needs of their populations, such as food, housing, health, education, etc. The head of this serpent, however, increasingly appears to be inflicted with a seizure. Since the early 1970s, symptoms of overurbanization, social anomie, ecological imbalance, political corruption, failure of governments to control national economies, and the subsequent economic instability have surfaced in the more developed world in ways that can no longer be ignored. These problems affect less developed countries as well.

The present problems of "Western modernization" of the more developed nations are an undeniable challenge to well-established presumptions of necessary positive development stages that less developed countries could attain by imitating more developed ones. These global problems have created a situation under which the concepts that worked for the old economic order are no longer capable of diagnosing and predicting the trends and development of the new phenomena. The old economic order is disappearing and the new international economic order is not yet with us.

The old economic order's "development model" has failed. It has proven to be wasteful and inefficient in overcoming underdevelopment. It has not been able to expand itself in the poor areas of the world. What role does sexism play, however, in such waste and inefficiency?

At least half of the poor are women, and as we will see, they tend to be the poorest of all. Little is known, however, about poor women's participation in socioeconomic development. Even less is known about their economic contribution to the family - a major part of women's hidden productivity. Enough data exist, however, to give preliminary answers to the questions posed in this paper and to identify policy initiatives that could help women among the poor, thus filling existing gaps in the identified objectives of the New International Economic Order.

Some predominant issues emerging from the World Conference of the International Women's Year (1975) were that economic growth and industrial expansion per se have failed to improve living conditions for low-income groups within which women are the majority, that participation of women in the development process accelerates the attainment of development goals, and that only minimal efforts have been made to integrate women into the development process of their countries.

Evaluating Women's Contribution to Development

Even those sensitive to this issue tend to emphasize one side of the coin, the welfare issue: "How are women affected by development?" and not the other half - the efficiency and growth issue: "How do women affect development?"

Women's plight may appear no more than a welfare issue at first glance. I hope that what follows will not only serve as an evaluation of women's contribution to development but that it will also make clear how it affects efficiency and growth in the overall economy.

The economic value of remunerated production

The principle of equal remuneration for work of equal value has by now been almost universally accepted. The application of the principle, however, is another matter. Statistical data relating to the differences between the average wages of men and women in the various sectors and occupations, at a comparable level of responsibility, skill, and other factors are meager and unreliable. They often cover the manufacturing industries, omitting the service sector, where so many women are employed. International Labor Organization studies of the situation in industrialized countries conclude that women's wages are about 50-80 percent of men's for the same work time.(5) The low level of wages that women accept tends to depress the general level of wages. Women are systematically segregated in lower paid and less skilled jobs, and they are expected to accept this situation as the natural consequence of their feminine nature. This is consistent with sexist attitudes that consider women second-class adults, dependent on their husbands for their support. These attitudes have long ceased to correspond with the reality that the majority of women do not seek employment to complement their husband's earnings. They work for exactly the same reasons men do: to support themselves and their dependents. It is difficult to accurately assess the percentages of women heads of households in the world because of polygamy, migration of husbands, widowhood, divorce, unwed motherhood, etc., and lack of data in many countries. It has been estimated, however, that 75 percent of women are heads of households in the Malagasy Republic, 63 percent in Nigeria, and 50 percent in Ghana, and that more than 25 percent of families are headed by women in Chile and Colombia.(6) Among taxpaying households in Lesotho, 25 percent are headed by females reflecting male migration to the mines of South Africa (see figure 6.1 for data on other countries). In Belo Horizonte, Brazil, male and female heads of households do not differ markedly in age or education; more than 50 percent of female heads, however, work in the informal sector, compared to 12 percent of male heads. Working

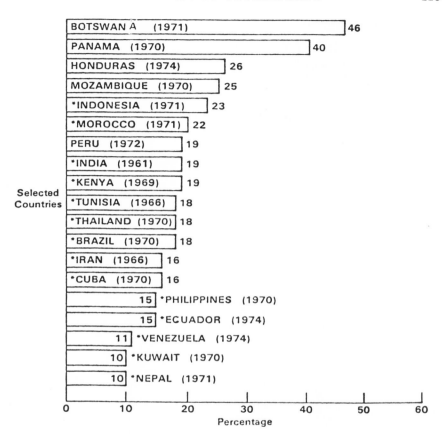

Figure 6.1. Percentage of "potential" heads of household
who are women, in selected countries

*Single mothers are not included as data were not available.

Notes: The magnitude of households that might be headed by women was defined by the percentage of "potential" women heads to "potential" total household heads. "Potential" women heads of household include all women who are widowed, divorced, separated, or single mothers. "Potential" total household heads include "potential" women heads of household plus men over the age of 20 who are not single.

Source: Myra Buvinic, and Nadia H. Youssef. "Women-headed Households in Third World Countries: An Overview." Paper presented at the International Center for Research on Women Workshop "Women in Poverty: What Do We Know?" Belmont Conference Center, Elkridge, Md., April 30–May 2, 1978 (table 2).

in the informal sector has a significant negative effect on male earnings, but the negative effect for females is twice as great.(7)   Furthermore, males earn more in the informal sector than females in the formal sector (see figure 6.2) and they earn a higher return to what education they have.   At least some of the earning power difference between men and women cannot be based on simple "economic" explanations.

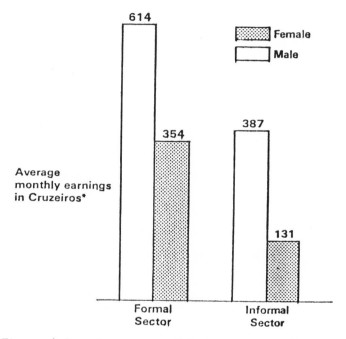

Figure 6.2.   Average monthly earnings in Cruzeiros of
male and female heads of households by
employment sector, Belo Horizonte, Brazil, 1972

*In 1972, the rate of exchange was about 6.25 Cruzeiros to U.S. $1.00.

Notes: The data are based on responses from 1,420 men and 226 women drawn from a representative sample of 2445 households in the Belo Horizonte metropolitan area.

Source: Thomas W. Merrick, and Marianne Schmink.   "Female Headed Households and Urban Poverty in Brazil."   Paper presented at the International Center for Research on Women Workshop on "Women in Poverty: What Do We Know?" Belmont Conference Center, Elkridge Md., April 30-May 2, 1978 (table 9).

As a result, female-headed households are much more likely to be poor than are male-headed households; An alarming 41 percent of all female-headed households in the Belo Horizonte sample had total income too low to satisfy the most fundamental needs, even by the government-established minimal standard. Of male-headed households, 27 percent were so classified.(8) A very similar picture appears for the Commonwealth Caribbean. About one-fifth of male-headed households had no income or none stated; 59 percent of female-headed households were so classified. Over half the male-headed households were in the high income category (more than $1,000), whereas only 13 percent of female-headed households had that high an income.(9) Furthermore, we are comparing monetary income; most female-headed households are worse off in terms of full income, having less adult time for child care and household work.

In Latin America, more women than men migrate to cities; households in Santiago, Chile, headed by migrant women had median incomes of 49 escudos monthly in 1962; for native women the figure was 84, for migrant and native men 93 and 109 escudos respectively.

Households with the most children have the lowest household income. For female-headed households in Belo Horizonte classified by income as poor, low, and middle/high, the dependency ratios are respectively 2.6, 1.2, and 1. For all Colombian households, the number of children per women is three times as high for the very poor as for the well-to-do. The poor have more children because they are poor, and they are poor because they have more children. This relationship holds for female-headed households as well as those with a male present.

Girls who are raised to raise children themselves choose occupations compatible with child raising; they do not acquire either the general education or the specific training required to command a higher wage rate. If they then end up raising children without the benefit of an income-earning partner, they and their children are caught in a vicious cycle of poverty.

For most countries, we have no information on the growth in the number of female-headed households. Official definitions differ; interviewer and respondent attitudes change; comparing the incidence from one time or place to the next is problematical. The number of households headed by women nearly doubled between 1960 and 1970 in Brazil; this trend probably prevails elsewhere in less developed countries. Migration at differential rates by sex is one cause. Female-headed households increased by 33 percent in Morocco between 1960 and 1971 (the number of male-headed households increased minimally), as Moroccan men migrated to Western Europe. In one district of Kenya, 40 percent of households sampled were headed by female farm managers.

Divorce rates suggest that numbers of female heads of families are extremely high even in more developed countries. In spite of this reality, however, in conformity with the dominant sexist attitudes, society tends not to take women's earning ability seriously, and it is very common for female and male experts to argue that women should not be employed when male unemployment rates are high.

As education and job opportunities have opened to women, they have opened precisely in the "feminine" - and much lower paid -areas of health, education, and welfare, extrapolations of the motherhood role to the arena of public affairs. It is specifically in these fields where job classification, comparison, and evaluation is most difficult for lack of reliable and objective means of measuring job content and determining job comparability. Women are usually automatically placed in the lowest grade, badly paid categories of "light work," which is often nonmechanized heavy work, while men are usually placed within the same factory in higher paid automated work which is not categorized as such.(10)

In a more developed economy, the labor force is relatively easy to identify since for the majority there is a clear link between their work and their income (pay or profits). In a less developed or basically agrarian economy, where many may work intermittently and without pay on family farms or in small enterprises, and where unemployment and underemployment may be widespread, it is particularly difficult in many cases to categorically classify a woman as "active" (in the labor force) or as "inactive" (outside the labor force). Women are more likely than men to be unpaid family workers, irregular or part-time workers, or unemployed but not actively seeking a job. In subsistence economies, and especially in nomadic societies, the labor force figures will inadequately reflect the true role of women in the economy.(11)

Women constitute the bulk of the part-time labor force throughout the world, with the consequences of curtailed or nonexistent social security benefits, job security, and career advancement brought about by their domestic and family responsibilities, generally not shared by men. This is so even in developed countries. Women are responsible for 80 percent of part-time employment in Australia, 85 percent in Japan, and 90 percent in Norway.(12)

Women's work in the demonstrably productive sectors, such as agriculture and marketing, has been amply documented.(13) Emphasis on women's market contribution, however, has led to relative neglect of the value of work in childrearing and household maintenance, perhaps reflecting a tendency to underrate the real work content of "housewifery" in capital-scarce economies.

Productivity   figures and women's unremunerated   economic activity

The International Labor Organization has estimated that for
1975 there are 198.3 million women economically active in the
more developed regions of the world, which constitutes 35.3
percent of their total economically active population; and there
are 363.3 million women economically active in the less developed regions, which constitute 64.7 percent of their total
economically active population.(14)   "Economically active,"
however, is defined in terms of remunerated production.   The
bulk of women's economic activity, that is, domestic work and
agricultural work for family or tribe consumption, remains
outside productivity figures.   In order for women's work to be
accounted for, the definition of "full employment" should
include not only the active labor force but also unused resources.

Domestic work.   The tradition of the "noneconomic" role of
women is deeply entrenched: in most households throughout
the world, the work performed by women is not valued in
economic terms and the same attitudes are reflected in the way
that governments define and measure women's work for purposes of national censuses.   By convention, the labor force
does not include housewives who work alongside men for only a
limited amount of their time – less than one-third of normal
working hours – even though they may also do heavy chores,
such as cooking for farm hands or carrying water from the
community well.   To be considered "economically active," a
worker or a member of the labor is expected to produce
significant amounts of economic (that is, marketable) goods, or
of visible income.   "Women's work" falls largely in the do-it-
yourself category and is not seen as work in the economic
sense, but, paradoxically, women who receive wages for
domestic work are called economically active.(15)
    With the gradual substitution of factories and offices for
the nuclear family, the family ceased to be the center of
production.   Socialized forms of production developed in
factories and offices, but not within the family.   Thus the two
distinct spheres of production developed.   Factory and office
work was done in a socialized manner in the public sphere,
and housework was performed in isolation in the private
sphere.

Housework is productive work.   The   "economically active"
population of the world needs clean clothes to wear that
either they or someone else has had to wash and iron; food
that either they or someone else has had to prepare; a com-
fortable dwelling that either they or someone else has had to
clean; and if they have children, either they, or someone else

has had to take care of them during the time of factory or office work. But housework is "invisible" because it is immediately consumed after it is produced, and its product is not brought into the market place and exchanged for money. Thus it has not been considered productive, or been given economic value, or been accounted for in the Gross National Product of any nation. Every place of production outside the home presupposes the productive work that is being carried on day after day within the home. If emphasis is placed on buying and selling and not on producing and consuming or on an attempt to satisfy human needs and to better the living standard of humankind, however, the productive value of housework will not be apparent.

Housework is productive in itself and it is essential to production in general. Yet because it has not been seen as an economic category, the woman who is not paid for her work has not been considered a true worker. She is caught up in a contradiction between doing more than a full-time job – depending on the number of her children – and appearing as someone who does not work, but concentrates on being beautiful, cheerful, and charming. To solve the contradiction, women from higher- and middle-income groups hire maids and buy electrical appliances. Increases in the demand for electrical appliances, however, may provide an increased incentive for the development of light industry at the expense of the heavy industry that may be necessary for economic development.

For poor women in poor countries, so-called housework involves physical labor in sowing and weeding, in fetching water, in grinding wheat and corn; it is also likely to require from some family members many more person-hours of child care, simply because there are more children. (16)

Much of this work of women is not subject to the marketplace of wages in which men place their services or the fruits of their labor. In censuses and employment surveys, where work has meant an activity producing cash income, women have been treated inconsistently or overlooked altogether. (17) The unpaid family worker is a small shop or farm was the first casualty of the misleading statistical categories "employed" and "unemployed."

Housework is relatively underdeveloped work.   Despite the existence of sophisticated electrical appliances that facilitate the tasks of housewives who can afford them, the method of production used in the private sphere does not reflect the highly sophisticated and efficient machinery that has been developed in, for example, outerspace technology or military industry. Production techniques have developed at a much greater rate in the public sphere than in the private sphere. Housework, because it is performed in isolation, uses individual methods that have been overcome long ago in the public sphere. Technological advances should be made available to humankind, all women and men.

The problem may well be that, if work is not remunerated by the hour, no one cares how long it takes a worker to do the work, and therefore, in sweeping, the majority of women still use brooms. While greater mechanization could improve the efficiency of specific services such as cooking, washing, and cleaning, it will not help women in their task of taking care of their children from the moment they are born until the time they are ready to go to school. The work day of housewives and mothers is unending, not because they have no machines, but because they are isolated.

Housework is a social service performed in isolation. The difference between social and socialized labor must be emphasized. Women's work is social, but women work in isolation and not in a socialized structure. Although the percentage of men who share in the performance of household tasks and in the care of children, especially young ones, may be steadily increasing, most of the housework and the nurturing and education of children is still basically carried out by females.

Agricultural work. Capital formation is not increased by the high activity rates of women in the economies of Asia and Africa because they tend to be engaged more in subsistence agriculture. Thus rural women are not only underremunerated but more often nonremunerated producers and therefore not consumers. Even though their situation varies from one region, country, and subregion to another according to level of "development," cultural attitudes, and traditions, etc., there is a basic communality: There is a heavy concentration of women in rural areas. Some are agricultural workers in tea and cotton plantations, etc., but most of them are an integral part of a subsistence, not a consumer, economy.

The majority of workers in the Philippines and Turkey are agricultural workers, and about 94 percent of these are women. The part rural women play in economic life is also very important in Latin America. Between 80 and 90 percent of African women live and work in the rural areas and between 60 and 80 percent of the agricultural work of the continent is carried out by women.(18) As a major source of agricultural workers in the world, whether they are remunerated or not, women should count as producers. According to the Food and Agriculture Organization of the United Nations,(19) women contribute 44 percent of the food supply as a worldwide average. Again the statistics are misleading because most of it is consumed, not sold.

In a few regions of West Africa, women virtually control large aspects of the food market. They produce, market, and distribute the food. This is local control. It is precisely in the regions where women control their agricultural production or sell their handicrafts in markets, where they enjoy higher status and respect. The more common situation for rural women, not only in Africa, but also in Asia and Latin America, however, is that traditional tribal and patrilineal systems give them little or no property rights in the land or its produce, and hence their economic status is almost totally subservient to the male members.

Regardless of the degree of control, rural women in the three continents work in conditions of real hardship, with primitive tools and virtually no exposure to modern methods of farming. René Dumont describes how in these economies, women undertake the role of beasts of burden (in Africa the loads are mainly carried on the head, in Asia on the shoulders by means of a yoke).(20) In some Moslem and Bengali villages, in regions where great famines have occurred, it has been considered dishonorable for women to work in the fields. Only the poorest women who had no choice would do so and thus be degraded and their virtue called into question.(21) In many African countries, aside from domestic chores and the care of children, women must perform all the agricultural work because it is considered feminine work. In the tropical forest zones of Africa, the entire burden of agriculture rests on the women. Agriculture is the main economic activity; yet men do no more than clear the forest. It has been pointed out by many that compulsory schooling for all girls in that region of the world would cause famine if educated people continued to refuse to do agricultural work. Yet many official educational systems in the area offer places in the agricultural colleges only to boys.(22)

Drudgery in the fields is combined with household drudgery. "Household" is a broader concept in these areas. Dwelling repairs and the maintenance of wells, for example, usually male tasks in the West, are the female's responsibility. Lack of water, very primitive and manual methods of housework and of producing and preparing food, and large families occupy rural women with heavy tasks from dawn to dusk. It is common for a woman to spend seven hours a day carrying water,(23) and three to four hours pounding manioc,(24) aside from putting in a full day's work out in the fields.

In rural households in the Philippines, for example, fathers garner the largest proportion of average household market income, but women and children together bring in almost 50 percent of this market income (see figure 6.3); when home production and school activities are included so that we are considering full income, mother contributes slightly more than father, and the average of four children per family, as a

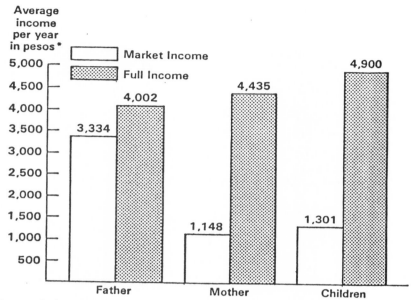

Figure 6.3. Market income and full income for family members, Laguna, Philippines, 1975-76

*In 1975 the rate of exchange was about 7.4 pesos to U.S. $1.00.

Notes: Market income is the value of market production. Full income is the total value of both market production and home production. Children's full income includes time spent in school. Excluding it, children's full income is equivalent to 3362 pesos per year.

The data are based on direct observations of a random sample of 99 rural households in Laguna in three separate 24-hour visits over an eight-month period.

Source: Elizabeth K. Quizon and Robert E. Evenson, "Time Allocation and Home Production in Philippine Rural Households," (Paper presented at the International Center for Research on Women Workshop on "Women in Poverty: What Do We Know?" Belmont Conference Center, Elkridge, Md., April 30-May 2, 1978 (table 9).

group, contribute more than either parent; full income is higher, by about 16 percent, in households where mothers are employed; the additional cash income of a working mother purchases, on the average, 145 calories and 3 grams of protein daily for each child; but since the time a mother spends with each child affects the child's height and weight at a given age, the gain to children from this additional food may be partially offset by the loss of mother's attention when she works away from home.

As in the Philippines, Malaysian women contribute about two-thirds of total family time to home activities – child care, washing, shopping, meal preparation, and housecleaning. Children contribute another 20 percent and husbands less than 10 percent. Husbands do even less in families with older children. Children do more when mother works for cash income.(25)

Similarly, in rural Peru mothers and children substitute for each other in cooking, hauling water, and animal care. Daughters are much more likely than sons to help with cooking and washing, and above age 10, to substitute for the mother on a meal-by-meal basis. Daughters are also more likely to haul water and collect wood. Animal raising is an important activity for women and children. Raising sheep, for example, is easier with a child at home, either to pasture full time, or to replace the mother in cooking and cleaning. In 11 percent of households, daughters raise sheep full time; sons do in only 2 percent of households. Girls attend fewer years of school than boys.(26)

Aid, technical assistance, and training. A tremendous imbalance exists between the participation of women in production on the one hand and the amount of assistance and training they have received on the other. The case of women and agricultural production in Africa is worth pointing out: 80 percent of food in Africa is produced and processed by women; yet more than 90 percent of agricultural aid has gone to men in this area, and it is precisely Africa which is bearing the cruelest load of suffering in the current food supply crises.(27) Policy-makers are very little aware of the knowledge, competence, and managerial skills of women and men in the lower ranks of the producing sectors. In particular, their image of women farmers has very little to do with the reality of these women's lives. So prevalent and persistent is the myth that women are economic parasites who, apart from raising children, contribute little to their family subsistence that Western development experts have been able to go into Third World countries to give development aid for food and agricultural production without consulting or assisting the major food producers and processors in the area: women. When agricultural training, credit, seeds, fertilizers, and improved agricultural tools and machines are made available, they go most often to men. Policy-makers do not seem to realize to what extent the solution of the world food problem may depend not on technological innovation alone but also on simultaneous improvement of the productivity of all workers.

They should be made more aware of the negative consequences of underutilizing women.

The history of development since the early 1950s, including the history of United Nations development organizations' programming policies, has produced an overwhelming concentration on the transfer of new technologies to men; on the provision of training in virtually all development fields - except domestic sciences and maternal and child health - to men; on the expansion of basic public schooling overwhelmingly for male children; and on the massive concentration of family planning persuasion upon girls and women, disregarding the generalized influence of men in decisions on fertility control.

Technology is human knowledge applied to human needs. It is not gender-related, but affects all people and all needs, from the most humble to the most sophisticated. Social and economic development cannot be successful without the participation of women, who make up half of humankind. All elements of society must be involved in the choice of science and technology for development; all must understand its limitations; and all must enjoy its benefits.(28)

A classic example of the negative effect of technology on women is the agricultural setting in which plowing (men's work) is mechanized, but the processes of cultivation, such as hoeing, weeding, and transplanting (women's work) are not. Women must work harder and longer than they did before mechanization in order to keep up with the increased plowing capacity. The development of simple technological aids for rural women has been recognized as essential in order to reduce the time they must spend in arduous, low-productivity labor, and to prevent the deterioration of their status as their male counterparts modernize.

The introduction of labor-saving devices threatens to separate women altogether from many of their traditional functions, or to leave them with only the drudgery. Pottery-making in Ghana, for example, was largely the work of women, but with the introduction of the potter's wheel, men took over the industry. Due to the lack of funds of their own, as well as lack of training in the new methods, women were unable to take advantage of the mechanized process. The spinning of yarn and preparation of looms, traditionally done by Muslim women in Kashmir, was threatened by a project that would have mechanized spinning completely, and displaced some 20,000 women for whom no other suitable employment was available. The widespread use of chemical sprays in agriculture in one province of India deprived women of an important source of income, since the majority of women of working age were employed four hours a day weeding the fields. Certain trade-offs must be made in choosing technologies, and some of these may have an adverse effect on women, but these should be anticipated and specific alternatives considered and built in.(29)

People: the unused or underutilized resource.   The old economic order's "development model" has been wasteful and
inefficient in overcoming underdevelopment because it suffers
from a strong tendency towards decreasing the number of
people - again, specially women - who participate in the
economic process, with the subsequent loss in capital formation, in spite of technological advancement.

Capital-intensive industrialization, which has been adopted
as the guiding strategy for economic growth in most less
developed countries, is unable to provide sufficient jobs.
There is a strong contradiction between the democratic participatory model of a free market on the one hand and the
increasing current trends towards globalization and concentration of production on the other.   Furthermore, global
corporations have steadily increased their degree of control of
business and economic mechanisms of the world market, being
to a large extent responsible for the strong trends towards
globalization and concentration of production.(30)   A major
consequence of this trend is decreasing opportunities for
women and other deprived groups to participate in the main-
stream of production and consumption and to benefit from the
fruits of development.   When production is channelled towards
exporting of raw materials and cash crops, very few employment opportunities are made available to women.

This has adverse consequences in the development process of industrialized as well as less developed countries, and
it should not be forgotten that more developed countries still
need development.

Adult women 15 years old and over participate less than
adult men in the economies of all countries, the discrepancy
between male and female participation rates being greatest in
the case of some countries in the Middle East, followed by the
majority of Latin American countries.   While the overall employment rates reflect the differences between the less developed and more developed areas, women's economic activity
rates do not.

Capital formation is not substantially increased by the
high rates of women's participation in developed countries of
Western Europe and North America.   Women are generally most
active in the nonindustrial, nonagricultural occupations, not as
administrative, executive, and managerial workers, but rather
in clerical and sales work or in services, such as domestic
work and as waitresses.   Some work in professions such as
teaching and nursing.   A few are lawyers and medical practitioners.

Increases in economic growth are not correlated with
greater participation, much less meaningful participation of
women in the labor force.   Taking into account changes in
activity rates, combined with changes in the age structure of
the female population, some recent ILO long-range projections

predict an increase in the overall labor force participation rate of the female population in the more developed regions from 33 percent in 1970 to about 35 percent by the year 2000. In the underdeveloped regions, however, the overall labor force participation rate of females is expected to continue to show a decline from about 26 percent in 1970 to about 24 percent in 2000.(31)

Margot Higgins argues that a larger role for women is not simply a matter of social justice but an indispensable condition for rapid economic development. While women's own potential for productivity is wasted, they will tend to perpetuate in their children those characteristics that are least conducive to development.(32)

Per Holmberg, a Swedish economist, has calculated that Sweden could increase her national product and income by about one-half if women were as productive and gainfully employed as men. He comes to the conclusion that the Swedish society is paying an exceedingly high price for the separate life roles of women and men, foregoing, in fact, almost one-third of the material standard of living which could be attained if those roles were the same.(33)

EQUITABLE SHARING OF RESOURCES IN THE NEW INTERNATIONAL ECONOMIC ORDER

Article 7 of the Charter of Economic Rights and Duties of States declares that

> each State has the right and responsibility to choose its means and goals of development, fully to mobilize and use its resources, to implement progressively economic and social reforms and to ensure the full participation of its people in the process and benefits of development.

How are these goals going to be achieved if 50 percent of human resources, women, are not appreciated in their contribution to development and are not fully utilized in more creative and productive ways? And yet, there is not one reference - explicit or indirect - throughout the Charter of Economic Rights and Duties of States or the New International Economic Order Declaration of its Programme of Action on the effects on the status of women on development and the participation of women in policy and planning for development. Significantly, even in the most direct internal references to the elimination of, for example, racial discrimination, apartheid, and neocolonialism, there is no mention of discrimination on account of sex,(34) although it has been fully substantiated that it is the most generalized form of discrimination.(35)

References to the World Conference of the International Women's Year and its Declaration and Plan of Action in the documents adopted at the Seventh Special Session of the United Nations General Assembly(36) certainly do not redress this imbalance. The new order should be a new international economic and social order where rapid industrialization, better terms of trade, and a balance of power between more developed and less developed countries will not result in worsening the situation of deprived groups and great numbers of women who are not protected by labor and social welfare legislation and may be used as cheap human resources.

A larger role for women and other deprived groups is not simply a matter of social justice. It is an indispensable condition for rapid economic development.

Principles and Guidelines for Action

Existing principles and guidelines that aid the process of attaining the equitable sharing of resources at all levels while seeking to eradicate sexism are:

1. Article 10 of the Declaration on the Elimination of Discrimination against Women (unanimously adopted by the General Assembly in 1967) and Article 11 of the Draft Convention on the same subject call for the application of all appropriate measures to ensure women equal rights with men in the field of economic and social life. Paragraph 9 of the Preamble of the Draft Convention states that the convention is "convinced that the establishment of a new, just and equitable international economic order will contribute significantly towards the promotion of equality between men and women." This text was adopted by the Working Group of the Whole on the Drafting of the Convention on the Elimination of Discrimination against Women at the thirty-second session of the General Assembly and forwarded to the Third Committee of the General Assembly accompanied by amendments.(37) The draft convention is expected to be adopted at the 34th Session. It may then very well be the first legally binding instrument of international law to mention the New International Economic Order.

2. Almost all the articles of the Declaration of Mexico on the Equality of Women and their contribution to development and peace (1975) have a bearing on the establishment of the New International Economic Order. It is in itself a far-reaching source of inspiration (E/CONF. 66/34, pp. 2-7).

3. The World Plan of Action for the Implementation of the Objectives of the International Women's Year (E/CONF. 66/34, pp. 8-43) and the programme for the first half of the decade (1976-1980) (E/5894), deal with action to be taken at the national, regional, and international levels that would help

achieve the equitable sharing of resources at all levels and the overall process towards the establishment of the New International Economic Order.

I feel very strongly that there is a tremendous need to synthesize existing legislation, principles, and guidelines for the further integration of women in development and the establishment of the New International Economic Order.

Implementing these Principles and Guidelines

The implementation of these guidelines and principles has been and will be under systematic scrutiny through a series of studies and reports on review and appraisal of progress achieved through their attainment. We are at the implementation stage of women's economic, social, and cultural rights. Some of these reports and studies are prepared in the context of the reporting system under the Declaration on the Elimination of Discrimination against Women, focusing on the situation of law and the situation in fact, including any obstacles that prevent the full implementation of the principles of the Declaration, and the review and appraisal of progress achieved in the implementation of the World Plan of Action under the International Development Strategy. The proposed 1980 World Conference of the United Nations Decade for Women will undertake a global review of progress achieved and possibly recommend reorientation of policies.

A comprehensive study of the participation of women in agriculture, trade, industry, and science and technology is in the process of preparation, which will constitute a step forward in the further investigation of the de facto enjoyment of the economic, social, and cultural rights of the poorest sector in the rural areas, i.e., women, where the institutionalization of these rights is rarely available - for example, water sanitation, daycare centers, participation of women in education, peasant unions, cooperatives.

A paper was prepared on Rural Women's Working Conditions: An Extreme Case of Unequal Exchange as a contribution to the Review and Appraisal for the World Conference on Agrarian Reform and Rural Development. Another paper on Appropriate Technology for Developing Countries and the Needs of Rural Women (ESA/ST/AC.7/CRP.3/Add.3) was prepared for ACAST, Ad Hoc Working Group on Appropriate Technology, Vienna, May 1977.

Policy Recommendations

As stated, the prevailing sexist attitudes consider women's work marginal to the process of production. This means not only that the functions of production, defense, and decision making are given much more power and prestige than the functions of reproduction and the care of home and children, but also that women's contribution to production is ignored or undervalued. Of course, women have also been helping to carry out the functions of production, but the myth prevails that women are economic parasites who bear children while men produce what is needed for their maintenance. Women do bear children and take care of them and their homes, but they are also producers and not just consumers. The majority of women throughout the world are overburdened with work precisely because of the double and triple shifts that are implied in carrying out all these tasks. Because of the myth, however, they are producing under much harder conditions than men.

Evaluate women's contribution to development

National development plans usually refer to the attainment of a higher quality of life for the population as a whole as a main objective. The focus of national plans, however, will not be improved by an approach that attempts to "integrate" women into the development process alone. An essential preliminary step is to evaluate women's contribution to development, that is to assess the extent to which women are already integrated and the extent to which their work and contribution is unremunerated or undervalued. Then effective planning can be carried out to increase women's level of education and training and their participation in production, art, and decision making. Continued planning without due consideration to the underlying values within which priorities are set and goals and objectives are established, while continued ignorance of women's concrete situations and continued perpetuations of the existing myths will continue to retard the development process.

Ease the Burden of Housework

Some groups of feminists in Italy and England say "pay us wages for housework."(38) Some have proposed bills to give a pension (not a wage) to women at home when they reach a certain age.(39) Both a wage and a pension, however, might only serve to institutionalize the role of women housewives. These measures will leave the structure of the family and work intact with their inequitable sharing of rights and responsibility between women and men. Others speak of the automation of housework and see it developing into a socialized industry. Socializing housework into an industry probably would allow for more efficiency and higher productivity, but the socialization of housework is a very distant goal, which may depend more on the economic development of each country than on policies and priorities.

Others have suggested that employers should pay an extra allowance to employees for the housework invested in them. The argument has been set forth that by the non-payment of a wage for housework, the figure of the boss or the employer is concealed behind that of the husband and children, who appear as the sole recipients of domestic services. The marriage contract legitimizes the appropriation of the housewife's work inside the home as a natural thing. Salaried housework, neighborhood collectivized housework, canteens, and personalized care centers and nurseries may be only stages in the process toward a more just society whose ultimate goal should be the full development of human potential in both the female and the male.

A careful check on how people in poor households use their time, would overcome the problems derived from distinctions such as "economically active-inactive" or "employed-unemployed."

Poor families have little schooling, few tools, virtually no capital, and often no land. In the way they use their time one finds the answer to who contributes to the household economy. Time budget surveys demonstrate indisputably what employment surveys previously barely implied: Women make an enormous contribution to the real income and well-being of the poor (see figure 6.4).

Data available for several poor countries shows that men devote almost all their work time to marketplace work, i.e., work done for wage income or income imputed from the value of agricultural production directly consumed. Men's work at home does not vary with the numbers, ages, and activities of household members. Women, in contrast, devote their work time to a combination of marketplace work (generating cash income or income-in-kind) and home maintenance, food preparation, and child care. Children share this work from about their fifth year onward. Children also do a considerable amount of marketplace work, usually only after their tenth year. Time allocation by women and children is flexible, changing with the number and ages of children and the annual cycle of agriculture and schooling (when children do go to school). As the demand for childrearing time and cash income increases over the household's life cycle, the burden falls primarily on the wife and to some extent on older children. When a mother works outside the home, her child-care time declines very little; leisure declines, hour-for-hour. Rural Filipino women working for cash income give up nearly four hours per day of leisure. Older children substitute for their mothers in home chores and care of siblings. When there are seven or more children, men actually reduce their child-care time (to about 10 minutes a day) and increase their leisure time: Older children reduce the father's but not the mother's work load. When the family is large, women enjoy significantly

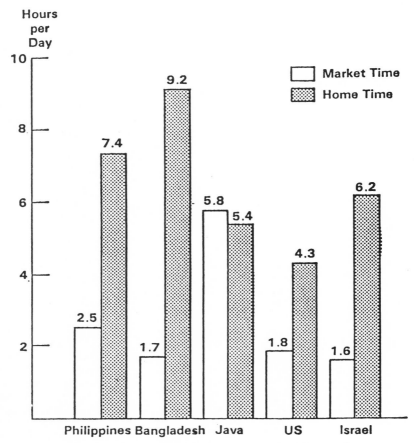

Figure 6.4.   Cross-country comparison of
women's use of time
(in hours per day)

Source: Elizabeth K. Quizon and Robert E. Evenson, "Time
Allocation and Home Production in Philippine Rural House-
holds," Paper presented at the International Center for
Research on Women Workshop on "Women in Poverty: What Do
We Know?" Belmont Conference Center, Elkridge, Md., April
30-May 2, 1978 (table 10).

less leisure than men; this is especially true if there is an
infant present, and especially true for women who work more
than six hours a day outside the home.(40)
    Market income (cash and subsistence crops consumed at
home) is not a good measure of household well-being because it

fails to measure the contribution of at-home work, estimated to be at least 40 percent of GNP in the United States and probably more in less monetized economies. Furthermore, women increase a family's market income at the cost of reducing either their leisure or the attention they can give to child care; the latter is in considerable measure an investment in human capital. The measurement of time use in rural households has for the first time made it possible to estimate full income, i.e., income measured by adding to market income payments family members would receive if child care, food preparation, breastfeeding, fetching water, chopping wood, and other home production activities were valued and paid for explicitly.

Underdevelopment will not be overcome while decisions on planning and policy are based on statistics that do not reflect women's contribution to the economy. Overall structural measures must be taken to accurately measure female labor.

Reduce All Workers' Working Hours and Dissolve Distinctions Between Public and Private Work

In order to eradicate prejudices that consider work performed in the private sphere inferior to that done in the public sphere, it may be necessary for all people to share in all functions. This may be a necessary transition period before a new and just balance is established.

Merging the public and the private sphere and socializing children to share in the care, comfort, defense, and support of each other may be necessary not only to overcome underdevelopment, but also to give children the opportunity to grow with healthy character structures and balanced personalities. Individual and small group solutions are possible. For all people to benefit, however, a restructuring of the family and work structures is necessary.

Let me give an example of a specific attempt to restructure the family: The Swedish government began an experiment more than fifteen years ago under which couples with young children were employed in three textile factories. Their children spent one-third of the day with their mother, one-third with the father, and one-third in day care centers where the personnel had been screened to choose adults who love children. Today these girls and boys - who were constantly surrounded by loving adults while they were awake - show a high degree of self-assurance, higher creativity than "normal,"(41) a high capacity to make rational and sound decisions and to resolve conflict under situations of stress and crisis, great adaptability to changing situations without losing their inner calm, and a great ease in satisfying basic needs of closeness, relatedness, and love.

The textile production also increased since there were three five-hour shifts rather than the standard eight-hour shifts when only men worked in the textile factories. Parents could give the best of themselves during the few hours they spent with their children, and they had extra leisure time to satisfy their own needs. If governments do not take the initiative, the proliferation of similar experiments seems very unlikely. The expense implied, however, may make them prohibitive in many countries.

The Swedish government has stated that

The division of functions as between the sexes must be changed in such a way that both the man and the woman in a family are afforded the same practical opportunities of participation in both active parenthood and gainful employment. A policy which attempts to give women an equal place with men in economic life while at the same time confirming woman's traditional responsibility for the care of home and children has no prospect of fulfilling the first of these aims. This aim can be realized only if the man is also educated and encouraged to take an active part in parenthood and is given the same rights and duties as the woman in his parental capacity. This will probably imply that the demands for performance at work on the man's part must be reduced: a continued shortening of working hours will therefore be of great importance . . . with a view to making it easier for husbands to do their share of work in the home. (42)

One of the characteristics of modern family development in Sweden is the weakening of sex-linkage in the allocation of tasks in the household and in government-sponsored nurseries where more and more tasks are allocated neutrally. The Swedish government has reformed tax structures in favor of two-income families in order to encourage women to take jobs. It has financed and set standards for preschools, it has experimented with part-time jobs for both parents of young children. Maternity benefits have become parenthood benefits, letting the father take the mother's place for some time within the framework of the six-month eligibility period. The decision is left to the couple. The change of maternity insurance to parenthood insurance is a notice on the part of the government that the father and the mother have a common responsibility for the care of their children. The dynamics of the Decade for Women: Equality, Development, and Peace, may encourage other governments to follow the example of this government.

NOTES

(1) Paulo Freyre, Pedagogy of the Oppressed (New York: Seabury, 1970).

(2) Unfortunately, being "centered" or "grounded" are rare qualities in people today. Yet a certain degree of self-centeredness is necessary for each person to know, accept, respect, and love her or himself and others.

(3) Cited by Sandra R. Herman, "The Liberated Women of Sweden," Center Magazine 7, no. 3 (May/June, 1974): 77.

(4) E/CONF.66/34.

(5) International Labor Organization, Equality of Opportunity and Treatment for Women Workers (Geneva, 1975) pp. 34, 36.

(6) Calculation by Elise Boulding's Women's Data Bank, Boulder, Colorado, based on data gathered by Ester Boserun's Women's Role in Economic Development (New York: St. Martin's Press, 1970) and on United Nations statistics.

(7) Thomas W. Merrick and Marianne Schmink, "Female Headed Households and Urban Poverty in Brazil" (Paper presented at the International Center for Research on Women, Workshop on "Women in Poverty: What Do We Know?" Belmont Conference Center, Elkridge, Md., April 30-May 2, 1978), (table 8).

(8) See Thomas Merrick, "Household Stucture and Poverty in Families Headed by Women: The Case of Belo Horizonte" (Paper presented at the 1977 meetings of the Latin American Studies Association, Houston, Texas).

(9) See Mayra Buvinic and Nadia H. Youssef, "Women-Headed Households: The Ignored Factor in Development Planning," (Paper presented for the Office of Women in Development, AID, Washington, D.C. 1978), table 12.

(10) This is extremely well documented in two excellent films for Argentina and Mexico in The Double Day, a color documentary on Women Working in Latin America, directed by Elena Solberg Ladd, produced by the International Women's Film Project, Tricontinental Film Center; and for India and Ghana in Outside the GNP, a color documentary directed and filmed by Bettina Corke.

(11) Woman Power: The World's Female Labour Force in 1975 and the Outlook for 2000 (Geneva: International Labour Office, 1975) p. 4.

(12) Woman Power, p. 15.

(13) See, for example, Ester Boserup, Woman's Role in Economic Development (London: George Allen & Unwin, 1970); also Signs: Journal of Women in Culture and Society 3, no. 1, (Autumn 1977), which includes papers given at the 1976 conference on Women and Development at Wellesley College.

(14) Woman Power, p. 4.

(15) In the international terminology, the economically active (or the labor force) include the employed (full- or part-time) and the unemployed. Subcategories comprise employers, persons working on their own account, salaried employees, wage-earners, members of producers' cooperatives, together with unpaid family workers. Unpaid family workers are predominantly females; they are counted in most censuses among the labor force - but the criteria used in identifying them differ from one country to another. One-third of the normal work period is the international standard for the minimum amount of work performed for a person to be counted as an economically active unpaid family worker (Woman Power, pp. 3-4).

(16) In Colombia, low-income families have nearly three times as many children as high-income families: See Joseph E. Potter, "The Distributional Consequences of Different Fertility Decline" (Paper delivered at 1978 meeting of the Population Association of America, Atlanta, Georgia), Table 1. In Nigeria, 70 percent of a sample of urban Yoruba women in the 25 to 34 age group had spent more than half of their adult lives either pregnant or breastfeeding; See Judith Harrington, "Some Micro-Socioeconomics of Female Status in Nigeria" (Paper presented at the International Center for Research on Women Policy Roundtable - (ICRWPR) - Washington, D.C., June 21, 1978), Tables 3 and 4.

(17) Elise Bowlding suggests that the census category "economically inactive housewife," still utilized in 34 countries, be abolished altogether. Forty-one percent of women in North Africa/Middle East and 37 percent in Latin America fall into the census category "unaccounted for" (see Boulding's paper presented at the ICRWPR "Productivity and Poverty Problems in Measurement for Third World Women," Table 2).

(18) Women Workers in a Changing World (Geneva: International Labour Office, 1973), p. 51.

(19) Food and Agriculture Organization of the United Nations, The Role of Women in Rural Development, E/Conf. 66/BP/11.

(20) René Dumont "Development and Mounting Famine: A Role for Women," International Labor Review 3, no. 6 (June 1975): 455.

(21) Dumont, p. 454.

(22) See for example Women Workers, p. 52 and p. 454.

(23) Elise Boulding, Women's DataBank, Boulder, Colorado.

(24) René Dumont refers to three hours pounding for a small family.

(25) Julie Da Vanzo and Donald L. P. Lee, "The Compatibility of Child Care with Labor Force Participation and Non-market Activities: Preliminary Evidence from Malaysian Time Budget Data," Paper prepared for the ICRWPR, tables 1, 2, 5, 6.

(26) Carmen Diana Deere, "Intra-familial Labor Deployment and the Formation of Peasant Household Income: A Case Study of the Peruvian Sierra" (Paper prepared for the ICRWPR).

(27) See Elise Boulding, Women, Work and Babies: Directing Work to Fifth World Farmers, International Women's Year Studies on Women, paper no. 4, Programme of Research on General Social and Economic Dynamics, Institute of Behavioral Sciences, University of Colorado, March 1975.

(28) Background discussion paper prepared by the NGO Committee on UNCSTD, of the Conference Group of NGOs in Consultative Status with ECOSOC, Mildred Robbins Leet, Chairperson: 54 Riverside Drive, New York, N.Y. 100024.

(29) NGO Task force's Background Discussion Paper, pp. 4-5.

(30) See Richard J. Barnet and Ronald E. Muller, Global Reach, the Power of the Multinational Corporation (New York: Simon & Schuster, Congressional Committee on Multinational's Reports on Mexico and Brazil, September 1975, and see United Nations Summary of the Hearings Before the Group of Eminent Persons to Study the Impact of Multinational Corporations on Development and on International Relations, ST/ESA/15 Sales No. E.74.II.A.9; Multinational Corporations on World Development, ST/ECA/190, Sales No. E.73.II.A.11, and The Impact of Multinational Corporations on Development and on International Relations, ST/ESA/11, Sales No. E.74.II.A.6.

(31) Women Workers in a Changing World (Geneva: International Labor Organization, 1973), pp. 6-7.

(32) Margot Higgins, "Women and Economic Development," Dialogue 6, no. 2 (1973) - a U.S.I.A. publication - pp. 78-81.

(33) Cited by Anna Greta Leijon, Swedish Women - Swedish Men (The Swedish Institute for Cultural Relations with Other Countries: 1968), p. 31.

(34) See Charter of Economic Rights and Duties of States, Article 16.1, and Declaration, Article 1.

(35) The basic principles of the elimination of discrimination against women and the participation of women on equal terms

with men in the political, economic, social, and cultural life of their countries have been the subject of a long list of conventions, declarations, resolutions, and recommendations adopted by the General Assembly during the last thirty years. A list may be obtained from the United Nation's Branch for the Advancement of Women.

(36) General Assembly Official Records: Seventh Special Session, Supplement No. 1 (A/10301), Resolution 3362 (S-VII).

(37) The amendments are as follows: Syrian Arabic Republic: Add the word "the" before the words "new international economic order;" Yugoslavia: Replace the word "a" by the word "the" before the words "new international economic order." Delete the words "just and equitable" before the words "international economic order." After these words add the words "based on equity and justice" (A/C. 3/33/WG. 1/CRP.1/Add. 1, p. 13).

(38) The Communist party in Italy proposed that both housewives and single women be given a pension when they reached 55 years of age. The bill was never passed.

(39) In the United States the Chase Manhattan Bank has calculated that the economic value of the housework carried out by a housewife in a middle-income family with two children is $160 a month. This implies that the U.S. economy saves $250 billion a year, because housework is not remunerated. (See Chase Manhattan Bank, What's a Wife Worth? - a leaflet published by the Public Relations Department, June 1970, 1 Chase Manhattan Plaza, New York, N.Y. 10005.)

(40) See Barry Popkin, "Women, Work and Child Welfare," table 3, and Robert Evenson and Elizabeth K. Quizon, "Time Allocation and Home Production in Philippine Rural Households," especially tables 3, 4, and 5 (Papers prepared for the ICRWPR).

(41) Piaget's research points to the fact that children's creativity basically grows through their exercise of choice.

(42) The Status of Women in Sweden; Report to the United Nations, 1968, (The Swedish Institute, Stockholm) pp. 4, 7, 8., cited in E/CN.6/384 p. 6.

7 Traditional Medicine as an Alternative for Health in Third World Countries

Xavier Lozoya
Carlos Zolla

INTRODUCTION

The problem of health is one of the most acute problems the so-called developing countries are facing at the moment. For some critics, the solution lies entirely in the correct exploitation of economic resources, while for others, it is precisely these very problems of health that weaken desired economic and productive advance. One way or another, the resulting vicious circle makes it impossible to outline and control effectively the level of health in the Third World countries.

As the World Health Organization (WHO) has recognized, Western medicine has not managed to cater for the needs of the ever increasing population of developing countries. The reasons argued are in turn a consequence of the socioeconomic realities of these countries, a phenomenon characterized by a variety of factors, such as the high cost of Western medical technology against low national budgets allocated to public health; technological dependence in the field of research into new appropriate medical means; insufficient numbers of physicians in relation to domestic demand; dependence for the supply of medicaments; imbalance in the distribution of medical services that range from high technical sophistication in cities to a complete lack of even the most basic services in rural areas; ignorance in scientific circles in industrialized societies of the problems and diseases of developing countries, which leads to disinterest in the development of new therapeutic techniques; inadequate medical training at the university level, combined with a tendency to discriminate against autochthonous medical and cultural values; a manifest alienation from traditional cultural patterns by the medical and paramedical students and junior practitioners who tend to migrate to the cities, etc.

The efforts being made to alleviate the critical health situations in developing countries are frequently directed towards medical systems and methods of providing services that have been modelled on those existing in highly industrialized countries, resulting in incongruity with the economic and cultural realities of poor countries. This process has been supported by the myth of "scientific and medical universality," which is yet another facet of cultural and economic colonialism.

With all this - and in spite of it - systems of traditional indigenous medicine survive in developing countries, even in those areas where people have access to modern medical services. These traditional systems, as their name suggests, are deeply rooted in popular culture and, forming an intimate part of this culture, supply medical assistance to the majority of people in developing countries.

On the other hand, this ancestral inheritance, the result of the development of empirical knowledge, has little importance for the domestic medical classes, trained in and inspired by Western medical culture. This results in a complete divorce between popular medical knowledge and an elitist medicine directed towards the wealthy.

In 1974, the authors of a joint study carried out by the United Nations Children's Fund (UNICEF) and WHO of the possible ways of satisfying the health needs of developing countries recommended the mobilization and training of all the professionals from the different systems of traditional indigenous systems, including nonprofessional midwives, in order to provide a basic health care service, this being the only real alternative in the solving of the problem. This same recommendation was endorsed by a resolution passed by the executive council of WHO, to which the World Health Assembly also gave its support. This resolution approved the formulated proposal to promote and develop pertinent investigations into traditional medicine in several Third World countries, and its incorporation into national health programmes. At the same time the Working Group for the Promotion and Development of Traditional Medicine was formed at the headquarters of WHO. Its programme has the following objectives:

- To encourage objective studies of all aspects of traditional indigenous systems of medicine in the world in order to promote them as part of the health services and in this way increase the efficiency of these services
- To examine the positive aspects of the traditional systems within the perspective of modern science as a first step towards achieving maximum diffusion of their usefulness and efficiency
- to promote the integration of knowledge and techniques of known value from Western medical science on the one hand and the traditional systems on the other

In the implementation of this programme, proposed by WHO, priority is given to the needs of developing countries, chiefly in respect to basic health services, taking into account national peculiarities in the political structure, economic resources, and development plans of each country.

Let us now analyze in more detail, the factors and characteristics that determine, on the one hand the existence of traditional medicine, and on the other the viability of applying such an alternative system to the development of health in Third World countries.

For this purpose, we will use as an example some aspects of health problems in Mexico, without, of course, assuming that the conditions in that country are necessarily identical to those in other developing countries, but because there are a sufficient number of common elements for Mexico's problems to be representative of the situation existing in the Third World, where a solution to the health problems of the people is badly needed.

THE PROBLEM OF HEALTH

The extension of capitalistic production on a world scale and the particular impact of the different policies planned from that moment brought to light a series of all kinds of problems for the dependent and colonized countries. Many of these problems did not fit into the usual categories of analysis and were of an atypical form, if not unknown till that time. The concept of social disease or of the social causes of disease started to become relevant when it was shown that many imbalances in health in the various countries did not correspond to well-known pathology in the narrow limits of clinical medicine.

For the West, contact with other cultures was, in more than one aspect, like a mirror of the situation its own policies of expansion had generated. From this point on, it is possible to show with endless examples from Latin America, Asia, and Africa, the repetition of the critical situations caused by colonialist and neocolonialist policies. It was possible to characterize the so-called Third World by its role of supplier of raw materials, its demographic explosion, and also for the deficiency in its sanitary conditions, starvation, and the fall in the life expectancy of its peoples.

The reasons for the fall in the population in the sixteenth century in the area known as Mexico today (to give an example of policies of expansion) was, in a sense, typical. Regardless of the prevailing conditions in Central America before the arrival of the Spaniards, we can reconstruct the phenomenon only in the light of the effects of the new economic, social, and cultural order established from 1521. The impact of the conquest was such that the population of Central Mexico fell from 25.2 million to 1.1 million in the period 1519 to 1603. Military causes are usually blamed for this phenomenon, but others that were in evidence in times of relative peace can be added, such as the introduction of new diseases into the area, the consequent alteration of the biological system, new patterns of land tenure, forced labor, the deterioration of sanitation, particularly in the towns, the decrease in the ration of food per person, and finally the unbalancing on a large scale of the ecology of the region.

Without doubt, the Mexican case, although serious, is not exceptional. Even today, despite the evident advance of underdeveloped countries on the international scene and the consequent weight they carry, this phenomenon still assumes the same typical forms. Uncontrolled exploitation of natural resources, ever-increasing overcrowding in the marginal areas around urban centers, deep social divisions and, in general, the exploitation of the lower classes in "poor" countries, all these factors generate situations in the specific area of health which only global policies can correct.

A good deal of the anthropological literature, a product (critical or condoning) of colonial expansion in the last centuries, bears witness to the clashes with various seemingly dormant societies, alienated from the dynamism of life in the societies that are today industrialized. This same literature has recorded, often with nostalgia, the rhythm of these unchronicled, "primitive" cultures, which were part of what is now the present-day developing world. In many parts of the world, it has become clear that more alarming than the apparent scarcity of resources and craftsmanship, is the developing world's seeming attempt to eliminate, irrationally, the modes of life and patterns of behavior it sees as frozen in time.

It is true that predictions relating to the ending of old customs do not seem incorrect if policies of exploiting people and obtaining raw materials irrationally are maintained. It is because these countries have such resources that we must, when all is said and done, doubt their classification as "poor countries."

What have the developing countries got in common from the point of view of health? In general terms, the existence of diseases of like etiology, linked to more or less comparable socioeconomic (and therefore sanitary, nutritional, educational, etc.) conditions.

At the forefront of these problems, also in general, it is not a question of resolving medical enigmas in order to effect a substantial improvement in the health conditions of underdeveloped countries. On the contrary, most of the ailments can be alleviated by known medical means. The fall in life expectancy, particularly in the rural areas, originates, in clinical terms, from illnesses which, since the last century, have been carefully studied and for which, in many cases, cures have been found.

All the same, as a consequence of social stratification in developing countries (the result of the aforementioned policies), the typical maladjustments of the great cities are repeated reproducing in the developing countries the same rates of sickness and mortality as in the big cities of wealthy countries. As a result of the growth of Mexico City, one of the fastest growing cities in the world, cases of degenerative diseases as well as heart disease have increased. While in the United States the highest continuous percentage increase since 1900 has been in these diseases, in Mexico, on the other hand, deaths from cardiovascular disease were not even counted among the main causes until the census of 1922, in which they were placed no higher than tenth. Such illnesses have increased parallel to the rate of urbanization: from fifth place among causes of death in 1963, to fourth in 1971, and third in 1974. Comparison with the rural situation continues to be significant: The number of deaths from cardiovascular disease per 100,000 inhabitants in 1974 was 14.1 in the country and 51.1 in the cities. These figures become relative, however, when cardiovascular problems in infants originating from rheumatic fever are taken into account. The Social Security Institute of Mexico estimates that of the 419,467 children examined between 1961 and 1970, 9,297 were rheumatic. The possible surgical solutions to these problems are uncostable and very highly technical. Once again, the solutions raise the social nature of the measures that have to be taken, particularly in the case of children who have access to schools. By observing the growth patterns in present-day Mexico, ever-increasing incidence of heart disease, ischemic heart disease, and cerebrovascular disease in general can be expected by the year 2000.

In the Mexican countryside, as in many parts of Latin America and the Third World, the picture is more dramatic. The picture is colored by unfavorable conditions in which pregnancies are ever-increasing, the implementation of adequate prophylactic measures are lacking, and diet is defficient. "Weight at birth," say Mexican specialists, "is an indicator of health at the time of conception, pregnancy, and confinement. Weight under 2,500 grams is considered premature, from 2,501 to 3,000 grams underweight, and above 3,000 grams desirable weight. Using this classification, of 2,113 newborn infants born alive in a hospital in the Federal District (Mexico City), the following distribution was recorded: 11.7 percent premature, 33.9 percent underweight, and the remaining 54.3 percent of desired weight." Furthermore,

The nature of most of the problems of illness and mortality in Mexico are such that solutions to them are not fundamentally medical. In the case of gastroenteritis and diarrhoea, the solution does not lie in doctors growing cultures, identifying germs, prescribing hydrant solutions and antibiotics in order to cure the patient. Nor is the solution to this problem within the reach of vaccines, which can only keep such diseases at bay for a time. So that the focus to these problems must remain within the much broader framework of socioeconomic development, education in hygiene, productivity and better living conditions.(1)

The numerous efforts being made towards increasing the level of sanitation, intensifying medical research, and generating new sources of professional training remain to a great extent aborted, in that education plans, specialization in research systems, selection of equipment, all this, simply reproduces the vices of the industrialized countries and neglects the peculiarities of a national model.

In the case of Mexico, these efforts have resulted in an increase in life expectancy, a lessening of a great number of illnesses, and a decrease in the number of previously incurable diseases.

Massive vaccination campaigns, the expansion of regional centers, as well as great advances in education and professional training are, among other factors, generating conditions in which more attention can be paid to health problems. However, if special attention is not given to national peculiarities, and a suitable framework is not found in which these phenomena and their variable conditions can appear, the resulting solutions will be extraneous.

The development of preventive medicine, for example, would considerably reduce, if not eradicate, illnesses such as poliomelitis, whooping cough, tetanus, etc., these being typical illnesses of large areas in Mexico. Surely there is also a need for specific treatments of illnesses such as onchocerciasis, trachoma, typhoid, amoebiasis, malaria, etc. Figures that estimate at a national level are indicators of the extent to which such diseases can be seen as typical of developing countries. Table 7.1 shows the causes of death per 100,000 inhabitants in Mexico, Central America, North America, and South America (1974):

Table 7.1.   Causes of Death per Thousand,
Western Hemisphere, 1974

	Mexico	Central America	North America	South America
Influenza and pneumonia	131.2	77.15	33.63	74.51
Enteritis and diarrhea	127.0	106.74	1.22	53.85
Heart disease	74.4	84.33	342.29	115.09
Accidents	54.9	42.24	57.37	49.38
Prenatal mortality	47.8			
Malignant tumors	36.5	56.93	158.95	80.31
Cerebrovascular disease	24.3	39.50	97.56	45.31
Cirrhosis	21.3	7.17	14.64	12.36
Acute respiratory infections	18.4	8.72	9.59	17.07
Homicides	15.9	13.05	8.40	7.32

The death rate, which fell in respect to previous years, was 7.7 per 1,000 inhabitants, of which a significant number were children. This appears dramatically illustrated if one compares the table of the most common infectious and parasitic diseases in Mexico in 1974 (table 7.2) to the death rate from these diseases according to age (see table 7.3).

Now, even though these examples give only a global and panoramic picture of the problem, we can evidently offer two hypotheses: either (a) Insofar as one makes a joint table in which disease appears as only one of the factors of general disequilibrium, and one provides solutions (medical, sanitary, nutritional, educational, etc.), human effort can be directed towards more specific objectives than are established at the moment; or (b) such efforts should consider both the medical resources available from modern science and the social base which, endowed as it is with a heritage and knowledge of traditional medical practices, is deeply imbedded and widely spread in Mexico, as in the other countries of the Third World.

Table 7.2.   Infections and Parasitic Diseases –
Mexico – 1974

	Deaths	Rate	% of total
1) Diarrheal diseases	50,842	90.0	63.8
2) Tuberculosis	7,660	13.4	9.0
3) Whooping cough	3,032	5.3	3.8
4) Typhoid fever	2,095	3.7	2.6
5) Amoebiasis	2,072	3.7	2.6
6) Tetanus	1,672	3.0	2.1
7) Paratyphoid	1,024	3.7	1.3
8) Helminthiasis	973	1.7	1.2
9) Infectious hepatitis	492	0.3	0.6
10) Measles	447	0.8	0.6

Table 7.3.   Death Rates According to Age

Region	under 5 years	5-14 years	15-44 years	45-64 years	over 65 years
Mexico	911.5	54.2	50.6	143.3	541.2
North America	87.5	1.3	2.4	9.7	32.9
Central America and the Caribbean	713.6	70.9	41.0	115.1	365.1
South America	586.7	27.8	27.8	73.0	196.7

TRADITIONAL MEDICINE AS AN ALTERNATIVE

The countless traditional healers who practice today in the majority of countries and who live primarily in distant communities where they are closely knit to local customs and enjoy the confidence of the people, have a popular knowledge that has many forms. A great store of practical knowledge, ability, and real wisdom has resulted from the empirical learning passed down from generation to generation throughout the centuries. It is therefore these health workers who, with their cultural background, can contribute their experience and, in turn, through contact with modern medical science can enrich their activities. The aim of extending a point of communication between at least two conceptions of medicine, from different backgrounds, must begin with mutual understanding of the principles, resources, and potential each one offers and practices. The validation of traditional indigenous medicine involves a scientific analysis of the usefulness of its resources. However, this validation demands as an essential condition the development of its own scientific method, different from the one prevailing, which, steeped in dogma, has distorted the usefulness of science as an instrument of objective valuation.

We are faced with the need to develop an adequate medical technology together with methods that are linked to the economic and cultural reality around us. Western science, the product of the extraordinary development of technology, particularly in the industrialized societies, can and must provide methods of analysis, but it is far from furnishing definite criteria for the evaluation of medical knowledge. It is necessary, therefore, to choose from among existing Western techniques whatever can be most usefully employed in outlining new forms of evaluation suitable for empirical wisdom, which has reached its own conclusions through different but not necessarily erroneous ways.

This process of scientific evaluation of resources in traditional medicine revives the deep meaning of science, liberated from the grip of dogmatic measures into which it has fallen, above all in the field of medicine, which is now accepted as something absolute by those who have developed it to its limits. The case of the traditional use of medicinal plants is a good example of the atavistic processes that Western science is debating. The search for pharmaceutical products obtained from medicinal plants has limited its approach to the utilization of these plants as sources of raw materials for the manufacture of new drugs. At one stage in the chemical research into plants, it was believed that total synthesization of pharmaceutical products would soon erradicate the use of vegetable products. However, such hopes

were dashed, since 80 percent of medicines used in the world
are derived from medicinal plants; only 5 percent are of totally
synthetic origin. On the other hand, the difficulties in
isolating the pure substances contained in these plants have
only recently come to light, and these same drugs, manufactured by industrial processes, are beginning to show
disadvantages in their use in medicine. Industrialized societies
are already beginning to doubt the real and transcendent value
of many drugs which until recently were used as panaceas in
the treatment of old illnesses. It is the underdeveloped
countries that have become the market place for these well-
tried pharmaceutical products, while societies of the industrialized countries are beginning to venture into "green
medicine" in order to open up new dimensions in the market for
trendy remedies. Apart from this, traditional medicine also
makes use of medicinal plants. Plant-based infusions and
extracts offer alternative remedies which have been tried and
tested. However, for many spokesmen of Western science,
such remedies lack useful application as they do not possess
the characteristics required of pharmaceuticals by Western
medicine, that is to say their grade of purity, concentration,
and composition do not satisfy the requirements of transnational patents.

This explains why scientific research into such remedies
in developing countries should be directed towards highlighting
the effectiveness of medicines which, in principle, break the
rules established by others in conventional chemistry and
pharmacology, but which take on a meaningful social and
economic dimension in the real development of their economies.
The hitherto unknown value of popular information about the
uses of these plants should also be noted.

Traditional medicine has built up a store of useful plants
as a result of a long, slow process of testing the effectiveness
of the resources that surround man. The selection of such
resources reveals the existence of a most valuable system of
apprenticeship that contrasts with the influential attitude of
Western science that formulates plans impressive in scale but
inefficient in result. This is the case, for example, in the
search for plant-based drugs against cancer, which can only
be achieved through the analysis of hundreds of thousands of
plants that are collected, ordered, or stolen from the countries
of the Third World for the affluent and complex institutions of
industrialized countries whose investigations are impressive in
their cost but have proportionately disappointing results. It
is the plants, used by the people, with their own language
and interpretation, and supported by popular wisdom, that
possess the therapeutic properties and demand scientific
research.

The example of herbalism is valid for the majority of
therapeutic remedies used in traditional medicine today. Acu-

puncture could be given as another relevant example of the necessity of applying modern methods of technology to the investigation and development of a traditional form of therapy which until a few years ago brought only smiles to the faces of the West.

The process of validation is the starting point for the inclusion of traditional medicine into present and future health systems, but this process needs, in turn, to take a fresh look at its own objectives and methods.

THE POLITICAL DECISION

When pluricultural societies recognize the diversity of their origins and the consolidation of their nationality, they must make use of all forms of cultural expression and as a result, medicine will attain a new and balanced dimension. Political decisions are essential if autochthonous values are to be rescued, but nevertheless they are certainly not sufficient on their own. A political platform is needed, primarily so that the existing conditions, cultures, and processes may be properly accepted, in order to generate a slow but vigorous process of assimilation and valorization of each country's resources and values.

On the other hand, in order to consolidate political decisions, the support of reliable data is necessary, which, as in the case of medicine, can be found in scientific research. If, at the time of generating global policies, improvization, thoughtlessness, and the absence of reliable parameters cannot be avoided, no advance will have been made. Indeed, it should very probably fall once more into the repetition of foreign models which, when applied mechanically, provoke the long list of well-known disasters.

True, the Third World needs its own political road, but for this it also needs its science, the deepening of cultural values, and an exhaustive understanding of the historical progress of each society. In particular, Third World scientists must understand that the very material they have to offer as a base upon which to make political decisions, is already impregnated with particular concepts, rooted in the positive or negative assessment they have previously made of the set of variables that make their own societies into something always in need of specific reappraisal.

Resorting to traditional medicine as a subject of study helps one understand the cultural development that by and large comprises large social groups and colors long historical periods. When considering the potential of traditional medicine, the politician and the scientist must not just look at one source of data, but must take into account the particular social

sectors that possess significant medical knowledge and, through
it, the ability to improve the efficiency of sanitary applications.
    The politicians and scientists who take notice of the
phenomenon of traditional medicine, must also ask themselves
how this knowledge has survived, extended, and been applied.
They must also ask why societies with universities, higher
education centers, the most powerful technology, and a system
of advertising that doubles the cost of patent medicines, have
not been able to generate a pedagogical attitude from physician
to patient. They must question, in fact, why in developed
countries, patients are not taught and therefore cannot
understand their role in a process in which they are the very
protagonists.
    It is encouraging that, to a large extent, international
organizations are beginning to consider and value some of the
determining variables, in order to solve the health problems of
developing nations. It is for this reason that we will quote
extensively the words of the director general of WHO, Dr.
Hafdan Mahler:

> The separation and mutual antipathy which exists
> between the traditional systems of medicine and the
> so-called modern medicine, has lasted long enough.
> Aren't the goals the same for the one and the other:
> to improve the health of humanity and by this the
> quality of life? Only those blinded by arrogance
> could suppose that traditional medicine has nothing
> to teach modern medicine and vice versa.
>   Unfortunately, the divergence between the two
> systems finds its parallel, nearly exactly, in the
> division of the world between rich and poor. While
> the prosperous and privileged inhabitants of the
> large cities and urban nuclei generally have access
> to complex technology and the ultraperfection of the
> methods of modern science, for tens of millions of
> others, the only health agents available are healers,
> medicine men, herbalists and traditional midwives.
> In most rural areas in developing countries, not only
> is there a complete lack of physicians to whom to
> rush in case of sickness, but also the availability of
> health care is utterly insufficient: one assistant per
> 10,000 inhabitants on average. . . . But the whirl
> of political transformation which has swept the world
> in the last decade, has been accompanied by a
> hurricane of radical change in the attitude towards
> health in the community. The social conscience of
> the world has been awakened as has the demand that
> the disparity in health care between rich and poor
> nations and between the rich and poor of the same

country be progressively reduced until its complete disappearance. The underprivileged who make up 80 percent of the world population have as much right as the remaining 20 percent to receive health care, to protect their children against fatal diseases, to have basic services for mother and child, not to have their problems ignored, nor be denied treatment against diseases which humanity knows how to cure and control.

Two years ago, we gave our pledge to try and attain an ambitious goal which can be summarized as follows: health for everyone by the year 2000. Well, now, this goal is unattainable with the present systems of health service and the availability of people trained in methods of modern medicine. We only have 23 years to complete this enormous task, and it is obvious that we will have to resort to unorthodox solutions since, in such a short space of time, it is unimaginable that developing countries will be able to find enough people with orthodox training to resolve their problems. For some responsible politicians, the training of health auxiliaries, midwives and healers may be seen as a disagreeable solution, but if it succeeds in giving help to those who can hope for no other kind of help, it must be the correct policy and should not be considered simply as a convenient solution of inferior quality.

NOTE

(1) J. Kumate and L. Canedo, La salud de los mexicanos y la medicina en México, (México, Colegio Nacional, 1977).

8 Environmental and Urban Policies for the Human Habitat

Luis Sanchez-de-Carmona

Environmental and urban conditions all over the world, and especially in most of the Third World, cannot be separated from political, economic, and commercial considerations at an international level. The vital framework and living conditions of the population are closely linked to economic and political circumstances in different states and to relations among nations.

The quality of urban and rural environment is not only the result of economic development, but depends to a large extent on the ways and means of production within the habitat. This includes the ways in which people make use of the resources in their natural surroundings, the processes through which they transform them in order to build the artificial environment that will satisfy their needs and the social relations that give nuance to and make possible this constructive labor.

The New International Order must be much more than simply economic. It is not enough to deal with issues related to the quantification of goods and services, monetary disorder, unemployment, deterioration in the terms of exchange of Third World countries, and the intensification of problems derived from the foreign debt. We must consider, in dialectical fashion, the interrelation between natural, artificial, social, and political elements that condition the quality of the framework within which mankind develops. Consequently, parallel to a New International Economic Order a New International Ecological Order must be promoted that considers the relation between people and their natural resources at all levels, from local communities to international society.

Urban growth in Third World countries is characterized by regional disequilibrium, leading to excessive concentrations of people with no hopes of work or well-being. There is, in most cases, no correspondence between the location of natural resources and urban development, given that the centralizing tendency of liberal economies prevails over the regional utilization of natural resources. In this centralizing process of urbanization, the rural sector is impoverished and the cities become congested. Natural resources are irrationally exploited, and the pollution derived from urban areas affects extensive tracts of territory. With this type of urban growth, life in the large conurbations presents many inconveniences: air and water pollution, modifications of climate, difficulties in transportation, insufficient green zones and recreational spaces, as well as lack of employment opportunities - all of which generate violence.

Rural migration into the cities and high natural population growth rates in Third World countries have made the cities' popular sectors grow at an accelerated pace. These sectors generally lack basic public and sanitary services; that is, they suffer shortages of water, sewerage, housing, clinics, schools, etc. The settlement of inhabitants with scarce resources in countries where urban land is the subject of speculation is difficult, and for this reason land invasions appear as an alternative so as to live near the city. The unstable land tenure of these settlers prevents them from making gradual improvements in their dwellings, and the government does not normally carry out basic infrastructure projects in these zones with irregular tenure. The location of these precarious settlements bears no relation to the industrial and service zones where the economically active population works, this implying a great daily cost in time and money for transportation. The ecological conditions of the land where these settlements are made are generally hostile, since the better land is occupied by the population sectors with higher incomes. The unhealthiness of these areas, the lack of drinking water and sewerage, and the proximity of garbage dumps generate conditions that cause disease and child mortality.

The magnitude of the urban growth problem at a world scale is colossal. The United Nations Conference on Human Settlements (Habitat) pointed out that between 1970 and the year 2000, there will be 3.5 billion more people on this planet, most of whom will inhabit urban centers. This implies constructing the equivalent of 3,500 urban centers with one million inhabitants each. In 1976, there were fewer than 300 cities in the world with a population of one million. For those 3.5 billion people, a minimum of 600 million dwellings will be needed, more than those that existed in the entire world in 1976.

The global task of constructing the artificial environment where people live and evolve implies modifying a series of national and international structures to enable the world's population, particularly the Third World's, to construct its own dwellings. This, to a large extent, means allowing lower-income groups access, through their own efforts, to higher levels of welfare.

PRINCIPLES AND OBJECTIVES SET FORTH
BY THE UNITED NATIONS

The issue of housing has long received consideration within the framework of the United Nations. Three years after the United Nations was established, in the Universal Declaration of Human Rights approved and proclaimed by the General Assembly in 1948, it stated that all persons have the right to an adequate standard of living that assures them and their families, health and well-being, particularly nutrition, clothing, housing, medical assistance, and the necessary social services.

The notion of housing prevalent during the 1940s and 1950s sought to cover all human environmental and spatial dimensions. In this way national institutes and agencies for housing appeared in many different countries. Conferences were abundant and cooperation extensive in this field at an international level.

During the 1960s it was ascertained that housing problems, instead of disappearing, had increased in countries of the Third World. It was acknowledged that housing was only one of the elements in the urban system that conditioned a population's well-being. It became necessary to plan land use in the cities, to consider infrastructure, equipment, and urban services in cities and towns. It was then that national urban development agencies began to appear and international activities on the subject were begun.

In the 1970s, people became aware that urban development had to be considered in relation to the global environmental conditions of a country. The United Nations Conference on the Environment, convened in Stockholm in 1972, was a decisive step in world awareness of this matter. In 1976 (Habitat) sought, among other things, to promote understanding among the general public about the fact that the housing problem was related to many others, and it was no longer justified to speak of housing, transport and road administration, energy, social usage of land (particularly urban), water supply, drainage, health and education, and other social services as separate and independent entities. Rather than consider the urban and the rural as two different environments, we must understand them as a continuum embracing all human communities, from huge metropolitan areas, cities, and towns to the most insignificant village.

Different countries have begun reorganizing their administration in order to coordinate their activities around the environmental concept, considering it in its overall view of the interrelation between natural, urban, and sociocultural environment. Up to now, it has been the developed countries that have initiated this process, like England (Department of the Environment) and France (Ministère de l'Environment et du Cadre de Vie).

It is to be hoped that by the decade of the 1980s the concept of "environment" will be integrated into that of socioeconomic development planning, since an awareness has been achieved in understanding that environmental, urban, and housing conditions depend on the type of development in each country, and the interrelation among countries at the international level.

In accordance with this concept, the term "eco-development" appeared àt the conference in Stockholm, and was enriched at the Cocoyoc Conference, held in Mexico in 1974. This approach points out that the improvement of environmental conditions in a country implies modifying the objectives of economic development. It is suggested that production be not an end in itself, but rather that a new logic be implemented in making production a means of satisfying the basic needs of the population, respecting the environment, promoting maximum regional and local self-reliance, and making it possible for the population to solve its own problems.

The Charter of Economic Rights and Duties of States points out in its preface the hope of "contributing to the creation of conditions more favorable to: (point F) the protection, preservation, and improvement of the environment." Article 30 of this charter mentions all nations as sharing a common responsibility before the international community:

> The protection, preservation and improvement of the environment for present and future generations is the responsibility of all Nations. Every Nation must try to establish its own environmental and development policies in accordance with this responsibility. The environmental policies of all Nations should promote, and not adversely affect, the present and future development potential of the developing countries.

OBSTACLES TO APPLYING THE OBJECTIVES AND PRINCIPLES

The obstacles for achieving a vital framework more adequate for the world population have to do, in the final analysis, with fundamental economic and social issues, such as the redistribution of the costs and benefits of development among nations, countries, regions, and different social groups.

Even though progress has been made in understanding that development cannot be measured solely by economic growth, there is strong resistance to the idea that there can be economic and urban growth without development. This is verified in the widening of the gap between rich and poor in countries with growing gross national products. By the same token, it can be seen that industrial growth without adequate development policies greatly affects environment and natural resources, jeopardizing future development.

Traditional economic theory considers environmental problems as simple side effects of human activity, whose costs are not considered in national or international transactions.

One of the main causes of the inadequate use of resources in the countries of the Third World is the diverging interests of the different groups in national and international society. Economic motives, represented by consumer habits and the search for short-term economic benefits, are in contradiction with the adequate exploitation of resources and their preservation for future generations. Easy access to the utilization of natural resources and raw materials at a low price has accelerated economic growth in the industrialized countries and has been an obstacle to the development of the countries that export these products. The use of energetics in the developed countries causes pressure to be exerted for the irrational exploitation of resources in the Third World. For this reason environmental deterioration in Third World countries will continue despite significant changes in world level energy policies.

The influence of urban and architectonic patterns from the developed countries conditions in an important way the types and methods of urbanization in Third World countries and constitutes another important obstacle to solving the problems of the latter. These influences are generally transmitted through the dominant classes in Third World countries, which adapt easily to foreign models because they have a culture and an economic capacity similar to theirs.

This influence evidently draws us to the development models of developed countries, which the underdeveloped countries try to follow. The sole possibility, although remote, of becoming developed countries seems very distant and perhaps unattainable to the underdeveloped countries. Some authors analyze the availability and use of energy in our planet and estimate that the quantity of energetics in the world is insufficient to provide the entire world population with a level of well-being similar to that of developed countries. Furthermore, the pollution produced by the means of production necessary to attain this standard of living would so alter the global ecosystem as to make this possibility still more remote. It follows that the American pattern of having an individual house, with its own gas and electric appliances, and the availability of one or two automobiles is impossible for the countries of the Third World. Nonetheless, the Latin American people aspire to that. This urban and habitational pattern also generates monstrous cities that demand costly infrastructural works.

Environmental and urban policies have been inspired in those of developed countries despite the fact that the priority of problems in Third World countries is very different.

The planning of human settlements constitutes a new activity that faces a multitude of obstacles in every country. Urban and environmental criteria are often considered incompatible with economic policies and objectives, and this makes the former less effective. In addition, urban planning must go beyond the regulatory level that led to static documents inadequate to the events and circumstances where they were meant to apply.

Traditional urban development tends constantly towards utopia - it subjectively imagines ideal cities and spaces where people are to be inserted, independently of their real desires, necessities, and possibilities. It is forgotten that life, which gives cities their origin and shape, cannot be prefabricated, only promoted and encouraged. It can also be verified that actual urban development is applied to a narrow political and humanistic view, limiting itself to the application of partial techniques, be they related to construction, transit, and transportation, or to the environment, with a frequent loss of the overall view.

Cities and dwellings in a developing country cannot be simple commodities like those in industrialized countries, where capital wealth enables most of the population to "buy" its own dwelling. The construction of dwellings and cities should be important in the generation of wealth itself, rationally applying an abundant work force together with an adequate technology and a minimum of capital, thus providing multiple sources of employment.

Construction activity in Third World countries is presently monopolized to a great extent by large construction companies that possess the "technique" that can satisfy those who administer capital (private and public), while the common people are left to their own devices in building what they can. In this way, the possibility of access to better methods of construction and spatial arrangement is removed for the brunt of the population.

Within this system, housing and city lose their sense of use value, and their character of exchange value is accentuated. Thus, the beauty or personal utility of constructions is not important, but rather its commercial value. Thanks to this

logic, grey constructions standardized for the market proliferate, and the possibilities are limited for the creation of
works of art at a popular level, which would be a real expression of what the people want and not of what the speculators
sell.

The importation of technology related to planning and the
construction of urban and architectonic works and services
suffers in many cases from the adoption of norms and criteria
that correspond to the economic, social, and cultural conditions
of the developed countries, and when applied to underdeveloped countries, it produces a series of anomalies. In this
way the adoption of foreign models of development is increased
as pointed out above. One can easily verify how the adoption
of foreign standards and products for housing in poor countries makes it impossible for the majority of the population to
enjoy a proper dwelling. The constructions produced with
these standards turn out to be so costly that their purchase is
impossible for most people. In this manner "popular dwellings"
become accessible only to a middle class which in many Third
World countries represents 20 or 30 percent of the total
population. For the rest of the population, there is no
possiblity of taking care of their needs under those standards.

It goes without saying that the transfer of technology
associated with the export of goods and products of developed
countries affects the economy of the importing countries,
leading to the disappearance of foreign exchange and limiting
the exploitation of local resources and materials.

On the financial side, there exist a series of obstacles for
taking care of the environmental and urban needs of Third
World countries. Most of the credits issued by international
institutions that finance housing and urban development are
geared to investments that can offer all the commercial guar-
antees in the countries where they are applied. This means
that international support once again favors middle-income
groups, leaving most of the population without this kind of
benefit.

Urban issues have faced many obstacles for receiving
proper attention within the United Nations. The United
Nations became aware of the importance of mobilizing international support for the development of human settlements, and
thus convened the UN Conference for Human Settlements
(Habitat) in Vancouver, Canada, in 1976. The definition and
impact of this conference were far-reaching, leading to worldwide recognition of the urban development problem.

The recommendations of the conference were divided into
those with international applicability and those limited to the
national domain. As regards the former, it was not until
December 1977 that the 32nd General Assembly of the United
Nations resolved to implement them through the creation of a
Center for Human Settlements and a Commission for Human

Settlements, made up of representatives from 58 countries. The first meeting of the commission took place in April 1978, with little progress made because the executive director of the Habitat center had still not been named. This appointment was not made until the middle of this year, and it is to be hoped that the new center will be fully working next year at its Nairobi headquarters.

These delays mean that the recommendations for international action made at the Habitat conference of 1976 were not fully applied until 1979. Up to now it has been the Center for Housing, Construction and Planification, and the Foundation for Habitat and Human Settlements, both part of the UN network, that have applied the Habitat conference recommendations, as was specifically requested by the 31st Session of the UN General Assembly. However, the budget of both these institutions has been cut, thus minimizing the impact of the conference.

The mobilization of resources at a world level to support human settlement projects has been hindered by the low priority attributed to this field in credit and financial aid negotiations. In particular, funds from the UN Development Programme have not contributed substantial support in this field, since they are subject to explicit petitions from the different countries, where those responsible for economic development give no priority to human settlements.

STRATEGIES, POLICIES, AND RECOMMENDATIONS

The fundamental strategy for overcoming the obstacles that hamper the establishment of a new international urban and ecologic order consists in fully integrating these issues into the consideration of economic and social development, and finally, into the development model adopted at a national and international level.

First of all, the adoption of a development model that permits adequate conservation, exploitation, development, and regeneration of natural resources and the environment must be promoted. This presupposes an adequate relation between population and natural resources, both in terms of population distribution within the territory, and in the way that resources are put to use for social benefit, including technological and cultural considerations.

This type of development must be evaluated in terms of attention and solutions to basic human necessities and must be measured in terms of life quality, beginning with the assurance for all humanity of the minimum elements for survival. The indicators of development based on quantitative terms, such as Gross National Product, must be complemented by others of a qualitative nature, which are more important in the final analysis. Using this approach, the environmental and urban needs of the population must be reconsidered so as to promote the adequate and indispensable steps to take care of such necessities. Traditional solutions to urban issues (roads, housing, buildings, infrastructure), as they are normally offered, must be analyzed and modified in order to suit the needs of the majorities. For example, if the standard housing built in a particular country fails to satisfy the needs of the majority, it will be necessary to consider other housing alternatives.

It is of fundamental importance to make clear in all national and international forums that ecologic and urban development are not opposed to economic development, but on the contrary, support and promote it. Evidently, an adequate environmental and urban policy must be set out since otherwise there is the risk of truly hampering economic development.

Economic development implies the more rational exploitation of natural resources and proper ecological protection to insure a continuous development. These premises hold true for the exploitation and commercialization of resources and raw materials at both a national and an international level. In the second case, the continued exploitation of underdeveloped countries' natural resources for the benefit of the developed countries must be avoided, since this prevents Third World countries from using their resources and potential for a sustained development.

The conservation, exploitation, and development of resources at a world level must be approached with an integrated view of the world. The planet should be considered as a spaceship with limited resources, in which we are all travellers. The depredation and waste of resources and the contamination of the environment must worry all of humanity, so that each country, and the international community as a whole, must establish the means to impede it.

Present-day methods of resource exploitation remind us of the colonial structures that supposedly have been overcome. To absorb one region's resources and impoverish it for the benefit of another region constitutes the reproduction of the colonial exploitation methods so much fought against by the United Nations.

In order that the environmental consequences derived from resource exploitation, urban development, and public works be duly considered, it is hereby proposed that for all project, construction, or commercial transactions, the associated or derived environmental cost be considered. It is equally important to consider and measure the economic consequences for developing countries derived from the exploitation of nonrenewable resources, considering the future development of these regions once the resources presently in use have been exhausted.

It is particularly recommended that the norms and criteria for evaluating and quantifying the environmental effects of diverse international relations and transactions be formalized, even going as far as establishing international means for the evaluation of environmental impact.

It is especially important for every country to have an environmental and urban policy in agreement with its social, economic, political, and cultural situation. It would be convenient for such policies to be inscribed within a regional plan that supports and strengthens national positions and in turn defends the less developed countries from aggression and privileged positions taken up by the developed countries.

Environmental policies in Third World countries must be situated within the framework of priorities given by levels of development. In general, an adequate policy geared to preventing future environmental problems seems more adequate than seeking solutions to or combatting existing pollution. To do the latter would require great economic investments very difficult to apply in poor countries. Planning with ecological criteria, on the contrary, does not imply important monetary expenditures and makes it possible for the growth that characterizes developing countries to take place in an orderly fashion, thus constituting a real development with due consideration given to the environment.

Development of human settlements in Third World countries must be based on the aid to the settlement of those sectors with least resources that constitute the majority of the population. The application in Third World countries of formulas and urban recipes from developed countries is an impediment to taking care of the majority's needs, since norms and criteria applicable to rich countries generate housing solutions that can only be payed for by those sectors with the largest incomes.

In any case, it is recommended that one country should not imitate the solutions of another. The most it can do is adapt certain solutions that correspond to similar situations, but certainly not adopt foreign policies, since any difference, even in the political sphere, can substantially modify the results achieved under different circumstances.

Scientific and technological cooperation in environmental and urban matters is very useful. Countries can benefit from the experience of others to take advantage of the positive and not repeat old mistakes. However, this cooperation must be shed of all ideological, cultural, and commercial imposition, something that is not often accomplished.

When they transfer technology, developed countries introduce, consciously or unconsciously, the sale of their products and consequently their way of life and their social values. The purchase of these products by underdeveloped countries creates serious problems that obstruct the balanced development of weak economies that must guard their scarce resources and apply them in those areas most important for accomplishing the welfare of the majority of the population. Consequently, the transfer of technology and scientific cooperation must keep several aspects in mind. It would be convenient to increase cooperation among developing countries, exchanging experiences to widen the perspective of each country. As to cooperation on the part of developing countries, technological advances should be used, but only insofar as their application is limited by a policy that corresponds to the circumstances of each country, and which insures, in addition, that said technology is implemented with local capital, materials, and labor power.

As for the financial aid requested for these purposes, new channels of action must be opened and new norms and methods introduced. Presently, environmental and urban programme financing is limited basically to those aspects fully justified in investments within developed countries, as is the case with middle-class dwellings. Practically none of the environmental or urban needs of the marginal or precarious sectors of society receive financial aid, given the lack of security they can offer and the fact that the national and international banking system is not ready to act under terms different from those normally laid down.

Therefore it is recommended that the present international finance channels open new possibilities to support the efforts of the population with scarce resources to attain a better environment in which to live. It would be convenient to open up new financial channels to permit presently unsatisfied necessities to count on the minimum resources they request.

In order to strengthen environmental and urban actions inscribed in a New International Economic Order, an adequate promotion and coordination of resources and activities by the different international agencies that deal with these issues is requested. In establishing the UN Commission and Center for Human Settlements, its activities must be adequately linked to those of the UN Programme for the Environment. Environmental and urban activities are intimately related, so that plans and projects in both areas must have a complementary influence in the improvement of global and regional ecology.

Bases for action on the subject of human settlements were already established by the Habitat conference. Now international activity must be promoted with a basis in the new UN Center for Human Settlements, which must carry out a fostering and catalytic activity in order to mobilize world resources in support of programmes outlined by the aforementioned conference.

It is proposed to strengthen regional action in such a way as to have promotion, control, and outcome evaluation of specific projects carried out in close contact with the areas where the projects have been put into effect.

ENVIRONMENTAL AND URBAN PROGRESS

The New International Economic Order must equally propitiate an ecologic, environmental, and urban order in the United Nations and at a world level. Any program of action that does not consider environmental effects or settlement of the territory will remain truncated in its effects and will lead to negative situations that will affect the very results of those programs. Consequently, it is proposed that the policies mentioned in the paragraphs above be included in the principles and objectives of the New International Economic Order.

It is suggested that a charter be prepared that establishes basic policies at a world level conducive to the adequate conservation, utilization, development, and regeneration of natural resources and the environment. The considerations made in this charter should accompany all economic programmes or projects. It is also suggested that guidelines be drawn to promote an adequate population distribution in the territory, as well as the adequate location of the diverse industrial or urban installations, with the objective of creating a worldwide territorial order that leads to the rational exploitation of resources. In order to evaluate progress made in the world population's living conditions, it is suggested that qualitative aspects of the framework within which human life develops be taken into consideration. Welfare cannot be measured solely in monetary terms – the relation between needs and their satisfaction must be considered, taking into account the culture of all peoples.

In the exploitation of resources and their international trade, it will be necessary to take fully into account short-, medium-, and long-term environmental effects produced in the countries exporting raw materials. What is proposed is to make it obligatory to fill out reports and opinions on environmental and urban impact on all projects and constructions that have a significant effect on the environment in order to evaluate alternatives as far as their location and implementation.

It is recommended that every country prepare its national plan of ecologic and urban development, which must be considered closely linked to the socioeconomic development plan. In this way the congruence between economic and environmental objectives will be ensured.

Technical and scientific cooperation with regard to a country's experiences and advances in the aforementioned fields should be increased, avoiding all ideological, political, and commercial imposition.

It is considered necessary to open up new channels and ways for international financing destined to improve environmental conditions, thus propitiating nonconventional forms of financing that aid the efforts of the majorities with scarce resources.

Finally, it is recommended that the UN Programme of Action with respect to the environment and human settlements be strengthened on the basis of coordination among all departments and agencies having to do with these issues, so that during the 1980s, economic development will correspond to an environmental, territorial, and urban development that enables humanity to count on a better framework to develop its life.

9 The Environment as Viewed Within the Context of the NIEO
Charles A. Jeanneret-Grosjean

THE FAILURE OF A DEVELOPMENTAL MODEL

The evident failure of two Decades for International Development based on a promotion of economic growth in the West, as well as the stagnation of the North-South dialogue, are factors that have precipitated the calling into question of ways of development undertaken in the past.

In the South

The rapid growth of the Gross National Product (GNP) has not been on a par with social and economic development. Furthermore, the imitative development model imposed by the West on the rest of the world has not only reinforced the cultural, economic, and political dependence of developing countries,(1) but has also directly and dramatically increased economic and social inequalities between the countries themselves.

The increased social inequalities found in the peripheral countries have, in their turn, reinforced the degradation of the environment. This degradation is brought about through the general impact of a development model that centers on the indiscriminate exploitation of natural resources with a view to their direct valorization abroad, and without regard for maintaining a deposit of renewable national resources that would directly service national needs and the needs of generations to come.

This has resulted in the inevitable excessive use of the small quantity of natural resources accessible to the majority of the poor population (a situation further aggravated by anachronistic land systems) and, on the other hand, in the squandering of rare resources, the responsibility of a minority elite, the use of which requires an increasingly higher percentage of the national income.(2)

The close relationship between the deterioration of the environment and what one ought to call "the advance of underdevelopment" is today widely illustrated by phenomena such as the massive erosion of soils and the progressive disappearance of the humus layer, the growth of the population drain, the decrease in volume of national nonrenewable resources brought about by the unrestrained exploitation of these by a foreign market, the cut in national food supply due to the intensification of export agriculture, increasingly unproductive soils as a result of generalized uncontrolled use of weed-killers and insecticides to boost production of export crops, accelerated deforestation provoking the real energy crisis of rural areas, that is, the disappearance of firewood, the regression of genetic pools, and the alarming extinction of animal and vegetable species. The fundamental problem is the growing difficulty, often seen as the concrete impossibility, of satisfying the basic needs of the majority of the population at a national level.

The negative effects of Western development are not only to be found in the Third World, although such effects are a lot more serious in that region. The consequences of such a development reach beyond the geographical limits of particular areas and thus become global challenges.

In the North

The countries of the North are also undergoing a crisis. This crisis is by no means cyclical. It is fundamental because it is a development crisis that questions the mode of development itself. The maldevelopment of the North is immediately apparent, first, because there is an absence of generalized prosperity in spite of high growth rates, and second, because a large percentage of the population is experiencing growing impoverishment (a percentage that ranges between 15 and 35 percent in the industrialized countries and which is actually below the officially defined poverty line). Other factors involved in this maldevelopment are the progressive deterioration of the environment and the natural resources reserve (pollution, fear of resource shortages), alienation, and the impossibility of influencing, in a significant way, the factors conditioning the life of the people, the growing evidence of the negative effects of "consumerism," the increasing effects of mental illness, the portents of a trend towards fascism, and the deepening disillusionment with the official paradigm, etc.

It is particularly significant and symptomatic that the terms presently used to describe the state of things in the world, terms such as "stagflation," the growth generated by underdevelopment, the fear of an accelerated shortage of resources, sociopolitical upheavals, and the ungovernable nature of democracies, are in evident contradiction with the conventional wisdom of economic theories, political behavior, and social aspirations. Such terms, nonetheless have been the quintessence of reflection on development.

One could, therefore, postulate the existence of a kind of crisis that goes beyond what has been termed the "crisis of accumulation." In this context, it must not be forgotten that the rapid unprecedented accumulation of wealth in the north-west portion of the globe has been possible thanks to the old order, that is, an international economic system fashioned during the last two or three centuries, by interests servicing economies of the center and conferring on these economies privileged access to cheap human, natural, and particularly, energy resources. The periphery was thus used as a residual market for these center countries' national productions and as a way of overcoming contradictory fluctuations within the capitalist economic system between under- and over-productive and/or consumption capacity.(3)

The Global Crisis of Civilization

The serious existential problems presently facing humanity and the general malaise in which the dialogue on development is carried out have allowed the uncovering of a kind of civilization that is characterized, at a global level, by the network of domination, exploitation, and violence, and which is sufficient testimony of existing contradictions, and in the final analysis, of general failure.

The essence of the conflicts for power and domination that afflict different human societies has now become a global concern, since what is at stake, be it economic, cultural, or political, is the appropriation and control of access to resources on a world scale, and the supremacy of technology to which only the already most powerful have access, together with the domination of the international trade network.

This global crisis, faced today by both the South and the North, may lead finally to the systematic breakdown in existential relations between human beings and nature. In effect, such a crisis is the result of an antagonistic approach to the concept of harmony between people and nature, an approach in which the mechanisms are founded on dependence with respect to an industrial arsenal of machinery and artificial structures, and which results in humanity's hostile and aggressive attitude to nature. In the final analysis, such as an approach is considered rather an obstacle than an asset. The proof is that in economic calculations, ecological nuisances are seen as the inevitable price to be paid for rapid economic growth rates. In other words, the growth of GNP, due to the perverse effect stemming from the logic of the system itself, benefits precisely from the progressive destruction of the natural patrimony.

Inequalities and injustices – on a national as well as an international scale – provoked by the indiscriminate recourse to modern technology, today denounce the myth of an endless exponential progress, the disappearance of the scarcity of resources, and the advent of a peaceful and harmonious world.

The disregard for ecological imperatives and, therefore, for the close and complex relations between ecosystems and the human societies making up these systems, is not only reflected in the material deterioration of basic global resources – the colonization of nature – due to endless growing needs in raw materials and energy. This disregard has also favored a kind of social organization in which the human being's role is increasingly less important. Rajni Kothari has expressed this idea in the following way:

> The result is that there are in this world millions and millions of what are known as "marginal" men and women, people for whom society has no use. The upshot is that man himself has become super-fluous and obsolescent; he is being looked upon as a burden not just on nature, but also on society. Paradoxical though it may sound, the system that modern man has produced is one in which the most dispensable element is man himself.(4)

To examine the deep causes of this situation would be to go beyond the scope of this brief synthetic analysis. Such causes have to do with the positivist, fragmentary, empiricist, and anthropocentric aspect of the Western point of view.

The effect of positivism on the orientation of science and technology has been particularly disastrous. It has reduced the natural patrimony and the interactions between the econ-omy of societies and the economy of nature to dependent variables, and has provoked technological decisions that will have irreversible consequences on future generations. As a result, this dangerously limits the choice of options in the future by denying generations to come the possibility and right of determining their own life style. The severe diag-nosis of the state of development in the world is not sur-prising. The lack of a new social paradigm is pressing. The questioning of conventional points of view is itself global. It transcends traditional scientific practices and acquired life styles. It puts foreward an overall vision that must finally surpass human activities as a whole. The only means of carrying out such a questioning will be by restoring the relations of people with the environment to a central place of concern; in other words, the 'Environment Development' problem. The only worthwhile development is that of people, not of things.(5)

ENVIRONMENT/DEVELOPMENT PROBLEMS

Global Challenges for the Distant Future

The deterioration of the global environment is one of the major potential forces of rupture of the world system. It is important to quickly outline some of the challenges where global problems seem to be particularly explosive when we consider them within a long-term perspective that involves the "basic needs - resource availability" dialectic.

The possible exhaustion of certain renewable resources (not exactly in the immediate future, since the present assessment of these resources hardly justifies the alarming opinions of certain politicians or of those responsible for multinational enterprises), the apparent decrease in volume of protein resources resulting from the overexploitation of fishing resources, the contamination of the food chain, and the deterioration of the ozone layer necessary to maintain the earth's ecosystem - all these are topics that are often underlined.

From here on, we will briefly analyze a certain number of particular environmental problems related to the long-term possibility of the earth's resources satisfying humanity's basic needs in the future.

One of the first consequences, at a global level of ecological deterioration, is certainly the progressive disappearance of tropical rain forests. We are here dealing with the earth's oldest and richest ecosystem, of which only approximately 24 percent remains today. It is estimated that annually 11 million hectares of what remains of rain forests are being burnt or cut down, that is, some 30,000 hectares daily, or 20 hectares every minute. In Africa, for example, more than half of the original rain forests have already disappeared. In the Indies, in Sri Lanka, in Burma, we are talking about two-thirds. Plant resources in southern Asia are considered the richest in the world. It is feared, however, that those of the Philippines and Malaysia will disappear in the course of the next decade.(6)

More than 90 percent of the plant resources capable of contributing towards human or animal feeding are to be found in the tropics. The destruction of this major ecosystem will clearly diminish, in an alarming manner, a leading potential resource for the future satisfaction of food needs. It is not

solely a question of ecological problems in themselves, brought
about by the destruction of that ecosystem (such as the
siltation of rivers and watersheds, erosion, and landslides due
to the disappearance of forests), but also of economic and
social problems provoked by the disappearance of a vital
resource for most of the world's population, that is, trees, the
scarcity of wood and paper, charcoal - essential energy source
of poor rural areas with intolerable living conditions.

Deforestation is in evidence throughout the world and,
with the exception of China, perhaps, it has spread to practically all countries of the South, particularly in Central
America, the Middle East, and Northern Africa. The multinational corporations, together with national forestry companies, are presently cutting down the rarest tree species at
an uncontrollable rate, thus preventing any possibility of
forest regeneration. This is undoubtedly carried out in the
name of gross income growth - always considered, although
falsely so, the most important indication of development - above
all in satisfying the voracious appetite of the industrialized
countries for wood. In this way, the Third World countries
are deprived of a basic resource from which they are apparently unable to draw great advantage.

The rapid spread of the population drain phenomenon is
another major global concern.(7) More than one-third of all
dry land is arid or semiarid. Approximately 20 percent is so
arid that human beings cannot live there. Every year,
however, additional stretches of land are lost, and desert land
increases in Africa, Australia, Asia, and the Americas. According to Brown and Eckholm, "the production capacity of
vast dry regions in both rich and poor countries is fall-
ing."(8)

Behind the population drain, we find ecological changes
that deprive the land of its capacity for maintaining a sustained agriculture and for supporting human settlements.
Again according to Eckholm and Brown, an ever more critical
threat to humanity would consist in "the deterioration of
patches of range land and crop land throughout the world's
arid and semiarid zones."(9) Once again, it is hardly a
question of the result of a natural process. Population drain
is the result of the economic effects of export agriculture,
overgrazing, deforestation, and demographic growth, as well
as the widespread use of chemical fertilizers, weed-killers, and
insecticides, which, in the middle and long term, contribute to
the sterilization of the soils. Although it is primarily an
ecological phenomenon, population drain has economic and
social implications: The perspectives for food production in
desert zones are becoming increasingly gloomier.(10) In spite
of irrigation systems set up to favor increased agricultural
production in the arid zones, experience shows that in many
irrigated areas, productivity falls due to inadequate hydraulic
administration and other factors.

Another crucial global area of concern fomented by the degradation of the world ecosystem is the genetic regression and progressive extinction of the earth's plant and animal species.(11) If, on the one hand, the extinction of plant and animal species does not appear to have an immediate impact on the deterioration of humanity's well-being (contrary, for example, to growing desert areas, or to air and water pollution), on the other, the regression of the genetic pool, that is, the decrease in the diversity of forms of life, must be of greater concern. E. Eckhold in "The Age of Extinction," estimates that "more than half the known animal extinctions of the last two thousand years, that is, since the first recorded extinction of the European lion around A.D. 80, have occurred since 1900. An average of about one animal species or subspecies is believed to have disappeared during the 350 years leading up to the mid-twentieth century."(12) Today, it is estimated that there is an average annual loss of one animal species or subspecies. The major factor in the reduction of wildlife has been destructive human intervention. Following the reduced efficiency of DDT, the use of other pesticides, the highly lethal phosphate-based chemicals, particularly malathion and parathion, have increased ecological and biological threats.(13)

The extinction of plants is ecologically even more significant. It is estimated that the disappearance of a plant brings with it the disappearance of between 10 and 30 species dependent on it, species such as insects and even other plants.(14)

The reduction of biological diversity has serious effects on the potential advancement of agriculture. Eckholm quotes the case where "a locally evolved strain in some remote corner of the earth may hold a genetic key to an important agricultural breakthrough."(15) The possibility of using available genetic reservoirs in the tropics as a deposit for future resources is likewise in the process of being dangerously reduced.

All humanity's basic foodstuffs presently depend on 20 plant crops, 12 of which feed approximately 80 percent of the human population. Many thousands of other plants, however, are equally edible and could contribute to the satisfaction of tomorrow's food needs. There is the danger, however, that such plants will disappear forever.

In the same way, mention should be made of the oceans and other salt water areas. With respect to energy, foodstuffs, raw materials, etc., these oceans comprise the globe's major potential deposit. Here we once again encounter short-term interests concerned with immediate profit and generated by rapid and massive exploitation due to sophisticated technology. These interests weaken such an essential deposit of future resources for humanity.

Nonetheless, it is not only the future needs in energy and foodstuffs that are thus threatened by the regression of the genetic pool of animal and plant species. What must also be pointed out is the importance of maintaining a resources deposit when considering the medical, pharmaceutical, and industrial areas. More and more medicaments contain natural ingredients. However, only 7 percent of world plant potential has been analyzed in relation to its medical and pharmaceutical value.(16) The potential use of troical rain forests as a leading raw material for an alternative organization of the Third World, induced by plant chemistry and "chimurgie," runs the same risk of being endangered.

Finally, mention should be made of the field of energy resources. In the final analysis, oil supply is limited, even if the oil companies plot to artificially exploit the shortage to their advantage and add to the confusion carefully preserved by them concerning the true energy problems. Nonetheless, most of humanity uses firewood as a major energy resource, together with charcoal, plant residues, and animal excrement. When comparing the high demographic growth rate in many parts of the Third World, particularly in Africa, Central America, and Southeast Asia, with the rate of plantation of new trees, we observe that the prices of firewood and charcoal have considerably increased, above all in the poorest regions. However, the time required by a family to collect the daily ration of wood is multiplied by a phenomenon that makes the wood even costlier, that is, the evident reduction of time available for the production activities necessary for the physical survival of these communities and all that survival entails. Cow dung, initially used as a natural manure for cultivation, is increasingly becoming a substitute for fire-wood. This implies a major risk of a breakdown in the fragile equilibrium of production from soils in these zones. E. Eck-holm, whose writings have helped draw the attention of the world to these vital issues, mentions that the use of other kinds of fuel such as leaves, branches, etc., is an equally important cause of soil erosion.(17)

The consequence of this environmental degradation due to the harm brought about by a technocratic kind of development in which the accumulation of wealth for some is necessarily carried out to the detriment of others, is twofold. On the one hand, the worsening of the real energy crisis, that of fire-wood, affects half the world's poor population and threatens the global ecosystem. On the other hand, the specter of more than a thousand million human beings living in ecologically degraded regions of the world, without any way to satisfy their energy and food needs, implies the risk of provoking fascist reactions that could lead to economic apartheid on a world scale.(18)

If we view the situation on the other side of the fence it is no absurd irony to see that the abusive use of fossil fuel tends towards what has been called the "greenhouse effect," provoking a rise in the temperature that can set off major ecological catalysts.(19)

It would be beyond the scope of this essay to analyze each case and the essential part that reverts to the application of "modern" Western technologies. The technological causes - in the case of the increase in infections, other diseases, malnutrition, and child mortality in the Third World, or the contamination of the food chain - are sufficiently well known in our day.(20)

The Slow Awareness of What is at Stake

Although the official concern for the environment as expressed above arose some ten years ago, it has to be recognized that in spite of great efforts - the organization of a United Nations summit conference (Stockholm 1972), preceded by the Founex Meeting and followed by the setting up of the United Nations Environmental Program (UNEP), along with a whole series of events, reports, and declarations - environment in relation to development strategies are far from holding the place of importance they merit in the reflections on development and its practice.

A certain official mistrust - North and South - can be seen when the discussions touch on the specific implications of healthy ecological development. Even the idea of a global society that should be resolutely involved in the search for development alternatives - North and South - seems to go against the general trend.

We can distinguish three conceptual phases in the awareness of the importance of ecological considerations. To a certain extent, these phases received their credentials at the Stockholm Conference.

In the first place, the negative effects are delineated - the nuisances of industrialization policies that have impressed public opinion. Considering these effects as a necessary cost to pay for the carrying out of rapid GNP growth, the struggle against air and water pollution was thus the leading topic of concern. This initial perception favored an approach to the problem, and consisted in counteracting the unpleasant effects seen as inevitable. The production process or the final contaminating product is overlapped by an antipollution element or by recommending measures to circumscribe or avoid a recorded nuisance. Better still, this struggle against pollution has itself given way to the appearance of industries based on the production of antipollution or protective devices (such as masks) which in their turn contribute towards stimulating the GNP growth rate.(21) In this way, GNP growth was to benefit once again from the environment's degradation.

Later, the perception of environment within the economic development process finds expression, under the impact of the Club of Rome reports and, subsequently, as a result of the world readjustment in oil prices, in an approach that sees the integrated administration of the natural resources as a priority task. Here we are no long dealing with a questioning of the economic development and industrialization model pursued in the past, but rather with a coordinated administration of natural resources in a given context, and with efforts to reduce waste.(22) The question of knowing whether a more integrated administration of resources is sufficient to compensate for the inherent deficiencies in the industrialization system adopted, is always evaded. This is on account of the exclusive interest shown for the supply side without at all questioning the demand side, that is, life styles, etc.

It is precisely for these reasons that a redefinition of the parameters and strategies of development is imperative. The final conceptual phase is concerned with this challenge. It deals with environmental and development problems and considers environment no longer an exogenous variable of the economic model but rather the basis itself of all future development and industrialization policies. The concept of environment has itself stretched beyond the notions of pollution or integrated administration of resources. In its most global sense it presently encompasses the totality of local, regional and national ecosystems, the close interaction between these and the human societies that inhabit them, as well as the effects of these interactions between humans and nature both on people and on their natural environment.(23)

The present debate on environment and development can no longer be reduced or rendered trivial by technical considerations such as pollution control, elementary public health precautions, or a responsible administration of resources. These factors are desirable, often necessary. Nevertheless, the environmental dimension of development, that is to say, environment as an integrated factor of all human development endeavors, raises questions that are wider and a lot more fundamental.

Among these questions, the choice of the social development model occupies a privileged position along with the strategies leading to self-reliant development, that is, a development capable of promoting a sustained ability of development with a view to the advent of a sustainable global society. We are thus dealing with an internalized mode of development that implicitly suggests a wide variety of models, precisely because of different ecosystems and an infinitely varied number of cultural, psychological, and social realities that characterize different societies. In fact, it is the definite and final rejection of the idea of a universal development model, standardized and homogenized in the Rostow tradition.

Synthesis: The Concept of Eco-development

The concept of ecodevelopment, proposed by M. Strong, the former Executive Director of UNEP, in June 1973, expresses the consensus reached since the United Nations Conference on Environment, that is, that environment and development are interdependent and that development must be "ecologically healthy." Otherwise there will be no development. The eco-development concept, moreover, reflects the proposals of global development as set out by the Cocoyoc Declaration (1974), the Charter of Rights and Duties of the States, and the Dag Hammerskjöld report "What now?" What is more, this theme has inspired the Bariloche model.(24)

The ecodevelopment concept is operational. It is neither a utopian scheme nor a panacea. It is a guide that must be applied to the countries of the North as well as the South. It proposes a new kind of growth. The fundamental characteristics of eco-development have been better outlined by Ignacy Sachs in his most remarkable synthesis study "Environment and Development" - new concepts for the formulation of national policies and international cooperation strategies - and in G. Francis's report, "Environment and Development - Phase III - Prospective and Eco-Development" - action strategies.(25) The essence of the eco-development concept in these two papers rests fundamentally on three main postulates:

• The efforts of society must center first and foremost on the real fundamental needs of their populations and particularly on the improvement of human potential rather than on economic growth as an end in itself.

• Self-reliance is an objective towards which humanity as a whole must continually tend, that is, a process founded largely on the autonomy of decision making; the capacity to list their problems and find solutions for them is the only means of obtaining true interdependence on a world scale.

• It is necessary to search for a real symbiosis between human beings and their milieu, founded on understanding of, as well as respect for the ecological need of maintaining systems of survival and variable resources. Only under this condition can it be possible to protect present and future generations and collaborate in the instauration of viable human societies.

To establish or reestablish this necessary harmony between development and environment, it is essential to work at the same time on the levers of supply and demand, implying life styles and consumer structures, particularly in the advanced industrialized countries. The supply side implies a new reflection on the means and priorities to be brought into play when dealing with renewable resources to be exploited, appropriate technologies to be developed for each situation, and human settlement.

Let us borrow Ignacy Sach's synoptic table.(26)   Eco-development is

•   a development approach with the aim of reconciling socioeconomic objectives and an ecologically healthy administration, in a spirit of solidarity with future generations
•   based on self-reliance, the satisfaction of basic needs, and a symbiosis of man and nature
•   another form of qualitative growth that is neither a zero growth nor a negative growth.

Eco-development requires:

•   harmonization of modes of consumption, time planning, and life styles
•   adequate technologies and schemes adapted to the milieu
•   reduction in energy consumption and the promotion of renewable energy capital
•   new uses of environmental resources
•   careful administration of resources and their recycling
•   ecological principles for human settlements and land use
•   collective planning and grass roots participation

Eco-development is applicable as much to industrialized countries as to the developing world.

With respect to the question raised, decision making arising from the social and political pyramid is viewed as difficult.   Such questions imply rather a constant research based on open-mindedness and dialogue between the people and the decision-makers, a process aimed at creating by consensus the kind of society sought after.   The concept of self-reliance can, in this context, play a leading role since it allows for the expression of desires, hopes, and objectives at a number of regional and local levels.   These questions require serious consideration of phenomena pertaining to history, culture, and geography.   A revision must also be carried out of the production techniques presently in service to satisfy basic material needs.

The durability of products, the minimization of production waste, recycling, the dosage of the quality and quantity of energy in terms of its ultimate use, and the transition efforts towards an economy that centers on resources and renewable energy forms are components in the preparation and application of a viable mode of development.

The concept of self-reliance is not at all equivalent to autarchy or integral self-sufficiency.   With the exception of a certain self-sufficiency in food production, indispensable for obvious reasons, self-reliance is perfectly compatible with the importing of technology, know-how, and equipment. In every age even the greatest civilizations have imported knowledge. Moreover, "self-reliance" does not impede international trade, provided its present almost exclusively vertical nature is questioned and all unequal exchange anticipated. (27)

The three elements - satisfaction of real needs, harmony with nature, and self-reliance - are closely linked when it is a question of converting eco-development into an approach for development planning.

To what extent an eco-development approach to planning differs from the conventional model of technocratic planning is shown by (a) the implicit acceptance of a vast diversity of concrete solutions that vary from case to case, and the subsequent rejection of the imported imitative model; (b) the emphasis placed on rethinking the development objectives themselves; (c) the return to grass roots, that is, to people concerned with a project, a programme, using their resourcefulness within their own ecosystem, thus reducing the North-South dependence syndrome; and (d) the need to explore and to develop alternatives, for the most part aspects of human activities, such as energy production, human settlements, institutional models, and priority of scientific research.

ENVIRONMENT, DEVELOPMENT, AND THE NEW INTERNATIONAL ORDER

A new international economic order, like a new international development strategy, should give priority to the global restructuring of relations between people and their environment.

The Crux of the Problem

This restructuring should, logically and psychologically, begin with (1) the demystification of conventional diagnostics which support the current explanation of the underdevelopment in the world (28) and (2) the demystification of the modernity doctrine.

At the heart of the problem we find an irresponsible life style, involving waste and the excessive tappping of global resources. Rajni Kothari sets out this fundamental problem as follows:

> The primary cause for large areas of underdevelopment and inequity is to be found in the global

> structuring of man-resource relations in which a
> minority of nations have, in pursuit of a parasitic
> and wasteful life-style, shared out the large bulk of
> world resources. The spread of the same life style
> among the élites of the countries of the Third World
> has also meant that they remain divided, both within
> each of them and between them severally. . . .
> This, in effect, means that the richer segments of
> both "developed" and "developing" nations continue
> to indulge in life styles that result in perpetuating
> global inequity, depleting world resources and
> unsettling nature's balance.(29)

If our diagnosis is exact and the approach inspired by eco-development principles has become imperative, we must also recognize that the formulas of the past will no longer be valid. More of the same policies will not be enough. Nevertheless, most governmental policies showing obvious signs of exhaustion continue to be applied to manage the crisis by clinging to policies of the past. It is precisely the pursuit of these policies that will reinforce the obstacles raised with respect to the implementation of a new international order.(30)

Thus the industrialization policies pursued actually reduce employment possibilities through the intermediary of technological advancements (for example, microelectronics, micro processors), reinforce social inequalities, and create growing numbers of persons who are becoming superfluous, as much from the production as from the consumption point of view. In favoring consumer methods that go against the production of socially useful goods (the arms industry, etc.) these policies are founded on technologies, as we have attempted to illustrate, that sap the planet's deposit of resources.

In the same way, the official policies to reduce underemployment are another example of "self-defeating" and counterproductive policies in relation to the establishment of a new international order.

Eco-development is concerned both with ecology and economy. It must be the fundamental inspiration of the new economy, harmonizing the advent of a new economic order by promoting the concept of use value rather than exchange value.

Shared Implications for North and South

To convert environment into the most important resource for a better development of human societies - the primary proposal for a new order among peoples - implies the following:

- a reformulation of development objectives
- a redefinition of the political economy for natural resources
- a reorientation of science and national technologies
- a progressive detachment of the structure of international
  economic power

The new objectives for development will be somewhat concerned with the concentration of efforts on the direct satisfaction of domestic needs of the vast majority of the urban and rural population, through participatory and global planning, as well as through guaranteed access to particular basic resources, which would favorably allow access to family self-reliance by removing these resources from the strength relations to be found in the market. These new objectives will be founded on an ecologically healthy approach, with a view to maintaining the resources stock, by using renewable flows, and by greatly reducing the economic production cycles so as to adapt them to local and regional realities.

The first consequence of these new objectives will be the necessary redefinition of the political economy for natural resources, in that the stress will be placed on the use of renewable resources where possible, and the bioconversion of solar energy, since we are dealing here with an almost inexhaustible energy source.

We must dedicate considerable efforts to the study and exploration of resources inherent in every ecosystem, resources that have been little exploited until now.

Ignacy Sachs has made a remarkable summary of the potentialities to be found in the tropical rain forest ecosystem: (31)

> It finds its vocation in cultivations carried out in the shadow of the trees rather than in monocultivations in open fields; less in cereals than in tubers; more so in agriculture producing fish, shellfish and fodder, in semiintensive or intensive animal breeding with silvicolous and aquatic fodders, than in extensive breeding practiced in the pastures obtained from the inconsiderate destruction of the forest. . . . How many are the possibilities, in the manipulation of tropical chains, for transforming the enormous bio-mass of invertebrates into a source of proteins for human consumption by using birds or fish as biological converters. How many new and cheap fodders can be got from the superabundant plant bio-mass, aided by relatively simple techniques and biological engineering, allowing for the intervention of micro-bodies and enzymes.

The great promise of the rain tropics for humanity as a whole is to be found precisely in its capacity to supply an immense potential of plant and animal materials as industrial raw material.(32)

The industrial promotion of the biomass becomes a major imperative in the elaboration of new industrialization strategies with a view to organic and self-supporting growth.(33)

Hand in hand with the redefinition of the political economy of natural resources we have the reorientation of science and domestic technology.

Most of the characteristics of environmental degradation may be directly or indirectly linked to inappropriate Western technologies.(34)   What is otherwise imperative is the elaboration of appropriate or adapted technology for each situation, and an appeal for the simplest techniques as well as the most advanced technologies, provided they are optimal for a specific situation.   These technologies easier to develop at a village level, imply nonetheless, major challenges when applied to industrial techniques.(35)

Scientific research, in particular, should receive greater impetus in the energy field (promotion of unconventional renewable energies) and in the use of the tropical biomass. The challenge of this reorientation can be measured when one recalls that 90 percent of research carried out on potential food-giving plants presently corresponds to 5 percent of the potential of industrialized countries, and that only 10 percent of research efforts focus on 95 percent of the world potential to be found in the tropics.

Greater emphasis must also be gvien to the development of the Environmental Knowledge Infrastructure (EKI) since the ignorance of large-scale environmental cycles and their subsequent destruction is frequently at the root of an incorrect use of the resources of a given ecosystem.   For example, the integrated administration of the ecosystem of mangroves, potentially a major resource deposit for large sectors of the population of many Central American countries, depends on the deepening of environmental knowledge.(36)

Within the eco-development vision, however, the reinforcing of the EKI will not be a question for a scientific elite detached from the population (which would correspond to the traditional approach), but rather scientific priorities will be determined in accordance with the objectives of the community and the needs defined by it.(37)

Following on from this, a certain freeing of the power structure of international economic domination is indispensable.

The growing integration of periphery economies into the central capitalist system is presently pursued by those who hold international economic power.   Such integration finds support in the theoretical positions of different United Nations organizations.

The reduction of the extraversion of Third World economies towards the setting up of national economies capable of directly satisfying the basic needs of the population, through judicious exploitation of renewable resources from their own ecosystems (local and national self-reliance) and by giving priority to contact and exchange between partner societies of similar ecosystems and comparable development levels (collective self-reliance), becomes a sine qua non condition.

In the same way, the countries of the Center should themselves be involved in the search for alternative development. It has been argued that the North's involvement in another development can be considered a prerequisite for fundamentally changing the present international economic structures with a view to overcoming global maldevelopment afflicting the world.

The next decade should lead the North itself along the path of self-reliance, an indispensable step in the long-term promotion of true global interdependence.

At a national level, political measures should permit the initiation of required structural changes. Such measures ought to include

- the conversion of industries to the production of socially useful goods - which in its turn should favor the birth of a new production ethic.
- the elimination of wasteful production patterns by using renewable and recyclable energies and resources - which should stimulate a new consumption ethic.
- support for smaller economic cycles that would favor the active participation of the people, the creation of new activities, the decentralization of decisions affecting the life of the community, local self-reliance.
- the alternative use of the national economy's productivity earnings, converting such earnings into a free time surplus rather than into a goods and services surplus. This would stimulate noneconomic values and behaviors, as well as activities not directed toward a market economy, thus weakening the latter in the very long term.

The path towards less maldevelopment in the North will demand considerable changes in present life styles and values. Those who benefit from the existing order will attempt to oppose such changes. The identification of the major obstacles to internal changes, be they legal, behavioral, educational, political, or informational, as well as the ways and means of reducing such obstacles - by giving priority to the participation of peoples and communities - will constitute a first essential step.

The legitimization of initiatives for alternative development experiences and the combined support of individuals, communities, and whole societies involved in seeking for alternatives or motivated by the same concerns (new alliances of progressive countries North and South, for example) are steps to be taken in the near future.

The new international order will be a step forward only when the environment subsequently becomes the basic resource and principal factor in the reorientation of the evolutionary process with a view to ridding the world of its maldevelopment.

NOTES

(1) It has become so commonplace to affirm that the growth of the GNP is not synonymous with development, etc., that one begins to seriously hesitate in affirming it. In reality, however, development policies continue to be the same as if nothing has happened.

(2) Cf. Jacques Bugnicourt, Basic Needs and Self-reliance in the Urban and Rural Environments, report of a seminar, prepared by Marc André Fredette, series prospective, vol. 4, Policy Branch, Hull; CIDA; and Ignacy Sachs: Environment and Development: A New Rationale for Domestic Policy Formulation and International Cooperation Strategies (Ottawa: Joint Project on Environment and Development, vol. 2, CIDA-DOE).

(3) Cf., for example Samin Amin L'accumulation a l'echelle-mondiale (Paris: Anthropos), and Imperialism and Unequal Development, Monthly Review Press, 1977.

(4) Rajni Kothari, "Environment and Development," keynote paper, Regional Seminar on Alternative Patterns of Development and Lifestyle in Asia and the Pacific, 1979.

(5) This effort of questioning is not detained even by philosophy: cf. the innovation studies of Jerzy A. Wojciechowski, The Ecology of Knowledge: On Science and Society - Past, Present and Future, N.H. Steinech, editor (Ann Arbor: University of Michigan Press, 1975) and Henry K. Skolimowski, Ecophilosophy: Designing New Tactics for Living - A Twenty-First Century Philosophy (London: Marion Boyers Publishers, 1979).

(6) Cf. Maurice Strong "International Community and the Environment," Environmental Conservation 4, no. 3 (Autumn 1977): 165-172.

(7) Cf. L. Brown and E. Eckholm, Spreading Deserts: The End of Man, World Watch Paper no. 13 (Washington, 1977); and Mazingira - The World Forum for Environment Development, no. 2, Man's Desert, (Pergamon Press, 1977).

(8) Ibid., p. 5.

(9) Ibid., p. 8.

(10) Cf. Collins and F. Moore Lappé, Food First (New York, 1977), for many examples in this respect.

(11) Cf. E. Eckholm, "The Age of Destruction," The Futurist (October 1978), and Disappearing Species: The Social Challenge, World Watch Paper no. 22 (July 1978). (The literature on this subject is fairly abundant; we mention only two references representing interesting syntheses.)

(12) Eckholm, "Age of Destruction," p. 287.

(13) Ernesto Lopez-Zepeda, Ecological Impact of Cotton Cultivation in El Salvador (Toronto: York University, Faculty of Environmental Studies, 1977).

(14) Cf. D. H. Raven, "Ethics and Attitudes," in J.B. Simmons et al., eds., Conservation of Threatened Plants (New York: Plenum Press, 1976), quoted in Eckholm, p. 6.

(15) E. Eckholm, "The Age of Destruction," p. 294 refers to two Purdy University scientists who in 1973 tried high protein sorghum and examined more than 9,000 varieties from all over the world before they discovered in the field of Ethiopian peasants two obscure strains of the quality they sought.

(16) The appeal by the World Health Organization, in favoring the reinstatement of the promises of so-called traditional medicine, runs the risk of remaining without a follow-up if the genetic pool continues to be exhausted at today's rates ("a species lost every hour").

(17) E. Eckholm, "The Other Energy Crisis: Firewood," World Watch Paper, no. 7, 1977.

(18) Is that apartheid not already a reality to a certain extent?

(19) See R. E. Munn's excellent study, "The Green House Effect," in Mazingira, 2 (1977).

(20) He refers the reader to the works of G.P. Mieton and Taghi Farvor, The Careless Technology: Ecology in International Cooperation (New York: Natural History Press) and to L. Mhlanga's study, "The Impact of Technology on the African Environment" (Dakar, ENDA Occasional Paper no. 7).

(21) Cf. the case of Japan.

(22) The origin, for example, of the "Conserver Society" concept must be placed within that effort to limit waste, but by essentially trying to end up with the same results with fewer resources.

(23) Cf. Strong, "International Community," and I. Sachs, "Environment and Style of Development," in W. H. Matthews,

Outer Limits and Human Needs (Uppsala; Dag Hammarskjöld Foundation, 1973), and G. Francis, Eco-Development, National Development and International Cooperation Policies (Ottawa: CIDA-DOE, 1977).

(24) A. O. Herrera (collective), Catastrophe or New Society, A Latin American World Model (Ottawa: CRDI, 1976).

(25) These texts form part of a series of publications on environment and development, directed by H. F. Fletcher (R. Durie) and Charles A. Jeanneret-Grosjean (Ottawa: CIDA-DOE, 1900).

(26) "The Salient Features of Eco-Development," in G. Francis, p.3a.

(27) Cf. J. Galtung, Self-reliance and Global Interdependence in Environment et Développement, 3 (1977)

(28) The unscientific explanations, because they are partial and prejudiced, are well known: demographic growth, aid diminution, weak education level, inadequate transfer of resources, lack of motivation, etc.

(29) Kothari, pp. 45-46.

(30) Cf. for example, Charles A. Jeanneret-Grosjean, "What Development in the North - Some Introductory Comments" (Paper given at the Scheneningen Symposium, "Towards a New International Development Strategy," July 1979.)

(31) Ignacy Sachs, "Vers une nouvelle civilisation industrielle des tropiques" (Paper given at the Sao Paulo Symposium, "Development Alternative: Solar Energy," November 20, 1975).

(32) J. J. Dreyon and D. Thery, "Eco-développement, Industrialisation: Rénouvelabilité et Nouveaux Usages de la Biomasse," Cahier de l'Écodéveloppement, vol. 3 Paris: CIRED.

(33) The present structure of world relative prices should be able, in particular, to stimulate three areas of industrialization through biomass: energy production, construction materials, and the chemistry of polymers.

(34) The case that has become a classic illustration of barriers.

(35) K. Vinaver and I. Sachs, "De l'Effect de Domination à la Self-réliance: Technologie Appropriée pour le Développement," in Mondes en Développement no. 15, (1976).

(36) Ibid., p. 20 and 112 ss.

(37) Ibid., p. 74.

10 The Role of the Military in the NIEO
Muzammel Huq

THE GLOBAL MILITARY STRUCTURE

Examining the military structures from a global perspective, we find that much of past thinking and analysis of the military turns out to be conventional and untenable wisdom. There exists a global military structure that is a historical development; it is an outgrowth of patterns of dominance and dependence it contains the sediment of past conflicts, and it is undergoing a self-sustained and irrational growth in organizational bureaucracy as well as aimless technological transformations.

Seen from a global perspective, the superpowers are found at the apex of the military hierarchy. Military apparatuses around the world occupy different positions in this structure that provides them with different functions. At the level of the superpowers, the military serves the function of international control for the preservation of established dominance. As we move down the hierarchy from the superpowers to the peripheral actors, the role of the national military becomes increasingly subordinate to and dependent on the great power aristocracy. This manifests itself not only in technological dependence on armament imports, military training, and advice, but also with regard to the functions of the military. In the industrialized countries, institutions other than the military have the responsibility of maintaining internal social control. The military has a secondary function of internal repression, more in potential than in actual use of force. In most Third World countries and also until recently in some peripheral European countries, the internal function of repression and violent coercion for the maintenance of social control has been the paramount role of the military. A major cause of this internal repression lies in the desire of ruling elites to have their countries adapt to the international division of labor. This requires cheap labor and a marginalized peasantry, plus the prevention of political participation of the masses including the labor and peasant organizations.

The military and economic expansion of the rich industrial countries of the North has irrevocably shaped the destinies of the countries of the Third World and brought about the present international system. The expansion of the European and North American powers between the sixteenth and early twentieth centuries was achieved as much by force of arms as by trade and investment, which in fact were two sides of the same coin. Yet the military dimension of that expansion and its continuing effects - both in the periphery and at the centers of the international system - has received remarkably little academic attention. Recent work carried out at the Stockholm International Peace Research Institute (SIPRI) has made it increasingly possible to describe the outward manifestations of the world military structure and the hierarchy within it.

A breakdown of the distribution of world military expenditures shows that industrialized countries - mainly the members of NATO and the Warsaw Pact countries - continue to account for over 80 percent (see table 10.1). But the share of developing countries has increased from 6 percent in 1955 to over 18 percent today. Clearly this trend reflects in part the great changes that have taken place in the international system as a result of decolonization. It is tempting to believe that the militarization of the Third World is a natural result of increasing sovereignty. The fact that after several decades of decolonization it has become necessary to start a major campaign to institute a new economic order should be enough to remind us that formal independence is necessary but not sufficient to break the chains of colonialism. It is legitimate, therefore, to enquire as to whether the increasing role of the military in the Third World is a function of increasing sovereignty or if it is a function of the military equivalent of neocolonialism.

In real terms the proportion of the world economy devoted to military activities is large and has a considerable impact on the rest of the economy. This impact has been summarized by Sivard as follows:

> An arms race out of control now commands close to $300 billion in public funds yearly. In addition to the growing potential for cataclysmic destruction, the arms build-up represents an immediate and heavy burden on the world economy. . . . It contributes to inflation, retards economic and social development, and diverts resources urgently needed for human

Table 10.1. Percentage Distribution of
World Military Expenditure 1955-1975

	1955	1960	1965	1970	1975
LDC[a]	6.1	7.5	11.2	13.4	18.6
Industrial	93.9	92.5	88.8	86.6	81.4

[a]Less developed countries, including China. In 1975 China, the Middle East, and the rest of the Third World accounted for very nearly one-third each of Third World military expenditures.

Source: Stockholm International Peace Research Institute, World Armaments and Disarmament, SIPRI Yearbook, 1976.

well-being. . . . Governments   spent   two-thirds more for military force than for the health care of 4 billion people.   Much could be done to promote economic and social progress and reduce the root causes of conflict through cooperative international effort.   So far that effort is dwarfed by the intense competition for arms.(1)

Sivard estimates that world military expenditures average $12,330 for each of some 22 million soldiers per year, while public expenditures for education amount to $219 per school-age child.   The governments of the developing countries spend as much on the military as on health and education combined. Thus every percent of a national budget devoted to military expenditures rather than investment in basic development reduces the chance of breaking out of the downward spiral of underdevelopment.   In   order   to   achieve   higher   levels   of investment in the national economies of poor countries, it is being increasingly felt that significant social and institutional changes are required.   And since important sectors of the economies of poor countries are tied to those of rich countries, internal social and institutional changes have important con-sequences for international and internal political relations.
It   is   argued   that   although   military   expenditures   are important in the world economy, purely economic considerations are of only secondary importance.   The crucial question is the role of the military in determining the social and institutional arrangements within countries and the degree of subordination

or autonomy of the poor countries in the global military and
economic dominance system established by the industrial
countries of the North.

THE ROLE OF THE MILITARY IN THE ESTABLISHMENT
OF THE PRESENT WORLD ECONOMIC ORDER

Military power played a vital role in the establishment of
economic orders in ancient civilizations. The Roman order was
based on a combination of military conquest and slavery. The
medieval period in Europe revolved around the military power
of nobles who were able on the one hand to subjugate their
serfs and on the other hand to combat each other or engage in
military expeditions to areas further afield.

The emergence of nation-states led to an increasing tendency to use the military resources of the state in the pursuit
of trading advantages and subsequently to obtain by conquest
the means of production, namely land, labor, and raw
materials.

Over a period of hundreds of years, there was a gradual
transition in the pattern of exploitation. As they moved inland
from the coastal enclaves, commercial companies were obliged to
recruit their own armed forces, and war became a commercial
proposition. But gradually the pattern of capital investment
shifted towards more tangible assets, such as plantations and
mines.

The discovery of riches to be obtained by sea gave rise
to the competition for control among the European powers,
bringing the Spanish and Portuguese to South America and the
British and French to North America, India, and Southeast
Asia. The Dutch established themselves in southern Africa
and in the East Indies, while the Danes controlled the trade
from the Atlantic coast of Morocco to parts of the Caribbean.

Gradually the mercantile economic order gave way to
an economic order based on mass production of plantation
products employing slave labor. Just as the mercantilists
depended upon the use of armed force in order to plunder
far-off regions of the world, so did the slave traders require
force in the pursuit of their profits.

Debate continues on the motives for this expansion and on
the question of whether trade follows the flag or vice versa.(2) In part the lack of consensus is due to that euphemism
"flag," for the fact is that even where commercial companies or
expeditions preceded the formal incorporation of territories by
the metropolitan powers, military force was the most important
factor in the expansion.

Marxist scholars(3) have pointed out that the late
nineteenth-century expansion was not merely a question of
expanding trade but also of overseas investment in railways,

mines, and plantations. Any investment requires some degree of security. Military force was therefore no longer required simply in order to seize valuable goods or slaves, it was also required to impose an alien political and economic system. This was achieved either by means of direct or indirect colonial rule or by means of "gunboat diplomacy." Networks of naval bases and coaling stations were established all around the world in order to support global military systems able to intervene anywhere in the empire and to protect shipping between the metropolis and the colonies. Writing of Delgoa Bay in 1899, Maguire said, "If this port fell into hostile hands our shipping in East African waters would be in grave peril" - an argument which is still to be heard today with regard to the Indian Ocean.(4)

In this way the colonial system became the basis of the world economic order that was established and maintained by military force.

In the present world economic order, military and economic considerations are integrally related in the minds of the leaders of the dominant powers.(5) Economic power is seen to depend upon military power and vice versa. Maintaining a lead in the strategic competition between great powers requires continued access to raw materials and markets in the Third World, and this in turn requires political control, achieved if need be by overt or covert military measures.

In considering the possibility of a new economic order, it is important to take account of the fact that the role of the military in the present-day global dominance system is essentially analogous to that of the military in the colonial period. They have the triple role of suppressing insurrections in metropolitan and periphery countries as well as preventing encroachment by competing industrial powers. Connected to the global military system are local military forces built up, trained, and equipped to a large degree by the dominant partner in the global system to maintain the present world economic order.

THE MILITARY AND THE WORLD ECONOMIC
ORDER SINCE WORLD WAR II

The present world is in part a reflection of the struggle for control of the world economic order. No effort to achieve a New International Economic Order (NIEO) can be successful unless it takes into account the military dimensions of the problem. One dimension of the problem is the establishment of worldwide military systems made up of land, air, and naval bases, transit and storage facilities, communications and navigation facilities, deep sea fleets, long-range transport and combat aircraft, satellite systems, and so on.

At one level these global systems are a function of the global competition between industrial systems, but at another level they are designed to facilitate control of the countries that provide the raw materials and markets so essential for the survival of some of the industrial economies in their present form. In both respects, therefore, the global military systems today have functions precisely analogous to those of the colonial epoch.

The colonial system was built up by a combination of military force and economic penetration. Colonial empires depended upon the establishment of navies and networks of military bases and staging posts around the world. Military forces were continually in action to subdue resistance or to support "friendly" local leaders. Dum-dum bullets, fragmentation bombs, and other forms of "superior" technology were used very early to "pacify" colonial peoples.(6) In some cases local military forces were recruited by the colonial powers, often from ethnic groups with martial traditions. Usually these forces were commanded by European officers.

The collapse of the colonial system may be attributed to a combination of political, economic, and military factors. The two World Wars - the greatest examples of the struggle between rival industrial systems - weakened some of the old imperial powers but strengthened others. In some of the old powers, the armed forces could no longer control the industrial working class, and revolutionary regimes were established. In others, the armed forces retained control but organized labor succeeded in obtaining improved working and living conditions. This increased the cost of labor but promoted the trend towards investment of capital in manufacturing industry in cheap-labor countries.

At the same time, colonial armies, in spite of modern technology (aircraft, communications systems, modern antipersonnel weapons, etc.), proved in the long run incapable of maintaining the old empires.

Remnants of the old colonial military systems remain to this day. However, much more striking has been the development of new global military systems in the post-World War II period.

It is hardly an exaggeration to say that during the period of decolonization, a new world military order(7) has been established. This is characterized not only by a global military system under the control of a great power but by the establishment of military governments, or military forces with influence on governments, in many countries of the world. The role of the military in government has been actively promoted as a means for industrial countries to retain control over the economies of the poor countries.

This strategy is made quite explicit in recent justifications for expanding great-power military budgets at a time when economic competition and shortages of raw materials are increasing. Thus, in an address before the National Convention of the Veterans of Foreign Wars in 1975, General George S. Brown, Chairman of the US Joint Chiefs of Staff, said:

> Our current commitments to forty-one foreign countries are entirely consistent with and reflect our dependence on free-flowing international trade, and the forward deployment of our military forces continues to support these important economic interests.(8)

In his address to the US Congress on the military budget for fiscal year 1977, General Brown provided a table showing that the United States is increasingly dependent upon imports of raw materials (see table 10.2). He described the intermixture of US military and economic interests in the Third World as follows:

> Africa: Any large-scale breach of the peace could destroy capital investment of American firms and interrupt US access to important raw materials such as aluminum, chromium, oil, manganese, tin, tungsten, copper, iron and lead. The rising Black African demand for US military equipment and training offers the United States both political and economic opportunities that should be evaluated as they arise. . . .

> Asia: US security interests in this area continue to place a premium on stable, independent governments favorably disposed toward the United States from the standpoint of naval operations, trade, access to raw materials, ports and military facilities, and of passage for maritime and airborne commerce, and the denial of political, economic and military advantages to major countries outside of the Communist powers.

> Latin America: The nations of Latin America are of significant importance to the United States. Their raw materials and industrial potential . . . could become critical for US defense. The importance of Latin America as a marketplace for US products should not be overlooked. In addition to imports of substantial quantities of raw materials from the United States, such as wheat and coal, the increasing industrialization drive in Latin America is creating new and enlarged opportunities for capital goods. As an example, US exports to Brazil were

Table 10.2. Dependence of the United States
on Imports of Strategic Raw Materials

Percent Imported	Mineral	Major Foreign Sources
100	Manganese	Brazil, Gabon, S. Africa, Zaire
97	Titanium	Australia, India
91	Chromium	USSR, S. Africa, Turkey, Philippines
86	Platinum	USSR, S. Africa, Canada
80	Nickel	Canada, Norway, USSR
88	Aluminum	Jamaica, Surinam, Dominican Republic
88	Tantalum	Australia, Canada, Zaire, Brazil
98	Cobalt	Zaire, Finland, Norway, Canada
86	Tin	Malaysia, Thailand, Bolivia
86	Fluorine	Mexico, Spain, Italy
60	Germanium-Indium	USSR, Canada, Japan
50	Beryllium	Brazil, S. Africa, Uganda
60	Tungsten	Canada, Bolivia, Peru, Mexico
50	Zirconium	Australia, Canada, S. Africa
40	Barite	Ireland, Peru, Mexico
23	Iron ore	Canada, Venezuela, Liberia, Brazil
21	Lead	Canada, Peru, Australia, Mexico
18	Copper	Canada, Peru, Chile, S. Africa

Source: United States Military Posture for FY 1977   (Washington, D.C.: Joint Chiefs of Staff, 1976).

valued at $3.1 billion in 1974, with a favorable trade balance of $1.4 billion.

Summary: Latin America is of strategic importance to the United States for political, economic and security reasons. Although many Latin Americans regard the United States with suspicion and distrust in so far as US political and economic activities are concerned, there remains a generally friendly rapport between representatives of the US Armed Forces and the Latin American military. Due to the unique leadership role of the Latin American military, I believe it is important that we further these traditional military-to-military relationships by being responsive to legitimate force modernization needs and thereby promote a favorable climate for attaining US political, economic and security goals in the hemisphere.(9)

On the basis of such reasoning, the United States has for many years promoted large-scale military assistance and training programmes. For its part, the Soviet Union has provided military assistance and weapons to a number of countries, some of which are now heavily in debt. It is less clear that the Soviet Union (which, as seen in table 10.2, is a major supplier of certain strategic raw materials to the United States) is motivated by economic rather than political and strategic considerations.

THE IMPACT OF GLOBAL MILITARY SYSTEMS
ON THE WORLD ECONOMIC ORDER

The global military systems have tremendous direct and indirect effects on the world economy. But more important is the question of their impact on the world economic order - that is, the system of economic relations between states.

It is estimated that about 6 percent of the world economy is devoted to military activities. Presumably, therefore, military activities account for a similar proportion of the consumption of resources and pollution. In wartime, however, these proportions change greatly. Not only are larger proportions of national economies devoted to military production, but the results of this production generate wide-scale destruction, and many of the effects are long term.

The great proportion of economic activity devoted to war is a major factor in inflation and increased taxation. The cost of past wars is a great burden on many national economies for a long time in the future. Though these economic effects are obvious, relatively little attention has been paid to them. Even less attention has been paid to the impact of the global military systems on the pattern of economic relations between states.

Global military systems established by nuclear powers are (or should be) of concern to nonnuclear states for several reasons. First, the global systems are dependent upon services rendered and facilities provided by nonnuclear states. In some cases these services are already directly damaging to the peoples concerned, as where nuclear tests have been carried out in occupied territories in North Africa and the Pacific, or where local populations have been deported in order to free their lands for military purposes, as in Diego Garcia in the Indian Ocean and Kwajalein Atoll in the Pacific. In other cases, providing facilities to nuclear powers will drag non-nuclear countries into the great power competition and possibly into a nuclear conflict - thus diminishing rather than increasing their national security.

Second, global military systems facilitate the use of military force to achieve political goals in other countries, either by means of direct intervention or by other overt or covert uses of military force. The goals sought may range from the desire to establish or maintain already established military facilities to the desire to establish or maintain a particular government.(10)

Third, global military systems today include massive military assistance and training programmes that aim to build up professional military elites in other countries.(11) Implicit in these programmes is the desire that these elites should remain loyal to the great power that provides the training and equipment.(12) Selected members of these are given special training in "civilian" administration, on the assumption that in many cases the military will take over the government - which in fact has often proved to be the case. This policy has often led to military coups (there have been more than 100 coups since World War II), the repression of civil rights, and the priority of military investment over investment in production, while opening the way to increased foreign economic penetration and dependency on foreign technology rather than to increased national sovereignty and social improvement.

The situation now is that probably a majority of the nations of the world - even many that are supposedly non-aligned - are one way or another involved in the global military systems of great powers. In some cases this involvement is open and takes the form of formal alliances; in many cases, it takes the form of secret agreements to provide certain facilities (for example, facilities for monitoring radio transmissions between other countries, satellite tracking and communications facilities, navigation facilities for nuclear submarines, aircraft, etc.). These facilities, individually, may be relatively innocuous from the point of view of the host country; but taken as a whole, they greatly extend the military capability of certain great powers to intervene in other countries in any part of the globe - as well as contributing to the global arms race between great powers.

In this way, global military systems are of the greatest relevance to the effort to achieve a more equitable world economy. Industrial countries are faced with increasing shortages of raw materials, as well as sharpened competition for world markets, as their economies slacken. These shortages and economic problems hit the great military establishments, which are confronted with shortages of oil, steel, paper and other materials. One answer to this problem is to reduce the size of the military establishments, but instead the military are arguing for increased capability to "protect" trade routes, offshore oil installations, etc., as well as for increased freedom in promoting "friendly" regimes abroad in order to ensure continued supplies of raw materials and access to markets. The great military establishments of some powers, therefore, have a direct interest in preventing a new world order and considerable capability to do so - capability reinforced by the facilities provided, inadvertently or not, by many smaller countries.

The prominent role of the military in the government of many countries raises the question of whether they are there to promote far-reaching internal changes - or to delay such changes. And do the global military systems exist to promote or to prevent changes in the world economic order? The social and economic consequences of the new military order depend upon the answers to these questions.

CONCLUSIONS

From the point of view of progressive global change, the struggle for the NIEO is perhaps the most fundamental issue of our time. NIEO has been the subject of a succession of important international conferences in which the raw material-producing countries have had some success in jointly formulating demands on the industrialized countries. The question of this new economic order has aroused the interest of many governmental and nongovernmental agencies and groups, but up to this stage, the debate has failed almost entirely to focus on one of the main barriers: military power. All the evidence of history suggests that most world economic orders have been established and maintained with the aid of military force, thus changing the economic order must take this into account.

The prevailing economic order operates essentially according to the interests of the advanced industrialized countries. This order, based on the so-called laws of supply and demand, reflects an imposed relationship - in particular, discrepancies in the strength of seller and buyer. The prices of manufactured goods, including armaments, tend to rise always more and faster than the prices raw materials can fetch on the world market. The uncertainties and setbacks generated by "free-market" forces play havoc with the efforts of developing countries, which depend mainly on exports of raw materials to plan for a steady economic development.

The highly industrialized Western powers depend upon cheap imports to sustain their economies, and they try to maintain the present system by promoting and supporting militarized governments in the Third World. Thus the militarization of the Third World reinforces the "old" economic order and has tremendous effects on the social and economic development of the developing countries.

The capacity of developing countries to import what is needed for agricultural development and industrialization is often drastically reduced by the importation of military technologies. The magnitude involved is such that in some countries, imports of arms reach one-third of total imports; in many cases, a substantial portion of other important technology is directly related to military activities.

The purchase of a modern weapons system of advanced technology for the armed forces induces a chain of supplementary import demands. Expenditure on spare parts and services will usually exceed initial procurement costs. Modern fighter aircraft, tanks, or naval units require expensive networks of support facilities to remain operational. Long after the introduction of such weapons, the presence of foreign specialists is required. The chain of imports required by the introduction of these weapons consists largely of advanced, capital-intensive technologies. Given the volume and the political priority of military activities in many developing countries, the imported arms have profound repercussions on the pattern of industrialization, on the utilization of natural and human resources, and hence on development in general.

In the Third World, a military system based on the importation of advanced training, technology, and weapons systems creates dependencies of its own, while reinforcing economic, political, and cultural dependence. The importation of sophisticated military equipment by developing countries deepens their dependence on supplies from industrialized countries. Most developing countries are still forced to import virtually all inputs for industrial production, but their import capacity is increasingly aborted by military oriented technology. These are imports which by definition do not promote development. Therefore, militarization and the proliferation of weapons must be considered a decisive factor in the continuation of unbalanced development or underdevelopment on a global scale.

Table 10.3. Dependence on Selected Imported Industrial Raw Materials, 1974
(Imports as a Percent of Consumption)

	United States	European Community	Japan		United States	European Community	Japan
Aluminium (ore and metal)	88	31	93	Manganese	98	99	87
Chromium	90	100	90	Natural rubber	100	100	100
Cobalt	99	100	100	Nickel	72	100	100
Copper	20	76	93	Phosphates	(a)	100	100
Iron (ore and metal)	17	59	100	Tin	92	87	90
Lead	19	70	67	Tungsten	64	100	100
				Zinc	59	73	74

(a) Net exporter

Source: International Economic Report of the President, March 1975, pp. 154-155.

NOTES

(1) R. L. Sivard, World Military and Social Expenditures 1976 (Leesburg, Virginia: WMS Publications, 1976), p. 5.

(2) T. K. Derry & T. T. Wiliams, A Short History of Technology (Oxford: Oxford University Press, 1960), p. 707. See also T. M. Maguire, Outlines of Military Geography (Cambridge, England: Cambridge University Press, 1899), pp. 137-38.

(3) V. I. Lenin, Imperialism, The Highest Stage of Capitalism (Moscow, 1916).

(4) See "Militarization of Indian Ocean," Patriot Magazine (New Delhi, March 1980), p. 4.

(5) See the RIO Report, Disarmament and Development (Rotterdam, June 1979), pp. 71-73.

(6) See Stockholm International Peace Research Institute, Antipersonnel Weapons (London: Taylor & Francis, 1977).

(7) The term a "new world military order" seems to have first been used by a Danish peace researcher, Jan Berg (Politiken, July 1, 1976).

(8) US Department of Defense News Release No. 410-75, August 21, 1975.

(9) United States Military Posture for FY 1977 (Washington, D.C.: US Joint Chiefs of Staff, 1976).

(10) See No. Stein, "The Pentagon's Proteges: US Training Programmes for Foreign Military Personnel," Latin America & Empire Report (North American Congress on Latin America), 10 (1) 1976, pp. 1-32. Using data recently released under the Freedom of Information Act, this paper publishes for the first time details of US foreign military training programmes.

(11) See B. Blechman and S. Kaplan, The Use of Military Forces as a Political Instrument (Washington, D.C.: Brookings Institution, 1976). This study calculates that military forces have been used as a political instrument to influence other countries on about 215 occasions by the USA and about 115 occasions by the USSR since 1945.

(12) See W. R. Kintener, "The Role of Military Assistance" Proceedings of US Naval Institute (March 1961), pp. 76-83.

Index

About the Contributors*

JORGE A. LOZOYA: UNITAR/CEESTEM Project Co-Director, Mexico City.

HAYDEE BIRGIN: CEESTEM, Mexico City.

IRMA GARCIA-CHAFARDET: UN Center for Social Development and Humanitarian Affairs, New York.

MUZAMMEL HUQ: Institute for the Study of Rural Resources, Kasherpar, Bangladesh.

CHARLES A. JEANNERET-GROSJEAN: University of Ottawa.

XAVIER LOZOYA: Instituto Mexicano para el Estudio de las Plantas Medicinales (IMEPLAM), Mexico City.

MIRCEA MALITZA: University of Bucharest.

PORFIRIO MUÑOZ-LEDO: Adviser to the President, Mexico City.

FERNANDO REYES-MATTA Instituto Latinoamericano de Estudios Transnacionales (ILET) Mexico City.

LUIS SANCHEZ-DE-CARMONA: Sociedad Mexicana de Ecologia Humana, Mexico City.

ANA MARIA SANDI: University of Bucharest.

(*) At the time of their contribution to the UNITAR/CEESTEM Project

JUAN SOMAVÍA: Instituto Latinoamericano de Estudios Transnacionales (ILET), Mexico City.

ALBERT TÉVOÉDJRÈ: International Institute for Labor Studies, Geneva.

CARLOS ZOLLA: Instituto Mexicano para el Estudio de las Plantas Medicinales (IMEPLAM), Mexico City.